CARY LIBRARY
VERMONT COLLEGE
36 COLLEGE STREET
MONTPELIER, VT 05602

WITHDRAWN

WITHDRAWN

Please remember that this is a library book,
and that it belongs only temporarily to each
person who uses it. Be considerate. Do
not write in this, or any, library book.

WITHDRAWN

Understanding Children's Art
for Better Teaching

Betty Lark-Horovitz

Hilda Lewis

Mark Luca

CHARLES E. MERRILL BOOKS, INC., COLUMBUS, OHIO

372.5
H816u
1967

Copyright © 1967 by Charles E. Merrill Books, Inc., Columbus, Ohio 43216. All rights reserved. No part of this book may be reproduced, by mimeograph or any other means, without permission in writing from the publisher.

Library of Congress Catalog Card Number 66-14404

Cover emblem: Man-drawing by school child of Minoan period, made on a slate over 3,000 years ago. Courtesy Chaponthier, F., "Une Árdoisé d'écolier a l'époque minoenne," *Revue des Etudes* Grecques (1925).

Jacket picture courtesy California school districts' contribution.

Printed in the United States of America

Preface

In *Understanding Children's Art for Better Teaching* the authors follow the course of development of artistic expression from its beginnings in the infant through adolescence, describing in detail changes in the representation of people, living things, and inanimate objects, and in the use of line, color, form, and composition, as well as various techniques. Characteristics of child art common to each developmental stage are described, and individual variation within developmental patterns are covered. The illustrations have been selected from the work of children between ages one and one-half through seventeen years from many countries, and they span a period of eighty years.

The book reports studies comparing child art with adult art of various epochs, and with the work of adults who are not artists. It deals with similarities and differences within and between ethnic and cultural groups. The findings of more than seven decades of research in a dozen countries provide a background which will enable the teacher to understand the needs of children in her class and set the stage for a natural unfolding of ability.

In dealing with development, creativity, and learning, the authors review research in all of these areas, explore their relationships, and propose a program for teaching art in the schools. Particular attention is given to the elementary school child, but pre-school and older children are also considered.

For many decades, the goal of research in child art was to describe and explain characteristics of children's pictures. At first, these pictures were studied as curious phenomena; later, they were interpreted as expessions of childen's emotional and imaginative life.

In recent years, child art has come to be used as an instrument with which to gain a greater understanding of the child's personality. Psychologists have found child art tremendously helpful in penetrating the child's mind. More recently, it has been used as a projective technique to gain deeper understanding of personality and the subconscious. Psychiatrists have found child art useful in clinical diagnosis and therapy; it has also been used as a means of assessing intelligence of younger children. Material concerning the use of child art in personality assessment, therapy, and mental measurement is briefly surveyed in this book to acquaint the reader with the conceptions underlying these applications. It is not intended to equip or encourage the reader to apply these techniques for similar purposes.

The final chapters of the volume present a teaching program based on research findings and successful classroom practices.

Illustrations

We find it advisable to point out various aspects useful in understanding the illustrative material.

Because there is a noticeable difference between the spontaneous art work of children and that of which is carried on in school, we have added "spontaneous" to the legends of those pictures which we felt reasonably sure were spontaneous.

The selection of the pictures was dictated by the necessity of providing examples for parts of the text which either directly, that is in particular cases, or indirectly illustrate the meaning of the text. The selection was also influenced by the desire to present as great a variety of examples as we could secure and thus to show drawing or painting phenomena. Therefore we have included a number of illustrations that show "poor" work of otherwise perfectly normal and intelligent children, but also samples of "excellence."

Many, if not most, of the illustrations serve as examples for more than one characteristic. However, we have usually emphasized the main characteristic which we wished to demonstrate more specifically than others, and which serves mainly, though not exclusively, for the section with which we are dealing.

A number of picture titles are in capitals. These titles were given by the children themselves in just these words. Other picture titles are not in capitals because they were either not given by the children, or we could not be certain about it.

Sex and age were usually given. If omitted, it is due to either lack of knowledge or uncertainty. Only non-American nationalities are indicated, except for occasions when we did it on purpose, because we felt it was fair to draw attention to talented American children, since the selections of non-American children always represent drawings by talented children. Whenever it seemed of interest and particularly when a child's work belonged to a past generation, we have added the year when it was made.

There exist very few developmental series by individual children through a significant number of years. This is particularly true of the present time. Therefore we felt fortunate in having access to one such individual developmental series through the Brooks collection, California. Besides the series itself (No. 49), Nos. 48, 35, 30 are by the same child.

No special group of illustrations has been assigned to the use of media, or techniques, though the medium is often mentioned. Media and techniques are especially pointed out in illustrations connected with "Learning." The following illustrations are indicative of treatment of medium: Nos. 31, 38, 48, 50, 54, 64, 75, 92, 94, 95, 97, 98, 99, 100, 101, 102, 115, 116, 121, 130, 131, 135, 141, 143, 144, 147, 154, 155, 174, 175, 177, 182, 183, 184, 185, 186, 187, 193, 212. We wish to point out the following in relation to specific color media: opaque paint—8; tempra—1, 16; water color—3, 5, 19, 21, 23, 31, 32, 34; crayons—7, 10, 35; papercuts and paste—15.

Acknowledgments

The literature that forms the background to this book has brought vividly to the mind of one of the authors her first art teacher, and the experiences connected with her. Betty Lark-Horovitz remembers in retrospect how well planned, how "modern," how free yet disciplined this teacher's approach was to her pupils and their work. To the memory of Annetta Pfaff, to her understanding of children's art development as it was discovered up to the first decade of this century, Betty Lark-Horovitz would like to pay affectionate respects. She also wishes to acknowledge the advantages offered to her in the 1930's by a Carnegie Grant for the study of literature on this subject.

We wish to express our gratitude and appreciation to Miss Dorothy Bennett for her friendly suggestions; to Mrs. Fanya Weingartner for her valuable help on the manuscript; and to Mrs. Mary Whipple for reading parts of the manuscript.

Mr. Manfred Cardwell was so kind to discuss certain personality aspects of children whose pictures appear in this book.

The San Francisco Chronicle opened its files—1961 to 1965—of children's drawings to us for the selection of much of the contemporary spontaneous child art. Mrs. Judy Weber of the San Francisco Chronicle's Promotion Department most generously helped us in this part of the work.

We wish to thank the California School Districts of Berkeley, Castro Valley, Danville, Oakland, Richmond, Sacramento, San Francisco and Walnut Creek for contributing samples of children's work.

The Berkeley Commercial Photo Company showed great patience, understanding and skill for our particular problems and needs, for which we express our appreciation. To Ruth McNitt and Rod MacConnell, San Francisco, our thanks for their excellent photographs of children at work and of exhibits of children's art work.

We wish to extend a special word of thanks to the International Child Center, San Francisco, for its assistance in obtaining and permitting us the use of art work by children in other countries. We want to thank Mrs. U. d'Alberque for the use of art work of Indian children in Africa.

We thank the teachers of Castro Valley for contributing practical suggestions for the classroom.

Contents

Teaching Children's Art

Children's Visual Expression

An understanding of the child's natural development in art is central to the successful guidance of children in this area. Therefore all experiences in art must grow out of the natural developmental course through which child art evolves.

Drawing comes naturally to the child. It begins with the discovery at about two or even earlier that certain substances leave marks on surfaces. These early marks evolve into scribbles, first random and disorganized, but more ordered as time goes by. The child has found an activity in which he can express *himself*.

Then one day the child becomes aware that in his drawing he expresses an idea. Once the child has discovered that simple forms can symbolize objects in the real world, he begins to build a graphic vocabulary in which shapes and lines are combined and modified with great versatility to stand for whatever he wishes.

The essential difference in the child's approach to art and to other subjects is that in *the goal is not to accelerate these stages, but to enlarge heighten awareness of forms*

speaking, reading, writing and ciphering he must master symbols and systems invented by others. In his art, however, the young child devises and uses his own symbols. Thus the child creates his own art language and uses it in his own way.

The teacher need only build upon what exists and help the child acquire greater competence in using art expressively.

omits creation of structure or order

The goal in teaching art to children is not to train artists but to offer experiences that contribute to the growth of the personality. Experience with art heightens his sensitivity to the physical world and leads to a greater appreciation of his environment. It helps him to give order to his sense impressions, and enlarges his capacity for enjoyment. It opens a way of expressing imagination and feeling.

Active participation in the arts is essential. This was the conviction of Franz Cižek, the great Austrian art educator, who insisted that every child understands and enjoys art only to the extent that he has acquired this understanding by his own efforts.

The child's stage of development is the teacher's point of departure. The teacher's task is to gauge the child's readiness and recognize his potential. The teacher must nourish and enrich each stage of the child's growth and aid him in his progress to the next step.

The aim of art education is not the production of works of art but the unity of the entire growing personality. Learning is not the incorporation of something alien, something imposed on the child. It is an increase in his capacity to bring forth what is within him.

Young children of today draw and paint with symbols mysteriously like those used by children of distant places and other times. It may even be that children's art of centuries ago was much like that of today.

There is, for instance, a sixteenth-century portrait which shows a small child holding a drawing of a man[10] which could also be a drawing by a contemporary child. The slate of a school child of the Minoan period of several thousand years ago shows a resemblance to the work of a child of our time.[11] This distinct character of child art, clearly recognizable through time, suggests that, for the child, "representation is not an end in itself, [but] rather a form of coming to terms with the world around him, which the child wants to make his own."[34] Studies have shown that children's drawings reflect their environment[1] and their culture.[46]

Figure 1. *A child of the early 16th century holds a schematic "man" drawing.*[5] *Portrait by Giovanni Francesco Caroto, Museo de Castelvecchio, Verona, Italy.*

and space relationships which are inate

The young child does not create works of art. He uses art as an avenue of expression. Therefore, a child's art must be evaluated in terms of the individual himself, his idea of "prettiness," and his stage of development in art expression.

There is a definite character to child art through the ages and around the world. There is also steadily growing evidence that all children progress through comparable stages of development in art expression. It is not merely a matter of interest for the parent and the teacher to be aware of this. It is a fundamental requirement for understanding and guiding children.

DEVELOPMENTAL STAGES OF CHILDREN'S ART

There are roughly three main stages of development in art expression through which all children pass. They follow one another in sequence, "step by step . . . the higher ones can only be reached by way of the lower ones. . . . Willful interference with this process creates disturbance."[2] These steps have been called *Scribble, Schematic,* and *True-to-appearance.* In order to observe intelligently the general characteristics of child art, the similarities and differences between the work of different children, and the class performance of even one child, it is essential to acquaint oneself with this natural progression.

Scribble Stage

The beginning of visual expression occurs roughly between the ages of one and four, when whatever the child endeavors to draw appears as a *scribble.* The child's scribble is the result of expressive activity

and has meaning for *him,* at the time, even though he finds it of only fleeting interest. Early scribbles usually escape adult interpretation, for they seem meaningless. The very term scribble carries an unfavorable connotation for adults, suggesting something unnecessary, born of impatience, or tension, or plain irritation. In discussing this first stage of drawing development, the word scribble is used as a strictly descriptive designation for the devices and symbols created by children in their first purposeful attempts to make marks.

A number of investigators have speculated on the nature and meaning of the scribble-character.

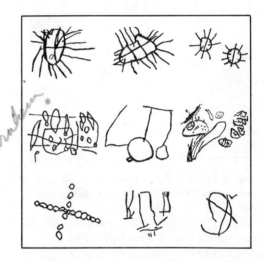

Figure 2. *There is great variety in children's scribbles.*[15]

Grötzinger suggests that "in its scribbling the child is walking over the paper as the flies walk over the wall. So in the spiral, the cross, the zigzag, we have in pictorial form three of the child's fundamental experiences: (1) floating, in which the child revolves on its own axis—the rotary sense of space; (2) standing, in which it experiences the perpendicular and horizontal positions and also the process of becoming erect—the primal cross; (3) walking—the zigzag."[18] The scribble has also been described as an experience of gestures that are given shape and so recorded.[2]

Figure 3. *A BIRD. Movement is shown by using scribble. Drawn during the primitive schematic stage. While drawing, the child commented, "He is my friend, I talk to him, he likes me, then he hopped about." Notice the face and enormous wings which sprout from the head.[19] Girl, age four, 1964, spontaneous drawing.*

The nature of the scribble has been interpreted in a number of other ways: for instance, as movements describing an action, and sounds in nature (wind, flight, animal movements).[30] It has been looked upon as imitative of adult performance.[7, 8] It has been considered the outcome of rhythmic movement,[25, 49] probably determined by tactile and motor sensations,[3] and as an experience leading the child to the dis-

covery of a causal relation between sign and movement.[25]

It has been regarded as a means of establishing direction[14] or as just one among other given patterns of action due to body activity.[9] Scribble has been analyzed as a typical early experience, and as a special form of behavior of hand-eye coordination. Pencils or other tools are, at first, nothing more than special objects used as a part of the child's total physical action (pounding, circling, darting back and forth, etc.).

Once the pencil and its trace are related, a whole series of conditional action is started: scribbling which is at first accidental becomes an intentional activity. It is simultaneously spontaneous expression and imitation.

Thousands of scribbles were examined by Rhoda Kellogg.[23] She distinguished twenty basic scribbles, single or combined. Curvy, zigzag, or looped lines and circles appear after age two; at about the age of three, certain shapes, called diagrams, evolve: squares, circles, triangles, odd-shaped areas, the Greek and the diagonal cross. According to her interpretation, pre-representational development culminates in the abstraction of the mandala design. The mandala, a doubly crossed circle, is a symbol in certain religious art, such as that of the Tibetans, and is often found in adult art around the world. Arnheim found that this type of abstraction seems to be used almost universally by children, perhaps as a kind of ordered and simple statement.[2]

During the scribble period the child begins to develop a tendency to close lines. Perhaps the closed figure represents "order" and "limitation," in a sense "protection," but does not yet represent shaping in a functional sense. In the attempt to close the lines or figures, the first shapes appear. Therefore, "formation of shapes . . . [is not the]

 *I disagree*

experiencing of formal or structural quali-ties, but rather the result of action."[34] One very significant interpretation considers the beginnings of children's drawings and paint-ings as an initial act of judgment on the part of the child, establishing the smear, scribble, and later shapes as meaningful, in contrast to the meaningless void or chaos around them.[6]

good

A large number of children talk while painting, drawing, or modeling. In spite of a variety of observations and interpretations, the extent to which the talk describes the child's art activity or only accompanies it re-mains uncertain. Only when the child starts to name what he produces or, still later, an-nounces his creative intentions in advance, can one be reasonably sure that the child is drawing with specific intention.

The early scribbles appear to the adult nothing but a wilderness of lines and smears. Later, shaped contours are produced but they, too, are apparently meaningless. How-ever, a complete collection of one child's scribble over a period of time reveals the evolutionary process that leads to the next stage, the primitive schematic stage.

Schematic Stage

The stage following the scribble is the *schematic stage*, a term derived from the Latin word *schema*, meaning outline. In a schema, outlined shapes have a degree of semblance to actual objects. Form is re-duced and simplified. Objects or figures are represented by outlined shapes which are used consistently, again and again, to designate the same objects. The schemata are repeated in much the same way as words are used. In this sense they are signs. Thus, in schematic representation, the same shapes repeated constantly come to express entire complexes of ideas.

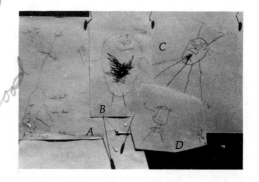

Figure 4. *Before drawing, this child announced his intended subjects. A. SANTA CLAUS and EASTER BUNNY. The boy described all the parts. B. THIS IS MY BROTHER. Scribble indi-cates his "tummy." C. A DEER. D. MAN.*[19] *Boy, age three (A) to age four (C, D), spontaneous, pencil drawing.*

Figure 5. *From scribble to schema, showing the development of "man." These drawings were made from age three on, over a period of a year and a half.*[36] *Boy, Germany, 1905-1906.*

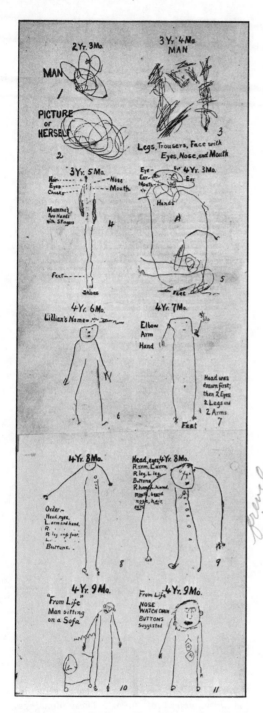

Figure 6. *From named scribble to primitive schema.*[25] *Girl, between ages two and five, American, 1897.*

The schema is at first primitive; few, if any details of the objects are shown and many parts of the objects are omitted or not completed. The primitive schematic stage marks the beginning of the transition from scribbles to a clearer visual statement.

Even though, from a given point of observation at a particular moment certain things cannot be seen, the child combines whatever seems of importance to him. It is as if he were on a tour of inspection, circling the object, looking down on it from above, from many angles or even through it, into its very interior. Although adults generally would not present both eyes in a profile, the child may do so. Objects are shown not from a fixed point of vantage but from many vantage points selected and combined so that each object or part of an object is presented in its most characteristic aspect. The child appears to ignore the way in which a fixed vantage point in nature obscures certain aspects of the object. For example, he may draw a table as though seen from above, and show all four legs sprawling out from the sides, even though they would be invisible from that vantage point. Many adults cannot even recognize the object in such a picture.

In a developmental series, there is, about age four, "a clearly defined state of transition from scribble to a variety of awkward drawings."[15] In the pre-schematic stage, only parts of the schemata have been completed; the schema is still fragmentary. For example, a man may be represented by only a round shape for the "head-man;" or by a shape "squeezed" into longish rounds roughly indicating head and body; or by a more structured head and body shape.[34]

In the earliest stages of modeling, comparable to the scribble, the child crumbles the clay or other plastic material. Later, he gives the material spherical, cylindrical, and flattened forms, parallel to the primitive schema in drawing.[4]

The schematic stage is reached when lines have a specific and understandable meaning in defining shapes, and when shapes have a very direct relation and resemblance to the essential features of objects. The shapes, so outlined, give the impression of diagrammatic notes to which children add their pictorial and often decorative comments. *The shapes are not reality but its schema.* The child accepts the difference between the object in nature and his own schematic equivalent.[2]

The nature and the characteristics of the schema and its meaning in relation to the child's personality and abilities have been widely explored and described. Various authorities have different views. One says the schema expresses the child's capacity to make objects and situations his own through pictures symbolic of an inner vision;[19] Mühle finds "it is not a sign or symbol that renders visible some concept behind it, but is actually different from the concept, because every expression, every shape is only meaningful for itself and for nothing more."[34]

However, Piaget's interesting conclusion is that the schema is not an expression of the perceived object, whether perceived visually or by touch, but rather an expression of the act of perceiving.[40]

The schema has also been regarded as an indication of mental pictures in which lines replace the actual object.[22] In its earlier phases of development, the schema makes note only of parts of objects: not until a later stage does it indicate relationships. Luquet, who through children's pictures probed so deeply into their reasoning, has described the schema as intended realism because of its logic in representing non-visible characteristics.[31] Adult realism in picturing is based on what he can see at one time, but the child also represents the invisible because he knows it is there and feels it belongs.

Children's urge to draw may be considered a phenomenon of development. It is a form of expression that appears at a certain phase of development and usually disappears later. It begins at a time when subject-object separation in the environment has not yet taken place. Child images expressed through drawing may be a more basic and immediate form of communication than language, which is still rudimentary. It may be that drawing loses its original function when it becomes inadequate for the delineation of experience and when

Figure 7. *EASTER MORNING. An imaginative schematic composition, with a scribbled groundline, a strip of sky and sun, and curved groundlines (they are not hills) on which are aligned trees, houses, and plants. On the left, eggs are lying on flat grassy ground. The child is in front of her Easter finery—large new shoes and hat, and a fancy hairdo. A diversity of graphic vocabulary, symmetrical arrangement, and ornamentation is shown.*[40] *Girl, age five, United States, 1963, spontaneous, pencil drawing.*

words become a much more useful avenue of communication.

It is as though schematic drawing fulfills a function in selecting the essential characteristics of the objects,[47] distinguishing parts or qualities of objects,[37] and thus developing perception.[24]

The variety of interpretation of the child's use of visual language is exceedingly wide.

None has been conclusively substantiated or rejected by research. The reader is invited to consider the validity of these views in the light of his own observation and experience.

It is generally agreed that modeling goes through much the same stages as drawing, but the relation of the two activities in direction and rate of development is still not clear. One investigator reported that the developmental stages follow one another more rapidly in modeling.[44] Another disagrees, noting that even at a time when the primitive schema has developed from "head-man" to bodiness, the modeling child makes, at best, thin pipes or flat strips to build a schema. This would indicate that in modeling, the child's visual development seems to lag behind.[41] Bakusinskij suggests that an "inner model governs both the two- and three-dimensional expression, and results in a parallel course and rate of development."[3] Corroborating evidence is supplied by Hoag in a study of construction by kindergarten children who began by using materials in a two-dimensional fashion and then proceeded to three-dimensional constructions of increasing complexity and realism as the experiment continued.[20]

This developmental course has also been discussed in terms of progression from recognition of the main dimension, length, to the concept of contoured two-dimensional flatness, then to a third dimension— modeling in the round.[41] Modeled shapes, and drawn or painted shapes of the primitive schema have been compared. In modeling, the child's shapes are roundish and egg-shaped, with a tendency toward flattening out the parts. Later, as in the schematic drawings, more attention is given to proportion and more correct joining of modeled parts.[32] The relief-like shapes, resembling gingerbread figures, common in the work of children, may originate from their

manner of drawing which they are unable to develop toward the less familiar three-dimensional material. By the age of eight, the child is making fewer flat shapes, and his work shows attempts at three-dimensional rounding, using simple shapes and little detail. However, the same child may alternately produce flat, schema-like figures and round sculptured figures at the same stage of development.[49]

True-to-appearance Stage

The developmental stage that follows that of schematic representation has been called the *true-to-appearance stage,* although the term is perhaps more characteristic of the aim throughout this period than of its achievement.

Figure 8. *True-to-appearance drawing in pen and ink. This was the child's first drawing in a new medium.*[41] *Boy, age fourteen.*

At this stage, objects and groups of objects are drawn as they are observed from a single point of vantage. Situation, position, or movement of living things is shown: bending of limbs, reasonably correct proportions among parts, and more "correct" color and light. The child gives proof of his awareness of the diminution of distant objects, of the line of the horizon. He begins to attempt perspective representation and

Figure 9. *VACATION. A pencil and crayon drawing made during mixed stage of development.*[30] *Boy, age twelve.*

Figure 10. *Harbor and docks. A schematic representation by a child in arrested development.*[41] *Boy, age fifteen, pencil drawing.*

foreshortening. Representation moves in the direction of photographic realism, toward the "natural" or "real" but rarely achieves this goal. Drawing ceases to evolve and loses the dynamic quality and originality of the child's earlier productions.[43] Frequently he abandons drawing which now causes more frustration than satisfaction.

Boutonier observed that by the time the child is eleven his work is seldom anymore "a spontaneous gesture, a sincere outcry, and thus it loses its essential qualities. Most frequently the taste for drawing, for graphic creativity disappears forever . . . the child

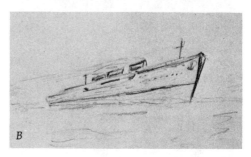

Figure 11. *Repetitious pencil drawings of ships which closely resemble each other, even in the representation of the "sea" space arrangement and technique.*[41] *Boy, age fifteen.*

in our society desists progressively from expressing himself freely in drawing."[5] Even those educators who have done remarkable work to promote and direct visual expression are forced to conclude with D'Amico that "this fine feeling for design seems to diminish as [children] grow up and it is at its lowest ebb at adolescence."[13]

When spontaneous drawing declines, the child often becomes adept at copying. At about ages eleven to twelve, technical skill in copying increases and reaches a peak in skill.[38]

On the other hand, twelve- and thirteen-year-olds may acquire moderate skill

Figure 12. *True-to-appearance crayon carica-ture of a cowboy. Motion is indicated by lines (hands and sleeves), and by attributes (lasso and "spittle").*[22] *Boy, age fourteen.*

in true-to-appearance representation from their observation of pictures and book il-lustrations. However, their drawings retain the rigidity and stiffness of the schema,[29] and liveliness of expression does not in-crease.[49] Caught between the desire to draw in adult fashion and the inability to do so, young teen-agers tend to remain fixed on a plateau, the threshold of realism. Drawings retain a number of characteristics from the previous stage and forecast, to a degree, the true-to-appearance stage yet to be reached. The relative occurrence of the characteris-

tics of the two stages indicates the stage of development.

Fewer than half of the fifteen-year-olds reach the true-to-appearance stage in their drawings.[35] This is even further reduced if the young people are faced with represent-ing unfamiliar objects.[27] The obvious diffi-culties encountered by children in the tran-sition from schema to true-to-appearance, and in the compromise stages between, have been the subject of much research. In adolescence, a child's development is often arrested and drawings may deteriorate. He may treat difficult parts of the object sketchily or omit them altogether. The child may persist in the schema, or may repeat his own drawings for as long as two years. The atrophy of his drawing ability may well be a reflection of his inability to express graph-ically the concerns of adolescence.[48] Ado-lescents who still draw spontaneously, favor caricatures and decoration of the printed word and show little interest in the human form or animals, even less in flowers and landscape.[21]

After sixteen, further development is neg-ligible, and whatever progress is evident is usually the result of instruction and practice. Drawing becomes a specialized ability rather than a general means of expression.[16, 36]

The teen-ager will often continue draw-ing, but without stimulating instruction most of them will not. The average teen-ager, like most adults, does not have facility in representation. He has gaps in his visual memory.[33] He is disturbed by unassimilated sensory perceptions, and as a result he can-not re-create true-to-life appearance as he would like to. For instance, he cannot render a landscape or cityscape to his satis-faction because he can not handle perspec-tive. Like the younger child, he cannot free himself of what he knows is there, even if it cannot be seen simultaneously, or he sees something differently from what he knows it to be.

Piaget's view that perception and operative representation are interfered with by assimilated images also holds for space representation because "geometrical space is not a perceptual continuum but an operational continuum due to the coordination and internalization of action."[39] In other words, what the child knows about the three-dimensional space he is trying to draw, for instance, the baseball pitcher's bent arm or the street that goes all around the block, is beyond his powers to translate into two-dimensional pictures.

Most interestingly, it has been shown that the drawings of half of all adults are at the schematic level,[17, 26] and can be compared to the schematic representations of six-to-ten-year-old children. Whether the adults had ever crossed the threshold to true-to-appearance drawing is not known. They may have regressed just because they had not made any effort to draw since they were children. Interestingly enough, marked regression to a former stage of visual expression is recognized as a characteristic of the mentally disturbed.[42]

Modeling in this developmental stage shows improvement in proportion and in position and movement of human and animal figures. Modeling from life shows better results and more improvements than drawing from life. This is perhaps due to the fact that in drawing one adjusts from three-dimensional observation to two-dimensional execution, whereas in modeling one observes and renders in three dimensions.[50] Special ability in modeling "is based on general sensations in the body . . . experienced in oneself."[49] A static frontal structure may be realized, but rarely is there a shift of the vertical axis direction to some other, dynamically necessitated change.[50] In other words, the modeled figure may present a good appearance from the front but not from all angles. A truly sculptural quality involving full use of three dimensions is seldom achieved.

Thus, in drawing and in modeling, the teen-ager falls short of his own goals in art expression, and far short of what is usually considered a successful level of performance for adults.

Child art is a phenomenon interesting for its own sake. It has been studied from many points of view. For example, it has been shown that there is a relationship between

Figure 13. *A. An adult's drawing of a man.*[20] *B. A ten-year-old's drawing of a man.*[37]

Figure 14. *A. An adult's drawing of a horse.*[21] *B. An eight-year-old boy's drawing of a horse.*[41]

Children's Visual Expression

chronological age, mental age, and what could be called drawing age, but that they correspond only roughly[28] (see Table I). Child art, undoubtedly, is a basis for further growth. However, the objective of teaching art to elementary school children is not to train artists, but to instill in children a sensitivity to aesthetic values.[12, 45]

Number of Drawings	Ages	Representational Level					% calculated from color drawings Use of Color							Size Proportions		Use of Medium			Line Treatment				Area Treatment								Compos. Arrangement		
		Primitive Schema	Schema	Mixed Stage	True-to-Appearance	Perspective	Local Color "True"	Local color varied	Organized color	Contrasting color	3 or less colors	4 or more colors	Monochromes	Correct (or fairly corr.)	Markedly incorrect	Consistent	Consist. & moderately effective	Consist. & remarkable	Hesitant or weak	Decisive	Subtle	Bold	Ragged & Smudgy	Smooth	Thick	Thin	Bold	Graded	Blended	Textured	Centered	Symmetrical or near-symm.	Planned Asymmetrical
166	6	26	73	1	—	—	74	—	5	12	10	82	8	14	64	33	8	—	7	22	—	—	36	19	6	—	—	—	—	—	94	26	7
186	7	8	90	1	—	—	85	—	4	9	8	92	—	16	58	42	14	2	9	30	—	1	22	35	6	4	3	—	—	—	88	27	10
200	8	6½	91	1½	—	—	77	½	2	5	14	85	½	26	49	63	13	1	25	27	—	—	43	22	8	3	—	1	—	—	91	28	6
202	9	½	88	11	—	—	82	3	—	5	16	82	2	31	42	67	14	—	12	29	—	1	26	38	½	—	—	2	4	4	91	22	10
200	10	1	72	20	5	1	88	3	4	8	20	69	11	42	34	59	16	5	12	29	1	1	21	37	9	10	4	6	—	12	95	10	11
184	11	—	61	30	17	1	76	4	5	6	36	60	4	41	23	57	25	6	9	33	1	3	14	49	11	8	5	2	10	15	86	13	14
230	12	—	48	35	14	2	64	2	—	1	25	71	4	42	21	50	25	4	11	31	1	1	17	52	6	10	1	3	6	16	92	12	8
188	13	—	57	35	7	—	69	½	2	2	29	62	9	46	23	59	16	2	22	22	1	—	16	45	3	10	—	—	—	12	80	9	8
174	14	—	41	29	29	1	85	3	2	2	28	55	17	62	13	29	43	5	22	30	4	4	10	55	33	53	—	2	2	23	88	14	17

Table I

Development Characteristics per Age Level
(in percentages)

Adapted from data of Munro, Lark-Horovitz, and Barnhart.[35]

CHAPTER ONE: TEXT REFERENCES

1. Appia, B., "La représentation humaine dans les dessins d'enfants noirs," *Bulletin de l'Institut Français d'Afrique noire*, I (1939), 405-411.

2. Arnheim, R., *Art and Visual Perception: A Psychology of the Creative Eye*, Berkeley: University of California Press, 1960.

3. Bakušinskij, A. B. A. W., "Das Kunstschaffen und die Kunsterziehung," Forschungsversuche über den Tatbestand der Raumkünste, Neu-Moskau, 1925, in: Wulff, O., "Kernfragen der Kinderkunst und des allgemeinen Kunstunterrichts der Schule," *Zeitschrift für Aesthetik und allgemeine Kunstwissenschaft*, XXVI, No. 1 (1932), 46-85.

4. Bergemann-Konitzer, M., *Das plastische Gestalten des Kleinkindes*, Weimar: H. Böhlaus Nachfolger, 1930.

5. Boutonier, J., *Les Dessins des Enfants*, Paris: Editions du Scarabée, 1953.

6. Britsch, G., *Theorie der bildenden Kunst*, edited by Egon Kornmann, Munich: Bruckmann, 1930, 2nd edition.

7. Brown, E. E., "Notes on children's drawings," *University of California Publications in Education*, II (1897), 1-75.

8. Bühler, K., *Die geistige Entwicklung des Kindes*, Jena: Verlag Fischer, 1922.

9. Cameron, N., "Individual and social factors in the development of graphic symbolization," *Journal of Psychology*, V (1938), 165-184.

10. Caroto, Giovanni Francesco, "Fanciullo con pupazzo," Verona, Italy: Museo di Castelvecchio.

11. Chaponthier, F., "Une 'Ardoise' d'écolier a l'époque minoenne," *Revue des Etudes Grecques*, (1925), 427-432.

12. Cižek, F., "Die Organisation und die kunstpaedagogischen Probleme des Jugendkurses." Spezialvortrag, 4. *Internationaler Kongress für Kunstunterricht, Zeichnen und angewandte Kunst*, Hauptbericht (1912), Dresden, 466-476.

13. D'Amico, V., *Creative Teaching in Art*, Scranton, Pa.: International Textbook Co., 1953.

14. Gesell, A. and L. B. Ames, "The development of directionality in drawing," *Journal of Genetic Psychology*, LXVIII, (1946), 45-61.

15. Ghesquière-Dierickx, B., "Comment dessinent les enfants: Evolution du dessin selon l'âge," *Enfance*, XI (1961), 179-182.

16. Goodenough, F. L., "Children's Drawings: A Handbook of Child Psychology, Worcester, Mass.: Clark University Press, 1931.

17. Graewe, H., "Untersuchung der Entwicklung des Zeichnens bei Kindern im Alter von 3-14 Jahren," Dissertation, University of Halle, 1932.

18. Grözinger, W., *Scribbling, Drawing, Painting: the Early Forms of the Child's Pictorial Creativeness*, New York: Frederick A. Praeger, Inc., 1955.

19. Hartlaub, G. F., *Der Genius im Kinde*, Breslau: Ferdinand Hirt, 1930.

20. Hoag, J., "Observational study of a kindergarten group using constructional material," unpublished doctoral dissertation, Berkeley: University of California, 1959.

21. Hurlock, E. B., "The spontaneous drawings of adolescents," *Journal of Genetic Psychology*, LXIII (1943), 141-156.

22. Hurlock, E. B. and J. L. Thomson, "Children's drawings: an experimental study of perception," *Child Development*, V (1934), 127-138.

23. Kellogg, R., *What Children Scribble and Why*, Palo Alto: National Press Publications, 1959.

24. Kerschensteiner, G., *Die Entwicklung der zeichnerischen Begabung*, Munich: Gerber, 1905.

25. Krötzsch, W., *Rhythmus und Form in der freien Kinderzeichnung*, Leipzig: Haase, 1917.

26. Lark-Horovitz, B., "Interlinkage of sensory memories in relation to training in drawing," *Journal of Genetic Psychology*, XLIX (1936), 69-89.

27. Lark-Horovitz, B., Unpublished work of "A visual memory experiment," carried out at the Cleveland Museum of Art, Cleveland, Ohio, 1941.

28. Lark-Horovitz, B. and J. Norton, "Children's art abilities: Developmental trends of art characteristics," *Child Development*, XXX (1959), 433-452.

29. Lombardo-Radice, G., I. "Il disegno infantile" (appunti d'una madre); II. "Documentazione," *L'Educazione Nazionale*, VII (1925), 1-21; 22-52.

30. Lukens, T., "A study of children's drawings in the early years," *Pedagogical Seminary*, IV (1896-97), 79-110.

31. Luquet, G.-H., "La narration graphique chez l'enfant," *Journal de Psychologie*, XXI (1924), 183-218.

32. Märtin, H., "Die plastische Darstellung der Menschengestalt beim jüngeren Schulkinde," *Zeitschrift für paedagogische Psychologie*, XXXIII (1932), 257-273.

33. Meumann, E., *Vorlesungen zur Einführung in die experimentelle Pädagogik*, 2nd ed., Leipzig: W. Engelmann, 1913, vol. 3.

34. Mühle, G., *Entwicklungspsychologie des zeichnerischen Gestaltens*, Grundlagen, Formen und Wege in der *Kinderzeichnung*, Munich: Ambrosius Barth, 1955.

35. Munro, T., B. Lark-Horovitz and E. N. Barnhart, "Children's art abilities: Studies at the Cleveland Museum of Art," *Journal of Experimental Education*, XI, No. 2 (1942), 97-155.

36. Oberlin, D. S., "Children who draw," *Delaware State Medical Journal*, X, No. 5, (1938), 111-115.

37. O'Shea, M. V., "Children's expression through drawing," *Proceedings of the National Education Association* (Asbury Park, N.J.) 1894, 1015-1023.

38. Osterrieth, P. A., "Le test de copie d'une figure complexe. Contribution à l'étude de la perception et de la mémoire," *Archives de Psychologie*, XXX, Nos. 119-120 (1945), 119-120; 205-253.

39. Piaget, J., "Perceptual and cognitive (or operational) structures in the development of space in the child," *Acta Psychologica*, XI (1955), 41-46.

40. Piaget, J. and B. Inhelder, *The Child's Conception of Space*, New York: Humanities Press, 1956.

41. Potpeschnigg, L., *Aus der Kindheit der bildenden Kunst*, Leipzig-Berlin: Seeman (Schriften für Erziehung und Unterricht), No. 2 (1912).

42. Prinzhorn, H., *Bildnerei der Geisteskranken*, Berlin: Springer, 1922.

43. Rey, A., "Epreuves de dessin, témoin du développement mental," *Archives de Psychologie*, XXXI, No. 124 (1946), 369-380.

44. Rouma, G., *Le Language Graphique de l'Enfant*, Brussels: Misch and Thron, 1913.

45. Ruttmann, W. J., "Bericht," 4. *Interntionaler Kongress für Kunstunterricht und angewandte Kunst*, Dresden, (1912).

46. Seeman, E., "Development of the pictorial aptitude in children," *Character and Personality*, II (1934), 209-221.

47. Sully, J., *Studies of Childhood*, New York: D. Appleton and Co., 1895.

48. Van der Horst, L., "Effect, expression and symbolic function in the drawings of children," in: *Feelings and Emotions: Mooseheart Symposium*, ed. by L. Reymert, New York: McGraw-Hill Book Co., 1950, 398-417.

49. Wulff, O., *Die Kunst des Kindes*, Stuttgart: Ferdinand Enke, 1927.

50. Wulff, O., "Kernfragen der Kinderkunst und des allgemeinen Kunstunterrichts der Schule," *Zeitschrift für Aesthetik und allgemeine Kunstwissenschaft*, XXVI, No. 1 (1932), 46-85.

CHAPTER TWO

Individual and Cultural Aspects

In his art activity, each child discovers anew what generations of children have discovered before him. He finds he can make marks, and he enjoys this outward expression of his inner urges. He sees a tree, the sun, a friendly bug, and tries to show them as he feels them. Later he observes the form and color of his world and tries to draw them as he sees them. Sun and sky, tree and bug, meet in the senses of boy and girl in every land. Their images move through the magic network of eye and ear, of body and brain, of heart and hand. The spontaneous art of children everywhere has certain distinctive and recognizable characteristics that spring from this natural flow of image, impulse and action. It also shows the imprint of the individual child, a kind of rudimentary personal style, from the earliest stages on.

Children's spontaneous art also describes in picture form the customs, daily living, plant and animal world of their surroundings. It draws attention to parallels between the child's and the adult's approach through visual means.

Figure 15. *Children of the Cameroon lowlands, on the coast of West Africa, draw animals (known in Western cultures only from visits to the zoo), such as the camel, much as an American child draws them.[44] Notice the cow and her calf.*

Figure 16. *Children of northern Liberia show important occupations, such as climbing coconut palms, and events in their society. For example, a mask-dancer on stilts (a member of a secret society) is drawn with a boy who must translate what "Mask" says. The boy carries a vessel of water in one hand and a wisp to sprinkle "Mask" and onlookers in the other hand.[8]*

CHILDREN'S ART IN DIFFERENT CULTURES

By the turn of the century, studies of child art had already been made in Europe and America. Since then, research has also been carried out in other parts of the world. Many studies by trained observers present evidence that the children of many Western nations draw in a similar manner and go through similar stages of development.[18] The child art of certain non-Western cultures[19] shows characteristics essentially the same as those of children's art from various countries in the Western world.[11]

Figure 17. *Drawing a "man" in Africa is the same as elsewhere in the world, but the customs of the European (left) are observed and distinguished from those of the native (right), who is shown here dressed in a loin cloth and playing ball.[8]*

Naturally, there are variations according to the outward manifestations of a way of life.[20] Differences in climate, landscape, animal and plant life are reflected in the drawings of children.[2] Differences of customs appear in children's art of various parts of the world.[1] Although the subject matter differs from culture to culture, the mode of representation itself reveals marked similarities of style regardless of where the child lives.

Figure 18. *The same objects were drawn by the same child with an interval of one year between drawing group A and group B.*[24] *Girl, age five (A), age six (B), 1934-1935, pencil.*

The course of drawing development is similar the world over. The familiar sequence occurs: scribble, primitive schema, fully developed schema with its characteristic details, and even the adolescent "plateau."[8]

Young children of very primitive populations, given the same materials for drawing, produce approximately the same kinds of drawings as do the children of the more highly developed regions of the world. This was recently confirmed by a study which concluded that "the African child [living in the many different parts of the African con-

tinent] passes through the same phases as the European child in his manner of representing the human body . . . racial features . . . are little accentuated . . . [and] distinction is more easily achieved by the kind of clothes."[3]

Children's art reflects the flow of life around them, including social changes and technological advances. As the horse gave way to the auto, the train to the airplane, these new elements in life were mirrored in children's drawings.[13] Electric light, the telephone, the mailman and the missionary are recorded by these naive historians. In addition, child art often makes note of not only the actual happening, but the attitude toward it. Just as an adult Yoruba woodcarver in Africa shows the missionary's umbrella, and makes the head of the British government officer disproportionately large under its sun-helmet, so children make social comments in their drawings.

INDIVIDUAL STYLE IN CHILDREN'S ART

Even in the earliest stages of development, a personal style can be observed in child art. This significant aspect is confirmed by Boutonier's extensive observations of a wide range of children. She finds that "all drawings carried out by the same child have the mark of his individual approach . . . whether the child draws a man, a house or a tree, the characteristics of the drawings remain the same."[5] Bried even claimed that a personal style can be observed at the scribble level.[6]

When children use the same subject for their pictures, and share much the same environment and level of development, their individual interpretations still differ. Although many of the same elements may be used in the pictures, their compositional arrangements will show a difference in the selection of details. One picture may barely indicate the shape of a person, another will be more definite, and a third may be enriched by a decorative treatment of details. Harris and many others since have found ample evidence that a child draws according to an individual pattern.[9] Unless taught otherwise, the child maintains an individual approach.

These individual variations in style arise from differences in temperament, emphasis or skill. Colors may be used hastily, especially if the nature of the medium is imperfectly understood or even disregarded, or the medium may be applied with care or even with special skill or insight into its na-

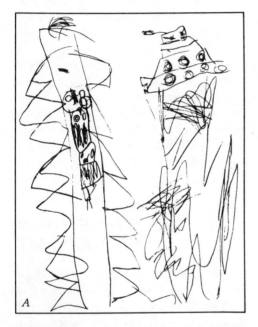

Figure 19. *Three spontaneous, pencil drawings done in one year reveal an individual manner of drawing. A. The boy is climbing a pine tree, followed by his younger brother. On the right is the family's summer cabin. The zig-zag scribble indicates running before climbing the tree. B. At the left is the town house in which the boy lives. He (largest face), his brother, and their cat (tail sticking out to left) peer through an upper window. Below, someone is coming through the door (he counted fingers and made a knob for the thumb). On the right, a tree and S-curve indicate a street and small square. Below the tree,* the house was "not right" and, therefore, scribbled over. C. A year later than picture A, the boy is back at the mountain cabin. He shows a treehouse containing himself, his brother, two visiting boys, and two visiting girls. Below the tree house, grandmother sits on a garden chair underneath a pine tree and reads a book. Very large pine cones are on the ground, while one falls from the tree. To the right is the cabin. Note the box-like treehouse and cabin, also the ladder leading to the treehouse.[19] Boy, age five, five-and-a-half, and six, 1962, 1963.

2. *GRANNY AND THE OLD HOUSE. True local colors. Schema, opaque paint, spontaneous. Girl, age 10, 1963.*[40]

ture. There are differences among children regarding the extent to which they seek to express their intense feelings through color or line, applying a pale or a saturated blue for the sky, a weak and hesitant line or a decisive one, or in the attention they give to proportion, or the emphasis they place on disproportion.

The universal sequence of development in art expression so clearly seen in children everywhere, can be likened to the general aspects of their physical growth. All chil-

Figure 20. *PEDDLERS. A. Turkish scarf peddler. The scarves flutter in the breeze and display their patterns and decor. B. The fruit and vegetable hawker is decorative because of the schematic repetition of her various wares. Both are done in tempera.*[19] *A. Boy, age ten, Austria, 1920's. B. Girl, age nine, Austria, 1925.*

dren go through it, yet all children differ in the manner in which it happens. The development of visual expression is part of the general pattern of growing up.

The art of children reflects their state of mind and their emotions. The success of the individual child in picturing his observations and in interpreting them relates to his development of skills and to his insight into the medium, and the extent to which he is able to give form to his inner vision.

Some investigators maintain that it is dif-

ficult to talk of levels of skill in the evolution of drawing, that the most important transformation seems to occur when "the child begins to be interested in his power over things [inanimate] and is drawn toward representing space in which his actions occur . . . [when] he becomes conscious of the world in which he is placed."[15]

In modeling, widely done in clay, mud, or other materials, it has been observed that characteristics of children's drawings do apply to modeling also, but relatively few experiments have been conducted on children's work in the plastic arts. The reason is rather obvious. Drawings and paintings can be studied at another time and in another place. Modeled pieces cannot be so readily stored—they must be treated and preserved if they are to be protected from shrinking or crumbling. They can be photographed, but three-dimensional objects must be shown from all sides to be fully interpreted. Lack of storage space and problems posed by time-consuming and costly photographic records have limited experimentation and the accumulation of research data in this area.

For a long time child art in America and other countries has been considered as a means of self-development and self-expression, closely related to the development of personality. Therefore, individual differences were, and still are, favorably received and encouraged.

In contrast, the Soviet Union seemed to consider "drawing . . . a means of acquiring knowledge, a translation as clear and profound as possible . . . of a world that is based on its historic content, and where it is agreed that perception of an objectively seen reality" is the main concern. "Drawing [in the U.S.S.R.] means drawing 'for others', and that is what a child must learn from its earliest years."[4]

CHILD ART AND ADULT ART

Both the child and the adult artist, through art, try to gain insight into the world and the self. The adult artist, through his art, tries to come to terms with the world around him, with his own feelings and convictions. Both child and adult use personifications to express themselves. The child gives to his objects a life of their own, endows them with, and at times subjects them to his own moral judgment. "The chair is naughty, the table is a good sort (well behaved), the ball runs away from me." These are the child's expressions. But "the woods are silent, the sun is smiling, the waves are whispering—so speaks the poet. The poet chooses carefully among his personifications, the child personifies everything indiscriminately."[21] Hence the adult often takes for intentional art what the child does or says or draws simply as an expression of his actual belief and interpretation regarding inanimate objects. Like the artist, the child feels the urge to visualize through picturing. His ultimate objective is to clarify, to order a world that must seem disturbingly chaotic. He wants to find his own place in it.

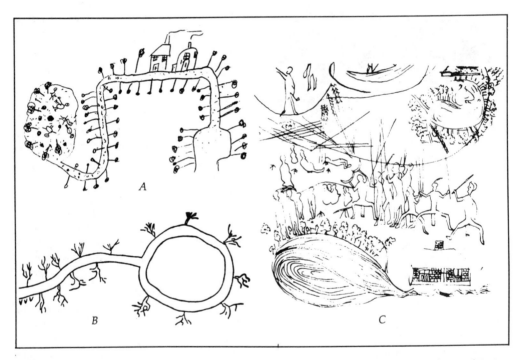

Figure 21. *The child tends to clarify his space concept by using a bird's-eye view. For example, a body of water or piece of ground is represented as a bird's-eye view, but is surrounded by profile trees as in A. Girl, age nine, ca 1900. Primitive Australian tribes show similar ways of dealing with this particular space problem, as in B. Here, the arrangement of profile view trees extending outward from the road is important because of the change in vantage point which is oriented toward the center. In a more complex manner, as in C, the flow of water has been illustrated (children also do this). The primitive Australian also represents objects differently than children do: note the representation of a house in C.*

Figure 22. *The adult of a primitive tribe is not forced to draw in a schematic style, but does so, apparently in adherence to custom or ritual, as can be seen in this cave painting by Bushmen in South Africa. They represent themselves in a highly stylized, schematic, and repetitive manner; yet, when they turn to the colonist of the Western world (right: couple, above: their houses), they can adopt a true-to-appearance representation.*[1]

Very gifted children have qualities that give their creations artistic power up to a point, but most children and most adults give form to their impressions, unable to reach an aesthetic level. "It cannot be pointed out often enough that the child does not create 'works of art' . . . but that he gives form to his impressions in a manner different from the artist and under different assumptions."[17]

Most adults have acquired only a limited facility for realistic representation. Their work, too, falls far short in aesthetic quality. The average adult has remained at the schematic stage of the child without the child's sincerity and immediacy of expression. A remarkable example to the contrary is Grandma Moses whose pictures are quite similar and sometimes almost identical to some schematic, fully developed compositions of older children.

Pictures in one study of adults of varied occupations and ages involving a variety of objects to draw (see Figures 13, 14, 125 and 126) showed "an overwhelming number of qualities of the schematic . . . stage, that is the drawings compare with the drawings of untrained children chiefly between the ages six and ten."[12] A more recent paper on this subject shows that the tendency toward schematic representation does not depend on age or ability, and that among the twenty-four adults observed, only two tried a "pictorial" approach in the expected adult manner, while the others tended toward a schematic representation.[16]

Certain aspects of child art show some similarity to the art of primitive tribes and to that of earlier art periods in history. For instance, certain characteristics are shared by the Western child and the adults of a contemporary primitive tribe.[10] It has been shown that primitive art and child art share certain parallels in their representation of the invisible. "The drawing [of the primitive] contains elements that cannot be seen but which, in the judgment of the artist, are indispensible. Inversely, he neglects elements of the model that his eye sees but which are of no interest for the [primitive] artist." Both the child and the primitive do not wish "to represent the actual object . . . but its essence."[14]

The child, in his art, is the center; everything revolves around him and must be brought into harmony with his self. His approach may be likened to a Ptolemaic system of the world. The adult artist's approach is more comparable to a Copernican concept, since he has already become a member of his group and culture. He expresses himself in complex terms due to his relationship to his own past, and the past and the present of his fellow men.

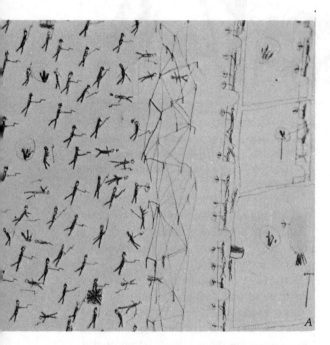

A

B

Figure 23. *The space representation that conceives of the bottom of the picture as being "close" and the top as being "distant," the adoption of man-schema, repeated innumerable times, as well as the simplified representation of movement by directionality of limbs (arms, spread of legs in running), and the division of space by a vertical axis to separate the groups in action are all striking resemblances between the "primitive's" and the child's pictorial expression. A. TRENCH-WAR[10] German boy, age ten. B. Bushmen battle cattle rustlers. The striking difference between this drawing and A is the realism of the animals.[1]*

CHAPTER TWO: TEXT REFERENCES

1. Anastasi, A. and J. Foley, Jr., "An analysis of spontaneous drawings by children in different cultures," *Journal of Applied Psychology*, XX (1936), 689-726.
2. Appia, B., "La représentation humaine dans les dessins d'enfants noirs," *Bulletin de l'Institut Français d'Afrique noire*, I (1939), 405-411.
3. Bardet, C., Moreigne, F. and J. Sénécal, "Application du test de Goodenough à des écoliers Africains de sept à quatorze ans, *Enfance*, XIII, No. 2 (1960), 199-208.
4. Baumstein-Heissler, N., "A propos du dessin: quelques opinions et traveaux soviétiques," *Enfance*, VIII, No. 4 (1955), 377-399.
5. Boutonier, J., *Les Dessins des Enfants*, Paris: Editions du Scarabée, 1953.
6. Bried, C., "Le dessin de l'enfant," Premières représentations humaines, *Enfance*, III, Nos. 3 and 4 (1950), 256-275.
7. Cižek, F., "Die Organisation und die kunstpaedagogischen Probleme des Jugendkurses," Spezialvortrag, *4. Internationaler Kongress für Kunstunterricht, Zeichnen und angewandte Kunst*, Hauptbericht (1912), Dresden, 466-476.
8. Germann, P., "Zeichnungen von Kindern und Jugendlichen aus dem Waldlande von Nord-Liberia," *Ethnologische Studien*, I (1929), 75-95.
9. Harris, D. B., "Intra-individual versus inter-individual consistency in children's drawings of a man," *American Psychologist*, V, No. 7 (1950), 293-294.
10. Kretzschmar, J., "Kinderkunst und Urzeitkunst," *Zeitschrift für paedagogische Psychologie*, XI, No. 1 (1910), 354-366.
11. Kretzschmar, J., "Die Kinderkunst bei den Völkern höherer und niederer Kultur," *Archiv für Paedagogik* (1913), 36-61.
12. Lark-Horovitz, B., "Interlinkage of sensory memories in relation to training in drawing," *Journal of Genetic Psychology*, XLIX (1936), 69-89.
13. Lark-Horovitz, B., "On learning abilities of children as recorded in a drawing experiment. I. Subject matter, II. Aesthetic and representational qualities," *Journal of Experimental Education*, IX, No. 4 (1941), 332-360.
14. Luquet, G. H., "Le réalism intellectuel dans l'art primitif, I. Figuration de l'invisible; II. Le rendu du visible, *Journal de Psychologie*, XXIV (1927), 765-797; 888-927.
15. Malrieu, Ph., "Observations sur quelques dessins libres chez l'enfant," *Journal de Psychologie normale et pathologique*, XLIII (1950), 239-244.
16. Maugé, G., "Représentation du movement et schématisation," *Journal de Psychologie normale et pathologique*, LII, No. 2 (1955), 243-252.
17. Mühle, G., *Entwicklungspsychologie des zeicherischen Gestaltens*. Grundlagen, Formen und Wege in der Kinderzeichung, Munich: Ambrosius Barth, 1955.
18. Papavassiliou, I., "Notes sur l'application du Test du bonhomme en Grèce," *Zeitschrift für Kinderpsychiatrie*, XVI (1950), 129-133; XVIII (1951), 65-87.
19. Probst, M., "Les dessins des enfants Kabyles," *Archives de Psychologie*, VI (1907), 131-140.
20. Seeman, E., "Development of the pictorial aptitude in children," *Character and Personality*, II (1934), 209-221.
21. Tezner, O., "Das Wunderkindphänomen in der Entwicklung des normalen Kindes," *Zeitschrift für Kinderpsychiatrie*, XVIII (1951), 257-266.

CHAPTER THREE

Subjects and Their Representation in Children's Art

In order to provide a background of information against which to evaluate the stage of development and performance of any particular child, we present at this point a discussion of more detailed findings on the progressive development of art expression in children generally. Familiarity with these materials will prepare the parent, teacher or other adult working with children.

If, for instance, one finds an unusually huge head, a curiously assembled body, or horses and turtles with smiling human faces in the drawings of six- to nine-year-olds, one should not be at all disturbed. And if an enormous variety of curious details and elaborations appear on some seemingly "unworthy" subject, this merely indicates a normal phase for a surprising number of children. Nor should the teacher who is hopefully guiding twelve- and thirteen-year-olds toward true-to-appearance representation be alarmed if a large number of her students fall short of the level of achievement for which she had hoped. She will see that this is typical not only of a large number of this age group but also of their parents.

Children are often influenced by the circumstances under which they make their drawings. Because of this, investigators have classified children's drawings into four distinct categories: *spontaneous* drawings,

Figure 24. *THE COUNTRY. A horizontal, schematic composition with several ground-lines to indicate the foreground, middle grounds, and distance. Notice the proportions of the man and house, the haystacks and birds behind the fence, the large sun, and the horizontal string of telephone poles.[40] Boy, age six, 1963, spontaneous pencil drawing.*

made on their own initiative as a play activity; *free* or *voluntary* drawings, made on request but with the children choosing their own subject; *directed* pictures for which the topic is proposed; *copied* or *to-be-completed drawings.*[8, 26]

Of these four types, spontaneous and free drawings are the most significant for understanding children's interest in drawing. It is important to distinguish between the *spontaneous drawing* where the initiative comes from the children, independent of adult supervision, and *free* drawing where the subject is also of their own choice, but where the activity is initiated by an adult and where specific materials are usually supplied.

SUBJECT MATTER: WHAT CHILDREN DRAW

An investigation of the 1890's dealt with the content of voluntary drawings by five- to seventeen-year-olds.[26] It was found that

humans, animals, and plants were the subjects most frequently selected for drawing up to age ten (Table II). Houses, the child's habitat and his intimate world, were also important subjects, although they ranked second to humans. In another investigation made in the early 1900's, houses, or houses in their gardens, ranked highest as the chief subject; next came animals and then people. After eleven, drawings of separate objects dominated.[18]

A review of the free subject choice of young children (kindergarten, first and second grades)[28] found humans to be the most frequently chosen, followed by houses and plants. However, a later analysis of drawings by the same children showed that drawings of nature ranked first in percentages, this trend increasing with age, while humans came next in decreasing percentages, and buildings ranked third increasing with age. An investigator in the 1930's studied a small group in grades one to four over a three-year period. From this longitudinal study he named the objects most often represented in the following order: (1) man, (2) house, and train, (3) airplane, and carriage, (4) boats, (5) automobiles, and (6) animals and plants.[27]

Recreation, games, and amusement have

Figure 25. *The fair is described entirely schematically by representing many people, objects, and animals.[42] Girl, age six, spontaneous pencil drawing.*

become popular subjects with the increase of leisure and prosperity, especially in the United States. Children's drawings reflect these interests, and also frequently show outdoor life, camping and playground activities. (see Figure 41)

Anastasi and Foley studied a collection of drawings and paintings by six- to twelve-year-old children from forty-one countries. These drawings revealed differences of choice in subject matter. The subjects chiefly selected depict much the same activities and occupations of everyday life: people, animals, plants, etc. However, the prominence given to certain objects differs according to the country. For example, American Indian children, as well as children of such countries as Greece, Brazil, Chile, favor outdoor settings in their drawings. Children of Denmark and Japan are more interested in interiors. Different animals may be more favored in one country than in another: the kangaroo in Australia, the camel in Africa, the tapir in South America. The kind of occupational activities depicted may vary according to how common and how important a particular occu-

Figure 27. *AT THE RACES. Racers are shown as they line up. The schematic space arrangement, though confusingly complex, is shown from various vantage points.[40] Boy, age seven, 1963, spontaneous pencil drawing.*

Figure 28. *PLAYLAND. A schematic presentation from different angles: bird's-eye view with the ferris wheel in profile.[40] Girl, age eight, 1963, spontaneous pencil drawing.*

pation is in a given nation—for example, the climbing of palms to pick coconuts or the use of camels for transportation. Drawings with imaginative content tend to reflect the religion, mythology, fables, or fairy tales of a particular country.[2] Tradition also influences subject matter in a given cultural group.[3]

It has been shown that younger children draw people most frequently but seldom alone. They draw them with other objects, with farm animals, pets or toys, in a setting

Figure 26. *THE CIRCUS. One of the rare treats all children especially enjoy and carefully observe is a circus. In this spontaneous, pencil drawing, the crowd of children, the parking lot for cars, and the elaborate entrance are shown with great clarity in a unique schematic space concept.[40] Boy, age eight, 1963.*

Ages	5-7	8-9	11-13	14-17
Men & Women	22	20	10	4
Houses	16	15	12	3½
Animals	11½	10½	9	8
Still life except flowers	20	24	31	27
Conventional design	3	6	5	2½
Transportation mechan. & invent. ...	4	6½	10	7
Ornament	1½	1	4	6½
Plant life	17	15	15	9½
Miscellaneous	5	1	1	—

Table II

Objects in Drawings (in percentages)

Adapted from Maitland, "What children draw to please themselves," 1895[26] (1,570 children).

of street, landscape, farm or playground. A knowledge of children's natural preferences may be helpful in teaching. For example, humans in their surroundings (Table III[23, 29]) is a subject children chose widely when asked to draw. (Similarly, it is noticeable that children draw the *entire* person at younger age levels within their surroundings, for example, in a landscape.) As these children grow older and find that schematic representation becomes less and less satisfactory, they find the human figure too difficult to draw. Simultaneously, their interest in faces and facial expression becomes stronger, and therefore they tend to confine themselves to drawing only the heads, omitting the rest of the body altogether (Table III).

Maitland's early study[26] analyzes a picture from the standpoint of its whole content—its theme or story, as distinguished from the single items included in it. Table IV shows her findings. Ballard's early study, (Table V[4]) on the other hand, classified picture content in such "items" as humans, animals, birds and insects, fishes, houses, and ships. This study concluded that boys and girls from

Ages (Total number: 864 children)	6	7	8	9	10	11	12	13	14
Figures by themselves	2	3	8	13	16	16	13	12	11
Heads by themselves	—	—	1	2	4	8	13	18	23
Animals only	1	3	3	4	4	3	3	3	4
Humans in Surroundings	55	47	33	23	15	9	8	3	2
Animals in Surroundings	—	6	10	5	4	3	3	4	4
Transportation by itself	1	4	5	9	13	18	20	21	16
Transportation in Surrounding	2	4	8	10	10	6	4	3	3
Still life (flowers, fruit, etc.)	2	3	4	7	10	14	13	12	12
Miscellaneous	—	—	—	1	1	—	1	2	4
Landscape by itself	37	30	28	26	23	23	22	22	21
Humans with or without Surroundings	57	50	42	38	35	33	34	33	36

Table III

Subject Matter (in percentages)

Adapted from the Cleveland Studies (1939).[23, 29] Subject: "Draw a picture of what you like best to draw."

the ages of three to fifteen like to draw living things. As they grow older, this interest, along with their interest in houses, decreases. But plant life remains a great favorite with girls, even with increasing age, while ships are featured more prominently in the pictures of boys, especially those between the ages of seven and eleven.[4]

Ages	5-7	8-9	11-13	14-17
Picture Stories	32	33	6	1
Landscapes	3	3	3	1
Objects by themselves	55	62	91	98
Miscellaneous	10	2	—	

Table IV
Subject Matter (in percentages)

Adapted from Maitland, "What children draw to please themselves," 1895.

There is little material on the free subject choices of adolescents. According to the existing evidence, however, their spontaneous drawings reflect interests different from those of young children.[17]

As far as modeling is concerned, children with no experience most often select objects of daily use, to a lesser degree humans and sometimes animals, as could also be seen in a quite recent child art exhibit of the Soviet Union. They work on single objects unless they are assigned a topic that calls for the groupings of several items.[2]

REPRESENTATION OF SINGLE OBJECTS

In order to examine the characteristics of children's art at various stages, the nature of the changes that occur with age, and the differences in the rate of development of particular characteristics, it will be useful to trace the development of the representation of single objects in detail.

Sex (B G)	B G	B G	B G	B G	B G	B G	B G	B G	B G	B G
Ages	4– 3	5	6	7	8	9	10	11	12	13–15
Humans	24 26	14 22	13 20	9 12	8 7	7 6	10 8	11 8	13 10	11 8
Animals	7 10	4 4	4 4	4 2	5 2	3 3	4 2	5 3	5 2	6 4
Birds, Insects	3 2	4 4	4 4	3 4	5 5	3 6	3 6	4 6	5 6	3 6
Fishes	1 1	1 1	1 1	2 1	2 2	3 2	3 2	2 2	3 2	2 2
Plant Life	7 14	13 22	12 27	14 37	15 37	16 41	15 40	13 40	13 38	15 39
Ships	10 5	19 4	20 10	27 10	27 9	26 7	24 6	18 4	13 5	10 3
Houses	11 13	15 16	12 18	13 20	14 23	12 18	12 16	12 15	12 12	11 8
Weapons, Instruments	9 4	4 3	4 1	2 1	2 2	3 1	4 2	6 1	4 1	5 1
Vehicles	11 2	17 4	22 5	15 2	9 1	9 1	7 1	6 1	6 1	6 1
Landscapes	— —	— —	— —	2 1	1 1	2 1	1 1	3 1	4 1	4 2
Miscellaneous	18 24	10 14	8 10	9 9	13 12	16 14	17 16	20 17	22 21	27 16

Table V
Subject Matter (in percentages)

Adapted from Ballard, "What London children like to draw," 1912 (nearly 20,000 children included in the study).[4]

Living Creatures

The evolution from scribble to schema followed by progression toward the true-to-appearance aspect can be readily observed in the representation of living things, especially humans, the foremost objects of interest (Table VI[19]).

Humans

Sometime during the scribble stage, the lines that once seemed so meaningless become a closed shape. It is at this point that one can observe the emergence of a primitive schema. Once the emerging schema develops, it has a number of characteristic details. The human being is drawn with a head that has a nose, a mouth, eyes, and ears (and sometimes other details[30])(Table VII[23]); and a body with a neck, chest, waist, legs, and feet as well as arms and hands. Each one of these parts is contoured as a shape by itself and fitted to another part.

The primitive schema often is based on a roundish shape to stand for a person. Features may be indicated. Lines attached directly to the head may be interpreted as legs. The primitive schema is gradually developed into the full schema, often carrying with it individual differences found in earlier work. For example, one can follow the development of the "head-man" schema to the ripened schematic stage and observe that the head continues to be oversized although to a lesser degree. On the other hand, the "leg-man" (with long, outsized legs and feet and a small head) retains, in the mature schema, some of the specific disproportion favored at an earlier stage of development.

The parts that make up the schematic representation of man are assembled by an additive process. The child adds, one by one, all the parts of the human figure that he deems necessary for his purpose, as he thinks of them. To the head, with all its details, is joined the body, sometimes but not always by a neck and chest, then come the legs and feet. A line may indicate the waist. Arms, eventually joined to the shoulders, were earlier joined at the chin or the ears, or the neck, and once in a while to the waist. Hands and feet are often omitted. When hands are pictured, they may assume the shape of dumplings, or look like a spray of three to seven short, fanlike strokes, similar to birds' feet. There seems to be a sequential order in which the various parts of a person appear in the drawings of children of average or superior intelligence.[1]

The human shape remains the same, regardless of the child artist's age or sex. Certain distinguishing attributes are added. Tie, belt, trousers, beard, pipe, or cigar for the man; hairdo, purse, jewelry, long eyelashes, high heels, skirt, or femininely shaped pants for the woman. Children may be drawn smaller than adults.

Every human figure is first represented

	Boys				Girls				
Grade	Schema	Mixed	True-to-Appearance	In the Round	Schema	Mixed	True-to-Appearance	In the Round	Age Level
1	98	2			98	2			6
2	90	10			98	2			7
3	78	21	1		95	5			8
4	59	36	5		87	11	2		9
5	48	46	6		79	19	2		10
6	16	59	18	7	66	31	3		11
7	7	52	28	13	52	38	7	3	12
8	3	44	32	21	57	35	8		13

Table VI

Representational Development of Humans: Father, Mother, and Child (in percentages)

Adapted from Kerschensteiner.[19]

Figure 29. *"Headmen," "legman," and other man schemata.*[30] *Boys, girls, ages six to eight.*

Figure 30. *Whatever the generation, the human schema consists of parts which the child has considered and then put together. A. Girl, age four, 1933,*[19] *papercut. B. Girl, age six, 1936.*[30] *C. Girl, age three, 1963.*

from a front view (Table VII[29]) which shows all the facial features in their most characteristic aspect. The head is roundish with dots or circles for eyes, line or double line for nose, and a wide horizontal line for the mouth, often with a grating for teeth. The schema of the human face, and its development, has a logic of structure and growth which is as clear in drawings from the last century as in those of the present time, and in this part of the world as in another.

Figure 31. *A FRIEND. Even when using different techniques, the human schema remains the same. Note the size of the head as compared to the chest, arms, and hands.*[13] *Boy, age seven, Japan, 1964, woodblock.*

	View of Figure and Face					Head						Figure							
Ages	Front	Back	Mixed Profile	Profile	Three-Fourth Turn	Hair	Eyebrows	Eye details	Ears	Nose detail	Chin	Neck	Shoulders	Waist	Chest	Hands	Fingers	Exactly 5 Fingers	Shoes or Toes
6	71	—	1	25	3	25	10	—	5	18	2	42	2	2	1	40	15	5	2
7	58	—	1	39	2	32	12	—	7	20	6	45	2	2	1	50	15	5	2
8	46	1	1	51	1	40	15	—	10	25	12	49	4	3	2	60	15	5	3
9	35	1	3	60	1	52	18	—	15	25	22	55	8	10	4	66	15	5	10
10	25	2	6	66	1	65	22	—	22	25	32	68	12	15	6	70	16	5	15
11	24	3	4	68	1	68	25	1	28	24	36	75	18	20	9	72	18	6	20
12	25	1	2	69	1	70	30	1	34	20	40	77	22	22	12	74	20	7	22
13	34	—	2	63	1	70	33	1	40	20	44	80	28	24	16	72	22	8	24
14	42	—	3	54	1	58	35	1	45	18	46	84	35	24	18	70	25	8	24
15	56		5	38	1	45	30	1	48	8	50	90	40	12	6	50	28	8	12

Table VII

Details of the Human Schema (in percentages)

Adapted from the Cleveland Studies, "Draw a picture of a man."[29]

The shape of the body tends to be oval, the neck a small circle or square wedged between head and body. Legs are made by single, later by double, lines and are similar to pieces of tubing. They hang straight down from the oval of the body with short tubes for feet. Arms are tubes, also, and thrust outward or hang limp on each side of the body unless holding something or demonstrating action. The hand is leaf-like with two to five more indentations.

In the front view presentation, the nose is the only feature that is not seen in its most characteristic aspect. Children observe this and often draw it by placing a side-view nose on the front-view face. The Italian art scholar, Corrado Ricci, who was a pioneer in interpreting people in children's drawings, tells that he himself became aware of them in the 1880's, while on his way to the university. He had to take shelter under the portico leading to the "Meloncallo" and noticed a number of uninhibited drawings, both natural and naughty. The lowest row was charming because it showed the expression of the youngest artists. And thus he began to study children's art. In regard to the double noses he explained: "After drawing a face with its nose in profile and eyes frontwise [children] stop to think and then add a second nose. This supernumerary nose is the result of their primitive logic . . . which reigns in all child art."[31] Children's convictions are deepseated, and although they may change their drawings in response to

Figure 32. *Schematic transparencies in which the child has shown as much as possible of what is important to him.*[33] *Child, ages five to six, Italy, 1885.*

Figure 33. *Sometimes the schema cannot be overcome and may be used throughout life.*[22] *Girl, age fifteen, crayon.*

adult suggestions, it offends their sense of what is right. Pipes and other attributes of man, seen more characteristically in profile, are drawn that way, so that for a time, a combination of front and side views prevails in children's drawings. "From then on there appears to be a hierarchy of motivations [for secondary aspects of the profile] and a unity of views must be constantly assumed to be part of the elaboration of the graphic theme."[14] Even adults of superior intelligence and often college training sometimes also mix up these views, apparently for similar reasons.[20]

Modeling the human figure, children shape it at first as a smaller (spherical) and a larger (long and cylindical) lump of clay which is set upright. Then details are worked out, such as roller-like arms, spread horizontally away from the trunk, then later down-

ward, flattened to the body. Still later the arms are bent forward or backward. Throughout, there is a symmetrical arrangement. Since legs in standing position pose technical problems, a sitting or reclining position is favored because these provide support for the figure.[7]

In the course of time children proceed to develop a full schematic profile in drawings. They do so with great economy of means. The outline of the body remains unchanged; it is still a near-round or oval. Arms and legs remain tubular, but are fastened to one side or extended in the direction toward which the profile looks, with the feet pointing in the same direction. The face is partly re-shaped to fit the profile, with the exception of the eye which usually retains the front aspect, Egyptian style. Certain details contribute to the profile's characterization, such

Figure 34. *Drawing done during the mixed state.*[30] *Girl, age nine.*

as the knot and strings of an apron on the right or left side of the waist. Most profiles face to the left as do most profile portraits made by adults through the ages, a fact that can be explained by the righthandedness of most people.

Once full maturity of the human schema has been reached, the child can produce almost automatically. For some children, development stops at this point. An avenue toward further development must be found if progress is to be made; otherwise the child will search for more satisfactory means of expression and may abandon drawing altogether.

Those children who continue their development, either on their own or with help, move through a mixed phase toward the true-to-appearance stage in their representation of humans. Representation of the head now predominates. This reflects a new interest in facial expression and an attempt to avoid the difficulties posed by trying to

Figure 35. *Portrait made in mixed stage.*[30] *Boy, age twelve.*

Figure 36. *The head and figure are true-to-appearance and individualized.*[30] *Girl, age fourteen.*

Figure 37. *True-to-appearance figures.*[30] *Girl, age fourteen.*

show the entire human figure. Correct proportion, reality of contour, and true appearance details are achieved up to a point, but the result is stiff, almost rigid.

Portraits by adolescents favor the "ideal" type, the athletic male or the alluring female. Continued repetition of the drawing with little variation makes it almost automatic. Boys and girls are almost able to produce such heads with their eyes closed, as if writing a number or word. Creative teaching at this stage will help the child expand and vary his pictures. Without such perceptive assistance, his further growth in visual expression may be blocked.

At this period the figures continue to have a two-dimensional look, like cardboard cutouts—in spite of attempts at true-to-appearance effects. Although the child may try to foreshorten arms and legs, especially if he wants to show movement or a three-fourth turn of the figure, the results mostly fall short of success and must be taken as an announcement of intention.

Animals

Animal figures, like human figures, are a frequent subject of children's art. The animal schema is developed as if it were human. Head and body have the lumpy roundishness and oval shapes of humans, but instead of being built up vertically, they are laid out horizontally. The animal's long legs resemble the tubular shapes or long single lines used for the legs of the human figure. The faces of animals are also shaped at first like the faces of humans. The schema developed by a given child is used almost unchanged for either human or animal faces, modified by such details as cats' whiskers or rabbits' pointed ears.

Since the profile view of the body is the most characteristic for an animal, the schema starts as a profile, although a front

Figure 38. *TWO WORKMEN. True-to-appearance portraits done by a talented child. Note the facial expressions.*[16] *Boy, age fifteen, German, ca 1900, pencil.*

Figure 39. *True-to-appearance "cliché" drawing of the ideal glamorous woman.*[30] *Girl, age nine.*

view is sometimes maintained for the face of horses, cats, and diverse other creatures. Some children show more concern for the characteristics of the animal body than for the human body. This may be due to the constantly observed motion of the animal body which therefore becomes as important as the animal's face. The child appears to focus on what is essential to him, a striking parallel to some primitive art in which the primitive artist "wishes to render from the real object not its aspect but its essence . . . Consequently, he chooses the exemplary aspect" (such as bird's-eye view of a turtle, profile view of quadrupeds and birds, or the front view of man). Just as the schematic rider drawn by the child often perches above the horse, so does the horseman drawn by the primitive tribesman.[25]

Identifying attributes of mammals, birds, or fish are selected and represented with amazing accuracy. Often the child hits upon the one characteristic above all that marks the animal unmistakably for what it is intended to be. For example, the nose of the dog or the whiskers of the cat will serve to distinguish the one from the other; or the child will make the bill of a duck so obviously flat and ducklike that it can be recognized instantly and thus distinguished from

Figure 40. *Various schemata of horses drawn during a period of developing schema.*[30] *Boys and girls, ages six to eight.*

Figure 41. *ZOO. Except for their tails, the monkeys have the same appearance as the visiting children in the schematic drawing.*[40] *Girl, age eight, spontaneous pencil drawing.*

Figure 42. *SIAMESE CAT WITH KITTENS.*[40] *Boy, age five, 1962, spontaneous drawing.*

Figure 43. *MY DOG AND NINE PUPPIES. Notice the similarity of representation of the cat and her kittens (Figure 42), and the dog and her puppies.*[40] *Boy, age eight, 1963, spontaneous pencil drawing.*

other birds, even when the body—and feet and tail—is just "bird." (Table VIII[19])

The animal schema follows the same developmental pattern as the human schema and sometimes results in such creatures as a human-faced bird, cat, butterfly or even turtle or bug.[13] However, if a new and strange animal is presented, the child may regress to an earlier phase. This was shown in an experiment using an unusual animal, a polar bear. In comparing the results with the children's other drawings, the investigator observed a retarding effect. There was a marked tendency toward a lower developmental status in the drawing of the unfamiliar subject.[22] (Graph I)

Many children who have reached the true-to-appearance stage in representing

				in Percent.					
	Boys				Girls				
Grade	Just "Animal"	Schema, but "horselike"	Mixed	True-to-Appearance	Just "Animal"	Schema, but "horselike"	Mixed	True-to-Appearance	Age level
1	89	9	2		98	2			6
2	66	31	2	1	95	5			7
3	57	39	3	1	86	14			8
4	45	43	10	2	73	25	2		9
5	31	56	11	2	70	30			10
6	32	56	12		62	37	1		11
7	19	43	28	9	57	35	7	1	12
8	12	36	35	17	67	33			13

Table VIII

Representational Development of Animals: The Horse

Adapted from Kerschensteiner.[19] At this time, horses pulled streetcars and carriages.

Figure 44. *ELEPHANT. Brush outline of the trunk (left to top), and an indication on the back of the animal. The tusk comes out of the trunk, horizontally to left edge of paper. Smears indicate the body. "He has no head, he has just a long trumpet to hide his head in, and that's all he needs." During a short period, the same child made many remarkably realistic elephant heads by kneading candle wax in warm water to model them.*[19] *Boy, age two years and two months, 1933, spontaneous brush drawing.*

humans will not necessarily draw animals in an equally advanced way. This may be due to lack of interest and consequent lack of observation, or it may be just a lack of

practice and confidence. Gifted children may handle people and animals with equal skill.

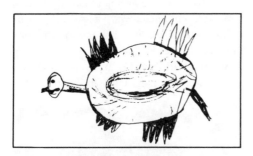

Figure 45. *Spontaneous pencil drawing of a land turtle.*[40] *Girl, age four.*

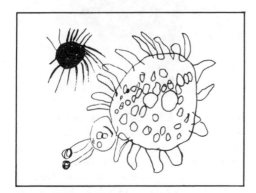

Figure 46. *Spontaneous pencil drawing of a mud turtle.*[40] *Girl, age five.*

Figure 48. *Mixed horse schemata. The "horse" characteristics are clearly recognizable.*[30] *A. Boy, age eight. B. Boy, age thirteen.*

Figure 47. *LADYBUG. Compare the similarity of shape and details with Figures 45 and 46 which are turtles. All three drawings have "faces."*[38] *Girl, age three, 1965, spontaneous pencil drawing.*

Figure 49. *True-to-appearance horse and rider.*[30] *Boy, age twelve.*

Figure 50. *Cow. A true-to-appearance wood-block by a highly talented child shows individual style.*[13] *Girl, age twelve, Japan, 1964.*

Plants

Trees and flowers are extensively represented in children's spontaneous drawings and are introduced frequently in drawings in which humans and animals are central. There is a distinctive development in the schemata of trees and flowers. In fact, the tree schema is of particular help in understanding the child's artistic logic, in that it provides clues to the interpretation of his depiction of directionality and disproportion, and of his portrayal of the parts of an object that are actually invisible.

Most children show trees with their roots, apparently because they know that these exist even though hidden. The visible part of the tree is developed into two kinds of schemata—the "morphological" tree schema and the "contour-appearance" tree schema. The morphologically inspired tree, as pointed out by the word "morphological," depicts the tree's structure and shows the child's awareness of roots, a trunk, branches, twigs, leaves, blossoms and fruit. All of these are clearly shown, whether visible or not. The contour-appearance tree displays the trunk and balloon-like or triangular outline for the top. Only occasionally are roots shown in this type of drawing.

The child, in his tree presentation, also reveals his endeavor to clarify directionality. The tree, as an entity, has an upward vertical direction, although the branches spread horizontally. At first only these two directions are sharply differentiated. Children's drawings do not show what exists in nature but the child's mental formulation and interpretation of it. The sharp contrast in direction, characteristic of early schemata, maintained rather rigidly at first, undergoes modification as the tree schema proceeds to develop. Wider differentiation of direction leads to a coherent concept of the whole.[9]

The younger child frequently omits the top of the tree entirely, finding the vertical thrust of the trunk an adequate symbol. This interesting phenomenon might also be explained by the child's lack of experience

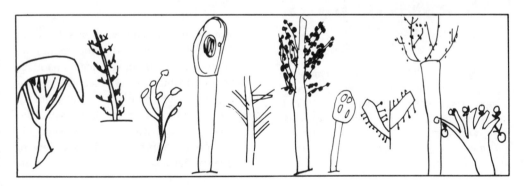

Figure 51. *Tree schemata.*[30] *Boys and girls, age six.*

with the far away tree top. Branches, twigs, leaves, blossoms and fruit are drawn singly and separately, a manifold repetition of his single schema for each.

The contour-type tree is characterized by a substantial trunk and a heavy mantle of leaves concealing the central branch structure. For example, an apple tree may show a lump-shaped roundish contour on which apple schemata are shown. Striving to reach a more realistic appearance, the child retains some of the structural fragments in a contour-shaped tree which he colors or shades.

In true-to-appearance representations of trees, the child tries to achieve correct and realistic proportions. He no longer carefully outlines single leaves, blossoms, or fruit but

Figure 53. *True-to-appearance tree.*[24] *Girl, age nine.*

Figure 54. *True-to-appearance tree as a plant study with clump of grass done by a talented child.*[40] *Boy, age seven, 1963, spontaneous pencil drawing.*

Figure 52. *TO YOU. A schematic composition in crayon which combines a "morphological" tree, showing branches and roots, with a "contour-appearance" tree. The overly large house is an example of making a "wrong" object but not erasing it.*[19] *Girl, age eight, 1965, spontaneous drawing.*

indicates them instead by color splashes or spots and dots. Like the development of the stereotyped true-to-appearance human face which leaves out whatever seems too difficult to master, the true-to-appearance plants are reduced to a few varieties in order to give a characteristic total impression.

Flowers are represented by a variety of schemata. Early studies classified them as:

(1) button schema: a dot and vertical short line underneath, (2) daisy schema: a heavy dot with a circle of smaller ones around it plus the short vertical line under it, and (3) the tulip schema: half-moon shaped and indented.[19] In the course of their development, children use first the simple schemata but later may add details and variations.

Schemata are also developed for the stem which is shown as one straight line, as a double line, or as a gently curved line. More advanced schemata have one or more leaves that emerge as longish shapes on the sides of the stem. To represent a field of flowers, the same schemata are repeated over and over, often in an orderly pattern.

Children differ in the degree to which they individualize their flower schemata. Some children are able to successfully create their own plant and fruit symbols that come close to true appearance.[32]

During the true-to-appearance stage, there is a preference for flower still lifes. The flowers are represented in a pot, a vase or other container. The main progression is toward the tighter grouping of a bouquet, a potted plant. Thus foliage, thickness of growth, and overlapping are elaborated, and quite frequently background or surroundings are indicated for the sake of realism. Nevertheless, the general impression is usually that of a two-dimensional object and setting. Many older children, particularly girls, prefer to draw flower still lifes because they present fewer difficulties and seemingly offer a greater chance of success than more complex subjects.

Nature: Mountains, Water, Fields

Children show mountains, rivers, lakes, fields, gardens and seashores in their schematic style. They reduce them to essentials

Figure 55. *Flower schemata.[35] Boys and girls, ages six and seven.*

Figure 56. *I LIKE TO DRAW FLOWERS. Notice the indication of a glass table and wallpaper in this true-to-appearance drawing.[30] Girl, age fourteen, color crayon drawing.*

Figure 57. *Mixed stage drawing of a country scene.*[35] *Boy, age thirteen, Spain, 1935.*

Figure 58. *NEGRO VILLAGE ON THE EDGE OF THE JUNGLE. A pen and ink schematic, fantasy landscape, perhaps suggested by stories of tropical forests and strange trees and birds. Note the very small figures.*[24] *Boy, age fourteen, Germany, ca 1900.*

that have meaning for the child from his observations and experiences in nature. More than that, the child sees a natural setting as his playground and an arena for his activities. Hence the characteristics of a landscape are set forth with certain details and emphasis, but also certain omissions and

Figure 59. *MOUNT SHASTA SCENE. The impressive height and loneliness of the mountain are shown in contrast to the tilled lowlands in the foreground and the hills of the middle ground. The drawing is entirely schematic, yet arranged with great topological order and the charm of schematic patternization. Notice the eternal snow on Mount Shasta and the enormity of the setting sun.*[40] *Boy, age eight, 1963, spontaneous pencil drawing.*

changes which may result from his fantasies. The child adopts the viewpoint which presents the most meaningful aspects of his subjects. Mountains are drawn as lumpy or spiky shapes; rivers, lakes and fields are represented in aerial view. The flow of a river is indicated by directional lines; the waves of a lake or the ocean are shown by curling, rhythmically repeated curves. Fields show the character of their cultivation and often bring to mind the details of Middle Age and Pre-Renaissance paintings (such as the neatly planted gardens and fields in a mural by Ambrogio Lorenzetti).

Landscapes are peopled with humans and animals, intersected by paths and roads, enlivened by cars and carriages, or automobiles, boats, airplanes, or spaceships. True to their schematic logic, children draw plants, people, animals, or vehicles singly, with ap-

Figure 60. *RIDING ON THE SNOWMOBILE. Both the pleasure of a winter ride and the pleasure of nature are expressed.*[42] *Boy, age eight, spontaneous pencil drawing.*

propriate repetitions to show that there are many or even masses of each.

Man-made Objects

Many man-made things attract the attention of children and are subjects for their drawings. Some appeal to the child because they are intimate and important; others because they are companions.

Houses and their interiors

The house is a longtime, universal favorite in children's art work. The loving attention children give to this subject suggests that a house is the symbol of the security connected with family life. Luquet, Eng, and Stern all report this pronounced interest which was clearly shown in their biographical studies of children.[24, 12, 32] It is corroborated by the predominance of houses in the drawings of war–refugee children.[5] This preference for buildings also appears in non-Western cultures where, in one instance boys drew as many buildings as humans, and girls drew far more buildings than humans.[10]

The house as a box soon emerges from the closed scribble. The box is favored in drawings of free and imaginative topics and apparently is an indispensable symbol of the home.[6] In the primitive schema, houses are frequently still "open," lacking a roof or one wall. The schematic representation of the house shows one to three sides, with the roof added smoothly to the topside of the rectangle, without overhang. The most important attributes of the schematic house are the door and the windows. The door is seldom forgotten. It is usually adorned with a knob or handle and may be decorated. The windows are smaller rectangles set in the wall, at first haphazardly and at irregular intervals. Later they are set in orderly and fairly regular fashion. The windows are detailed with curtains and shades, and may be subdivided into panes. The number of the windows follows the same logic as that of the number of fingers on the hand: three or seven or twelve—it all means the same, many.

Almost every house has a chimney, usually placed at right angles to the slope of the roof[15] and therefore not vertical and parallel to the walls of the house. Out of the chimney curls a black cloud of scribbled smoke. Chimneys and the smoke they blow arouse the imagination of children. As one little boy explained quite seriously: "That smoke is blown into the chimney by a lion who lives in the house and hides there." In recent years the television antenna is often added.

In schematic representations, houses are handled as if they were boxes, around which the child takes a walk, depicting what he observes. Sometimes the child will draw all four sides, despite the fact that in reality he cannot see simultaneously the front and the back.

Figure 61. *Schemata of houses in various stages of development.*[30] *Boys and girls, ages six and seven.*

Churches are treated in a manner similar to houses, but spires, towers, bells, and ornamental peculiarities are carefully noted and drawn. Drawings of houses and churches by the untrained adult show how little he has advanced in representation since childhood. He has, however, lost the child's lively observation and his interest in adding imaginative decoration.[20]

As the child moves beyond schematic representation, he restricts himself to the two walls of the house seen from a single point of vantage. He also tries to give a slant to one of the walls to suggest the meeting of walls at the corner of the building, yet

Figure 62. *House schema. Typically, the chimney is shown at an angle.*[30] *Boy, age six.*

he does not achieve the correct proportions. Only when he reaches the true-to-appearance stage is he able to give a three-dimensional appearance with correct perspective. By then the house is no longer a favored subject as it was at a younger age. For adolescent boys, this interest has passed entirely.[17]

Children do not often represent interiors. When they do, they picture the people or children and the furniture in the room space as though in a void.

Interiors present a difficult problem in spacial visualization and representation. Some children avoid interiors entirely.

Figure 64. *A true-to-appearance pencil drawing by a talented child showing a house in a setting of trees, like a "motif."*[26] *Girl, age fifteen.*

Others solve the problem by using a map-like approach or bird's-eye view. Some youngsters show one wall of the room with the furnishings in front of it. The drawing of interiors presents an interesting subject for research because it reveals a variety of solutions used to suggest distance: convergence, size-diminution, overlapping, and problems of grouping.

Transportation

In each generation children seem to delight in picturing all forms of transportation —horses, carriages, boats, trains, cars, planes, and spaceships. Even today, when the horse is no longer important for transportation and limited in use mainly for sport, the cowboy and his horse remain favorite subjects. Trains have strong appeal

Figure 63. *House schema with smoke blowing in three directions.*[30] *Girl, age six.*

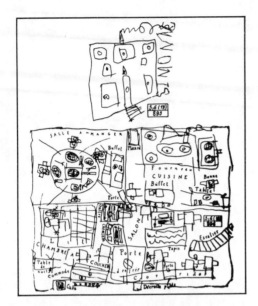

Figure 65. *The interior and exterior of a house, with a map-like plan of the rooms and furniture, combining front, side, and bird's-eye views. For example, the dining room (left top) has a circle for the table, with four radial legs, while the people seated around the table are shown in a front view.*[26] *Girl, age five, ca 1900, spontaneous pencil drawing.*

Figure 66. *An interior of a house, in which the people and all objects are schematic. There are many details. Note the astonishing variety of chair-representations. Interior space is indicated by the line of the wall in back and by the door and window.*[40] *Girl, age ten, 1963, spontaneous drawing.*

Figure 67. *Schematic pencil drawing of a ship with sailors going aboard. Note the water surface and the ship's position.*[41] *Girl, age seven.*

and many children specialize, for a time, in train pictures.[16]

During the primitive schematic stage and during the earlier phases of the schema, a train is essentially a series of boxes on wheels, the first box with a chimney belching smoke, very much like the chimneys of children's box-like houses. Trains are presented in side view on rails presented from a bird's-eye view, peopled with travelers who are often shown through seemingly transparent walls of the railroad carriages.

Once a child has worked out a schema for trains (much as he does for people and plants), he uses it over and over again.[16] As his observation improves, and he becomes more interested in realistic rendering, his drawings may reflect changes in designs of trains, cars, trucks and planes, showing more streamlined models. Lately, jets, rockets, spaceships, and satellites have become popular subjects in children's drawings, even though children seldom have occasion to "know" them as they do cars and must be guided by pictures.

Objects of immediate surroundings

The child's surroundings interest him and receive careful attention in his pictures. He

Figure 68. *These drawings were done by a child who specialized in drawing trains. From top to bottom, the drawings show the same character and individuality but an increasing facility with an increasing complexity of details. The last drawing indicates his love of trains and of his father. Trains, in this case, reveal distinct emotional involvement, also indicated by the front view of the engine, as if a front view of a person.*[10] *Boy, between ages four and six, 1930's.*

Figure 69. *A schematic train with box-like cars is competing with the airplane on which the pilot rides as if on a horse. This was the child's first pen and ink drawing.*[41] *Girl, age six, 1940.*

Figure 70. *A modern train drawn in the mixed schematic stage by a boy interested only in machines.*[41] *Boy, age nine, 1940.*

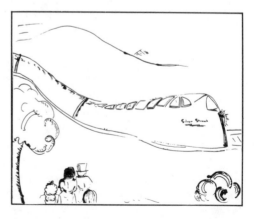

Figure 71. *The sinuous lines of this streamlined train indicate smooth movement.*[41] *Girl, age twelve, pen and ink drawing.*

works out schemata for a variety of objects, showing their most characteristic aspects. For instance, he shows the dinner table as seen from above but shows the legs as seen from a side view. He shows plates and saucers from above, knives and forks as if held in full front view, and cups and glasses in part profile. The child will draw toys,

Figure 72. *A pencil drawing of a schematic racing airplane which shows neither technical knowledge nor imagination.*[41] *Boy, age fourteen.*

Figure 74. *A sober, schematic drawing of tools that shows no imagination, in fact, indicates retarded development.*[41] *Boy, age fourteen, pencil drawing.*

Figure 73. *SMELTER. Lively interest in the function of machines and the daring of the workman, the child's father, is shown. Boy, age eight, a mixed schema, pencil drawing.*

tools, and machines in similar fashion to present their distinguishing features to best advantage.

When children approach the true-to-appearance stage, they strive for realism in presenting these man-made objects just as they do in representing living things. At this period, however, there is a decrease in the variety of objects that are shown, as well as in the variety of ways in which a single object is presented. As in the representation of living things, objects that are difficult to draw true to appearance are avoided. One study showed that the children in later developmental stages, especially, feel that they can draw machines with "realism," and that they like to do this. In striving for realism in drawing machines, just as in the case of other subjects, children establish a method of drawing, then use it repeatedly with little variation. Even after exposure to a variety of stimulus pictures of subjects involving machines, a large number of children of all ages seem unaffected and repeat their own first pictures without any effort to gain from this experience. Girls especially have only a slight interest unless the machines concern transportation, especially boats; then, it is not the steamship as a ma-

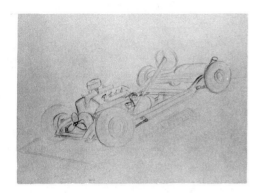

Figure 75. *An automobile—engine done in true-to-appearance, blueprint-like drawing.*[41] *Boy, age fourteen, pencil drawing.*

Figure 76. *This schematic drawing of a kitchen with a stove, towel rack, and rug is an example of arrested development.*[41] *Girl, age fifteen.*

chine-object, but rather the activities connected with a ship that catch their fancy.[21]

Through the years, the interest in machines continues, especially at certain age levels. The work of some boys, between the ages of seven and ten, has been interpreted as relating the human figure with machines and using the machine to represent themselves.[11]

Awareness of children's interest is essential to understanding and interpreting their development in art expression. Although a favored subject may be drawn more often and its representation more carefully developed than others, they all reflect the essential outlook of the child.

CHAPTER THREE: TEXT REFERENCES

1. Ames, L. B., "Free drawing and completion drawing: a comparative study of pre-school children," *Journal of Genetic Psychology*, LXVI, 1945), 161-165.

2. Anastasi, A., and J. Foley, Jr., "An analysis of spontaneous drawings by children in different cultures," *Journal of Applied Psychology*, XX (1936), 689-726.

3. Anastasi, A., and J. Foley, Jr., "A study of animal drawings by Indian children of the North Pacific Coast," *Journal of Social Psychology*, IX (1938), 363-374.

4. Ballard, P. B., "What London children like to draw," *Journal of Experimental Pedagogy* I, No. 3 (1912), March.

5. Baumgarten, F., "Die Hauszeichnungen von Kindern als Nachwirkung der Massenzerstörungen im Kriege," *Zeitschrift für Kinderpsychiatrie*, XVI (1949), 74-83.

6. Baumgarten, F., and M. Tramer, *Kinderzeichnungen in vergleichend psychologischer Beleuchtung*, 2nd ed.; Bern: Francke, 1952.

7. Bergemann-Konitzer, M., *Das plastiche Gestalten des Kleinkindes*, Weimar: H. Böhlaus Nachfolger, 1930.

8. Boutonier, J., *Les Dessins des Enfants*, Paris: Edition du Scarabée, 1953.

9. Britsch, G., *Theorie der bildenden Kunst*, edited by Egon Kornmann, 2nd ed.; Munich: Bruckmann, 1930.

10. Du Bois, C., *The People of Alor, A Social-Psychological Study of an East Indian Island*, Minneapolis: University of Minnesota Press, 1944.

11. Elkisch, P., "Significant relationship between the human figure and the machine in the drawings of boys," *American Orthopsychiatry*, XXII, No. 2 (1952), 379-385.

12. Eng, H., *The Psychology of Children's Drawings: from the First Stroke to the Colored Drawing*, London: Kegan Paul, French, Trubner & Co., 1931.

13. Graewe, H., "Das Tierzeichnen der Kinder," *Zeitschrift für paedagogische Psychologie und Jugendkunde*, XXXVI (1935), 251-256; 291-300.

14. Guillaumin, J., "Quelques faits et quelques réflexions à propos de l'orientation des profiles humains dans les dessins d'enfants," *Enfance*, XIV, No. 1 (1961), 57-75.

15. Hanfmann, E., "Some experiments on spatial position as a factor in children's perception and reproduction of simple figures," *Psychologische Forschung*, XVII (1933), 310-329.

16. Hildreth, G., *The Child's Mind in Evolution*, New York: King's Crown Press, 1941.

17. Hurlock, E. B., "The spontaneous drawings of adolescents," *Journal of Genetic Psychology*, LXIII (1943), 141-156.

18. Katzaroff, M. D., "Qu'est-ce que les enfants dessinent?" *Archives de Psychologie*, IX (1910), 125-133.

19. Kerschensteiner, G., *Die Entwicklung der zeichnerischen Begabung*, Munich: Gerber, 1905.

20. Lark-Horovitz, B., "Interlinkage of sensory memories in relation to training in drawing," *Journal of Genetic Psychology*, XLIX (1936), 69-89.

21. Lark-Horovitz, B., "On learning abilities of children as recorded in a drawing experiment. I. Subject matter, II. Aesthetic and representational qualities," *Journal of Experimental Education*, IX, No. 4 (1941), 332-360.

22. Lark-Horovitz, B., unpublished work of "A visual memory experiment," carried out at the Cleveland Museum of Art, Cleveland, Ohio, 194.

23. Lark-Horovitz, B., E. N. Barnhart and E. M. Sills, *Graphic Work-Sample Diagnosis. An Analytical Method of Estimating Children's Drawing Ability*, Cleveland: The Cleveland Museum of Art, 1939.

WILD DUCK. *Unusually light use of watercolors. Talented American girl, age 7, 1960.*[42]

4. *SANTA CLAUS. Composition in blues. Watercolor and pencil. Boy, age 9, Germany, ca 1927.*[9]

5. *HORSES. True local color, much varied. Grouped composition tending toward a central axis. Movement, clarity. Water colors, spontaneous. Talented girl, age 11, 1964.*[42]

6. *OUT THE WINDOW. Subtle colors, painting, spontaneous. Girl, age 13.*[40]

24. Luquet, G. H., *Les Dessins d'un Enfant*, Paris: Alcan, 1913.

25. Luquet, G. H., "Le réalism intellectual dans l'art primitif. I. Figuration de l'invisible; II. Le rendu du visible," *Journal de Psychologie*, XXIV (1927), 765-797; 888-927.

26. Maitland, L. M., "What children draw to please themselves," *The Inland Educator*, I (September 1895), 77-81.

27. Märtin, H., "Die Motivwahl und ihr Wandel in der freien Zeichnung des Grundschulkindes," Zeitschrift für paedagogische Psychologie, XL, Nos. 9/10 (1939), 231-241.

28. McCarty, S. A., *Children's Drawings, a Study of Interest and Abilities*, Baltimore: Williams and Wilkins Co., 1924.

29. Munro, T., B. Lark-Horovitz and E. N. Barnhart, "Children's art abilities: Studies at the Cleveland Museum of Art," *Journal of Experimental Education*, XI, No. 2, (1942), 97-155.

30. Partridge, L., "Children's drawings of men and women," *Studies in Education*, II, No. 5 (1902).

31. Ricci, C., *L'Arte dei Bambini*, Bologna: N. Zanichelli, 1887.

32. Stern, C. and W. Stern, "Die zeichnerische Entwicklung eines Knaben vom 4. bis zum 7. Jahr." *Zeitschrift für angewandte Psychologie*, III (1909-1910).

Some Characteristics of Art Development

A number of other interesting character-istics of children's drawings can be ob-served. Some of them appear for a short time and then disappear again. All of them are part of the development in children's art, interdependent qualities that are part of their growth in visual expression. They con-tribute significantly to the understanding and interpretation of the child's pictorial language.

TRANSPARENCY

Among the particular characteristics that indicate developmental change, one of the most curious is *transparency*, the way in which children draw a figure so that legs and arms show through their clothes. The child does not intend to indicate transpar-ency, but he produces that effect by draw-ing a figure first and then dressing it. It is as though the child is guided by feeling his own body through his clothes. Adults who have remained in the schematic stage, and struggle with drawing, occasionally also re-sort to transparency, apparently to build up by logic a shape that they are unable to visualize.[25]

There is a curiously similar use of trans-parency in the art of some primitive tribes. The drawing contains elements of the model

55

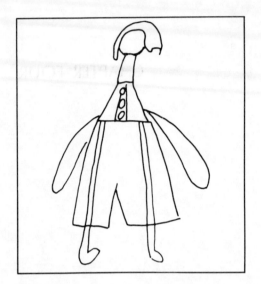

Figure 77. *Transparent schematic man.*[30] *Girl, age six.*

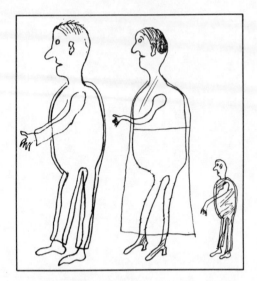

Figure 78. *Pencil drawing showing a transparent schematic man, woman, and child. Adult, ca forty years old, head of a machine shop.*[20]

that cannot be seen but which the artist considers indispensable; conversely, he neglects elements that are striking but of no interest to the artist. An especially astounding example is the build-up from invisible interior to exterior as in masks where one perceives the face under the mask.[37]

Transparency shows up in drawings in which houses are made as though seen from the outside, yet show the interior with the family at dinner or perhaps just the table, a symbol of home. A bellringer may be shown within the walls of a church tower or a train engineer on the inside of his cab; or the leg of a rider on the invisible side of the horse; or a person sitting inside a boat as seen through the sides.[53]

Studies dealing with the occurrence of transparencies show that they are relatively rare in the drawings of children under five, and occur most frequently in the work of children five to nine.[4] When asked to explain their transparencies, children gave such replies as: "because it is prettier," "because the man inside can look out." When their "errors" were pointed out, they did

Figure 79. *Color crayon drawing of a transparent house with "dinner on." Note that top of table is seen from above, while chairs and people are in profile but front-faced.*[30] *Girl, age eight.*

not admit them or make any move to correct them. After age nine, children make a spontaneous correction: "I used to do it that way," "I don't do it anymore with my new houses." (Table IX[4])

In general, transparency occurs in the work of relatively few children for any length of time. In fact, some authors regard it as being exceptional.[39] In a way, it is another form of the schematic tendency to show as much as possible of an object, whether or not the parts are visible at the time.

In countries where drawing is "taught" quite early, use of transparency is rare, even in kindergarten, because self-criticism is fostered at ages as early as four and five. Transparency rarely occurs in drawings of children instructed by teachers who stress "strict perception of reality and its usefulness to 'others'."[3] Children who have had rather formal art instruction would be unlikely to use this manner of drawing.

GRAPHIC VOCABULARY

A graphic vocabulary depends on a large number of objects and symbols describing a function or relationship (see Figures 7 and 100). Its development in children's drawings is most significant. Each object is developed until perfect within the phase and the limits of the child's ability at the time. In the next developmental stage its depiction is changed again.

Some children have a very limited *graphic* vocabulary. In the primitive stage, the same shape is frequently used for more than one object (see Figure 18). To find the meaning of the shape, it becomes necessary to observe an individual child closely and hear the child's own comments. In this period he may draw some objects carefully and in detail and continue to develop them while

not bothering to develop his drawing of others beyond a certain point. This is understandable when one considers that long practice is needed for the visual presentation of any object. The child does not develop graphic language as a goal in itself but as a means to an end. Therefore the graphic vocabulary changes as experience and the need for expression broaden.

When faced with new subject matter that needs new graphic symbols, many children entirely avoid drawing the unusual object or they represent it in the manner of an earlier developmental stage. Only after repeated efforts are children able to raise the level of their drawing of the new subject to the general level of their graphic development.[28, 43]

The graphic vocabulary of children increases during the schematic stage[38] but

Age	Boys	Girls
5	21	22
6	17	18
7	16	25
8	14	17
9	9	10
10	6	10
11	5	8
12	.5	8
13	.4	1

Table IX

Percentage of Transparency

Adapted from Boussion-Leroy.[4]

begins to decrease on entering the true-to-appearance stages. The reason may be found in the difference of graphic approach. The schematic approach makes use simultaneously of various aspects of a given object. It even uses symbolic lines and written words when the approach fails. On the other hand,

Figure 80. *BATTLE. A schematic painting in which movement is indicated by direction and position of figures.*[9] *Boy, age seven, Germany, 1920's.*

Figure 81. *BATTLE OF CHANCELORVILLE. An action drawing done by a child whose development is accelerated. Notice the diminishing size of figures in the background.*[40] *Boy, age four, 1962, spontaneous drawing.*

the true-to-appearance representation limits itself to a single point of view and to entirely visual characteristics of the objects. The youngster's general development at this time leads him to a sharper criticism of his own achievements and to a greater responsiveness to the sharper criticism which he now begins to receive from other children and adults. As a result he becomes more reluctant to undertake art work in which his success seems doubtful. Consequently, many children begin to lose confidence in themselves and become wary of situations which may invite criticism of their work.

PROPORTION

Any schematic picture shows incorrect proportions not only of objects in relation to one another, but also among the parts of single objects. (Table I) Sometimes parts of objects are not even connected, and sometimes they are drawn separately in some corner of the drawing.

Analysis of four drawings Per Child.

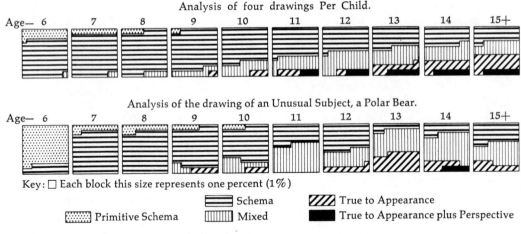

Analysis of the drawing of an Unusual Subject, a Polar Bear.

Key: □ Each block this size represents one percent (1%)

▤ Schema   ▨ True to Appearance

▦ Primitive Schema   ▥ Mixed   ■ True to Appearance plus Perspective

Graph 1: *Comparison of representational stages of various subjects*

Adapted from Munro, Lark-Horovitz, and Barnhart.[43]

This raises the question—how does the child consider parts of an object as related to the whole? When he draws a person as large as a church and a flower as large as a house, is he aware of the disproportion in his drawing? (Table I)

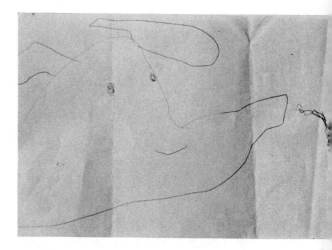

Figure 83. *BOY FEEDING ELEPHANT A PEANUT. On the right, a tiny boy with an arm twice his size feeds peanuts to an elephant.*[40] *Boy, age four, 1963, spontaneous pencil drawing.*

Figure 82. *A schematic color crayon drawing with unrealistic proportions.*[30] *Girl, age nine.*

There is no doubt that the child can correctly appraise both the actual sizes and proportions of familiar objects that are reasonably close to him, and that in the case of several objects, he can usually discern their size relationships. Indeed, children are able to describe and compare the sizes and relations of different objects at such early ages as three and four years. However, in his graphic presentation, the child ignores his observations and experiences. He tailors his pictorial creations not according to his knowledge of his environment, but according to the flow of his ideas and feelings. If a person is important in his picture, he may make him larger than the other figures, using size as an emphatic device, much

as the early Renaissance painters did. Similarly, the child may exaggerate a part of an object to stress its important function. Thus he may draw the signaling hand of the policeman three times as large as he would that of an ordinary man; or he may draw the throwing arm of a baseball pitcher far out of proportion to the rest of the player's body, and for further emphasis he may omit entirely the other arm that has no special function. But once in a while, the child may be so overcome by some gigantic size, such as an elephant, that he may picture himself in Lilliputian dimensions compared to the size of the animal and its threatening trunk.

Exaggeration, shrinking, or omission of parts may also express things that cannot be fulfilled in reality. The child knows quite well that the real object is actually different from what he has represented in his picture, but he has exaggerated or disregarded it to express an idea (see Figure 150). Similar artistic liberties are found in Western pre-Renaissance art, in Oriental art, and in tribal art. Unlike the child artist, who is motivated chiefly by personal feelings, the adult artist who uses disproportion is presumably guided by the accepted rules of his time and place.

Sometimes a child, absorbed in details, after drawing part of a figure may discover that its head is not large enough to properly accommodate all the necessary features. He solves the problem by crowding all the features into the small space that is available. As he proceeds, he may add a new object important to him but not planned for, and therefore unduly out of proportion with the rest of the picture.

Once the true-to-appearance stage has been reached, proportions are observed and rendered much as an adult perceives them, the degree of success depending, of course, on the child's ability. Details that cannot be mastered in their true proportion may be omitted or glossed over.

COMPOSITION

A composition presents a certain number of objects in some kind of arrangement. The arrangement usually reflects an idea, even though the drawing itself may not show clearly what the idea is. The child uses size and position in a manner meaningful to him. In the beginning, however, he shows a startling disregard of direction and sometimes continues to do so during the early school years, even to the third grade.

Orientation

A small child can often be seen "reading" a book upside down. Most young children can recognize objects in pictures and even printed letters on an inverted page or a page held sideways. In this they differ from adults who are highly dependent on directional orientation. Most adults are disturbed or confused by pictures viewed upside down or reading matter not oriented in the cus-

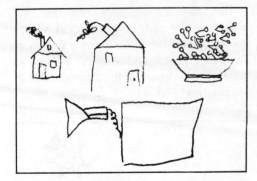

Figure 84. *Correct placement of objects is unimportant to a child in the schematic stage.*[4]

tomary manner. The left to right eye movement habitual in the Western reading pattern is a result of training and habit, and is so deeply ingrained that most adults find it difficult to accommodate to any other procedure. If the direction is reversed or unusual, they almost automatically slow up.[61]

In the scribble stage, directionality is usually lacking. Even after closed shapes have been developed and a meaning associated with them, top or bottom, left or right, have no significance. In the primitive schematic stage the orientation of objects or parts of an object seldom follow any apparent logic or pattern.[8] The pre-school child is still unaffected by directional orientation, but he is exposed to it as soon as he is given pre-reading activity in school.

It is rather startling to observe a child start by drawing the feet of his figure on top of a page and, adding the legs next, proceed without hesitation unerringly downward, finishing by drawing the head of the figure at the bottom of the page. He may also draw several objects on a page from various directions according to the turn he gives the page.[55] In placing objects, the child seems to be as much influenced by convenience and available space, as by any consideration for direction or spatial orientation. Until the child discovers the need for a given direction, corrective advice is of

Figure 85. *An unorganized composition in which there is no relation between objects; drawn when the schema has been lost, but the true-to-appearance cannot be achieved.*[22] *Boy, age fourteen, pencil drawing.*

little help until he grasps the uses and advantages of directional discipline.

In drawing at this early stage, up to ages five and even eight or nine, the child deals with each object as a separate entity. When he has drawn it, he is ready to move on to another object on another part of the paper —but he does not attempt to relate visibly the various items.[54] For instance, in first putting parts of humans or animals together, the child joins the limbs at the wrong place or puts both eyes on one side of the nose (see Figure 29). One might compare this stage with the period during which children can name numbers, but have not yet learned which number precedes or follows which,

nor why, nor how they relate to each other.

Certainly it must be assumed that the sense of orientation is acquired and not inborn,[55] and that the child must learn directional orientation such as left-right in reading and up-down in drawing. He moves from one object to another so that the drawing is merely an enumeration,[49] not an integrated grouping. Some children take a long time to grasp any kind of positional relationship. For example, the windows of houses may at first be placed outside the wall space of which they are a part, because the window exists as a unit separate from the unit "house."[55] Disorientations of this kind disappear by the time the schema has been fully developed. Some orientational problems still arise but by the time the true-to-appearance stage is reached, they have been solved.

Grouping and Arrangement

The young child knows the parts of his picture but cannot create a visual unit of several related parts. He can explain what the parts of one unit are, and how they fit together (like the features of the face), but he cannot yet arrange numerous objects into a meaningful whole.

The scribble of young children is sometimes a pleasing or even fascinating composition to the adult. The degree to which they are accidental or evidence of intentional design is an intriguing but unanswered question. Children tend to fill a page, turning it while drawing, putting on more lines and smears wherever there is room. It might be concluded that the motivating force is a compelling desire to fill an empty space rather than any intention to complete a composition.

In the early schematic period, the child scatters individual figures and objects over the paper with no visible connection between them. However, he sometimes

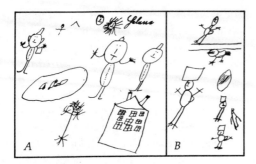

Figure 86. *In A, the objects are scattered. No relationship is shown, though it may exist. Primitive schema.*[24] *Girl, age eight, Germany, ca 1900. Objects are separately placed in B, but are related by a story they are supposed to illustrate.*[17] *Boy, age seven, Germany, ca 1900.*

Figure 87. *This space arrangement consists of three planes. There is a schematic sameness of the girls and trees on each side of the street.*[30] *Girl, age eight, color crayon drawing.*

bridges the obvious gaps in the picture by telling a story about what he is drawing. Another child may merely enumerate the separate objects. In each case the child fills in verbally what he is not able to achieve by

Figure 88. *CHINATOWN. The space layout of four planes, one placed above the other, is used to indicate the nearby and the distant. The first groundline shows shops (though they could not be seen from this vantage point) and a sidewalk; the second groundline indicates a street with cars; a third is the opposite sidewalk; and a fourth is the opposite houses. All people and objects are schematic.*[40] *Girl, age nine, spontaneous pencil drawing.*

drawing.

By the time the child reaches the schematic stage, he has made an important step toward composition by using the standline. He conceives of the world as the earth on which people stand and objects are placed. He makes a line at the bottom of the page (or sometimes uses the lower edge of the paper) to indicate the ground. On it "stand" people, plants, mountains and man-made objects, usually side by side in a row. The same organizing principle is adhered to in a more complex manner when two or three baselines are drawn one above the other (see Figure 7). These multiple standlines, indicating a space-distance relationship, show successive planes in the distance. If the child wants to show a mass of objects, like the myriad trees of a forest, he may use the same device—several standlines, one above the other. The arrangement along a stand-

A

B

A

B

Figure 89. *Schematic compositions of masses of figures in relation to the house and door. A. In FIRE DRILL, a central axis divides and balances the house (left) and figures (right). Two suns are symmetrically placed in the corners. Boy, first grade, 1961. B. THE LITTLE DEVIL. A central axis—the door—divides the two parts of the picture: St. Peter (and angels), and the little devil positioned against a crowd of people and angels. A nearly symmetrical drawing of great clarity and balance.[9] Girl, age nine, Germany, 1920's.*

line is similar to the pictographs of some primitive cultures.

When a child of four or five draws several figures, he forms a family. Influenced by his associations and experience, he relates the separate figures to each other and creates a group. Associations seem most influential in groupings made by young children. Later, other factors provide some ordering principle of group arrangement. Van der Horst suggests that while "grouping and arrangement of images [occur] initially un-

Figure 90. *Early schematic attempts to show two figures that "belong" together. A. SISTER AND BROTHER GO TO SCHOOL.[32] Girl, age five, Germany, 1919. B. MAN AND WOMAN. The child explained in detail that the woman has her head turned sideways because she is flirting; she wears slacks, a fashionable coat and hat. Her lips are red: "one swings this way and the low lip the other way." Notice details on the eye-glasses of the man (the child wears glasses). The man's profile legs indicate that he is stepping toward the woman. Notice the transparent clothes.[19] Girl, age five, spontaneous color crayon drawing.*

Figure 91. *A group of people and animals.*[30] *Girl age twelve, color crayon drawings.*

Figure 92. *WAR. This highly developed schema shows a sensitive and decorative composition with delicate details. Clear, clean lines give the topology of the countryside.*[35] *Boy, age eleven, Spain, ca 1935.*

Figure 93. *THE FARMERS WORK ON WITH-OUT LET-UP. A bomb is exploding in the clouds, but below, the farm wagons, loaded with hay, move homeward between patches of woods. Schematic, exact repetition of groups (farmwagon, woods).*[35] *Boy, age twelve, Spain, 1935.*

Figure 94. *PLAYING SOLDIER. In this unusually complex grouping, a central axis and three standlines are used. The shapes of faces, hands, and leaves have been repeated. Note the surprising foreshortening of the boy in the lower right corner.*[38] *Girl, age nine, Austria, 1919-1920, linoleum cut.*

der purely emotional guidance and on the basis of undifferentiated experiences, [they] begin to give way to principles of classification."[59]

At seven or eight the child responds to a central theme such as "a house and garden," and arranges the details in relation to the whole. After eleven, he becomes quite concerned about the arrangement or layout of his pictorial units and their de-

tails.[17] At this stage, however, there is very little organized grouping. Only a small number of children of this age ever achieve meaningful composition, and the majority of those who do are gifted children (Graphs 2 and 3). Even when children have reached a true-to-appearance stage for their single figures and objects, composition remains loosely organized.[30]

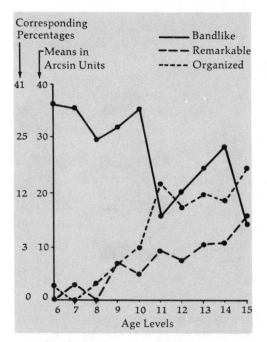

Corresponding
Percentages

Means in
Arcsin Units

Bandlike
Remarkable
Organized

Age Levels

Graph 2: *Developmental trends in terms of chronological age: Grouping*

Adapted from Lark-Horovitz and Norton.[30]

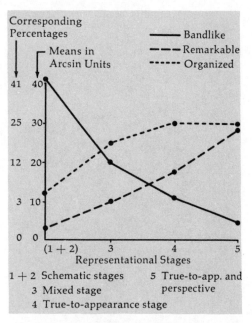

Corresponding
Percentages

Means in
Arcsin Units

Bandlike
Remarkable
Organized

Representational Stages

1 + 2 Schematic stages
3 Mixed stage
4 True-to-appearance stage

5 True-to-app. and
perspective

Graph 3: *Developmental trends in terms of representational stage: Grouping*

Adapted from Lark-Horovitz and Norton.[30]

Symmetry

One striking characteristic in the compositions of children's pictures is the tendency toward symmetrical arrangement around a central vertical axis. This is probably founded on the symmetrical build of the body, and on the experience of balanced movements such as jumping. The two sides of the axis can be complementary rather than identical as in walking, when movements are not simultaneous but alternating. There is also the possibility that the child, the center of his own universe, tends to arrange all other objects in balanced symmetry around himself.

In early childhood, the tendency toward symmetry is strong and contributes markedly to the decorative effect of schematic composition. After twelve, children sometimes deliberately introduce asymmetry in their compositions. A large number of their arrangements, however, lack organization and show little evidence of planned composition (Graphs 4 and 5).

Figure 95. *A group of horses with a portrait-like head in center. This true-to-appearance, spontaneous drawing was done by a talented American child using a line and brush technique.*[42] *Girl, age eleven, 1965.*

Figure 96. *The careful schematic, symmetrical decorativeness of the Christmas tree is enhanced by exact repetition of branches and needles, decorations and lighted candles.[32] Boy, age eleven, Germany, 1920's.*

Figure 97. *JUMPING ROPE. This symmetrical arrangement is a typical schematic composition: groundline, sun with a face like those of the children. Large black shoes indicate the importance and joy of jumping. Note that the girls who turn the rope have only the one arm needed to hold the rope.[30] Girl, aged nine, color crayon drawing.*

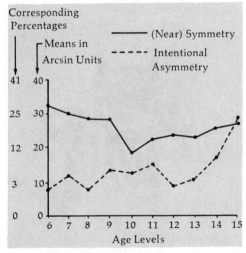

Graph 4: *Developmental trends in terms of chronological age: Arrangement in composition—symmetry and asymmetry*

Adapted from Lark-Horovitz and Norton.[30]

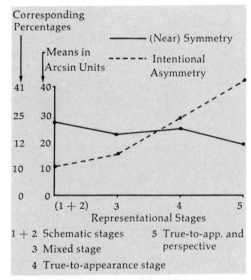

Graph 5: *Developmental trends in terms of representational stage: Arrangement in composition—symmetry and asymmetry*

Adapted from Lark-Horovitz and Norton.[30]

Clarity

During the schematic stage the child strives toward clarity by drawing each object against an empty background. In this approach the child achieves the clearest possible distinction between the form of the "figure" and the "ground" on which it is drawn.[5] This phenomenon can be explained to advantage as a "Gestalt" phenomenon, "Gestalt" in the sense of form, figures, shapes and their interrelationships in a configuration. In other words, a separate element is not only an addition to a configuration but changes its total function. The term "Gestalt" implies a functional interrelationship of all parts.

The concept of the figure-ground relationship is useful in describing the developmental process in drawing. In the light of this interpretation,[5] the child's first blotches or smears of color, or scribble, define an existing "figure" in contrast to the surrounding undefined background. The child proceeds to contour his objects, establishing

Figure 99. *FOG OVER THE GOLDEN GATE. The carefully drawn, decorative clouds are typical of the "high" fog of the West Coast. The mountains and houses, and bridge and cars, and the boat below are done with loving care.[40] Girl, age eight, spontaneous pencil drawing.*

Figure 98. *COCK. The decorative quality of this pencil line drawing, made with great economy, was achieved mainly by the size and stylization of the cock.[32] Boy, age thirteen, Germany, ca 1920's.*

Figure 100. *Fully developed schema at a comparatively late age, but an outstandingly decorative composition. Note the graphic vocabulary and the meticulous arrangement of objects. Each particular object is schematic and repeated over and over. Patternization puts impact on the decorativeness.[32] Girl, age fourteen, Germany, ca 1920.*

them clearly as figures set apart from the ground. The figure-ground relationship constantly needs clarification as the number of small units drawn increases.

Figure 101. *CITY. An elaborate, detailed schema showing the closeness of buildings and streets in Europe.[19] Girl, age twelve, Austria, 1925, pen and ink drawing.*

Figure 102. *BALL CARRYING RACE. A sports event showing children in action and a crowd of spectators is portrayed. Note the amazing arrangement of the crowd, schematically showing individuals, and the impressive black and white balance.[13] Boy, age ten, Japan, 1964, woodblock.*

Children, aged nine to ten, attempt to fit their contoured representations into a grid as a means of clarification.[39] At ages fourteen and fifteen, the youngsters no longer set each figure off against empty background, but overlap them on each other.

In the true-to-appearance stage other techniques assist in achieving clarity: better understanding of composition, more skill in establishing spatial relationships through color and perspective, and increased mastery of media.

Story Telling Through Time-Sequence Pictures

The composition of story-telling pictures is adapted to their purpose, namely the illustration of a series of events. In a picture of this kind, several episodes are portrayed, featuring the same figure in repeated appearances in the same or a different setting. Luquet, in his remarkable day-by-day study of his daughter's drawing development, shows a number of these episodic pictures. In one of them the same lady shopper and clerk appear several times as the lady proceeds on her shopping tour.[35] Young children will use this story-telling approach both around the time when they are emerging from the primitive schematic stage[36] and later when their schematic vocabulary has already reached a highly developed state.[33]

In play, the child of six to nine clings to a world of his earlier childhood in which he and inanimate objects had a life together —when he could scold a rock for hurting his foot or talk to a tree as to a friend. In drawing, at this time, he creates a symbolic world where he lives on the paper, ordering and arranging the relationship of objects and people. This is a real experience for him and serves an important purpose in helping him to become objective, no longer tied to the early subject-object interpretation.[59]

Figure 103. *The story of a shopping expedition is illustrated. A and B appear several times, at counters, at the door, on the street. The store is shown in a map-like manner, with counters and displays shown from various angles.*[26] *Girl, age five, France, ca 1900.*

By the true-to-appearance stage, story-telling pictures can be compared to certain book illustrations in which the artist crams a multitude of story-telling details into one picture, related to a specific incident in a story, or to some of Breughel's paintings, such as "Children's Games," in which a score of simultaneous scenes are united in one composition.

SPACE AND DEPTH

The visual presentation of space is one of the most interesting aspects of art the world over. Representation of space by children is not only fascinating in itself but also sheds light on the mental development of the child. Some investigations have shown that long before a child can use perspective in his drawing, he can correctly interpret pictures in perspective.[56] Even in the scribble stage, the child may indicate verbally that space and distance have some role in the idea expressed by the scribble, although the scribble itself gives no evidence of this.

Figure 104. *ALICE IN WONDERLAND. This drawing was made six weeks after the child saw the movie. From left to right: Alice; the baby who turned into a pig; tree with Cheshire cat; mockturtle; Alice opening the many doors; the tea table which is set; the March hare who jumped on the table, (to left on the tiny chair is the little hare, to right on small chair is Alice); above the tea table, Alice swims behind the rat in the pool made of her tears (wavy lines indicate water).*[19] *Girl, age five, 1934, spontaneous, primitive schema, pencil drawing.*

Figure 105. *TO THE BOTTOM OF THE SEA. A combination of modern science and folklore (mermaid) is illustrated in this schematic drawing.*[40] *Boy, age six, 1965.*

Figure 106. *THE CROW AND THE FOX. Story illustration done during the schematic stage.*[12] *A. Boy, age eight, Switzerland, ca 1909. B. Girl, age eight, Switzerland, ca 1909.*

Although skill in spatial representation develops slowly, even younger children may be aware of the artist's skill in showing space and distance in a picture and wonder how it is done. One five-year-old asked:

Figure 107. *This picture illustrates a story the child made up herself: "He suddenly ran behind a bush when he saw a large herd of horses coming. He began running home fast to spread the news. He was very, very startled. A herd of pinto horses, which are called clouds because of their spots, came charging from the south. And so did real thunderclouds." There is an astounding grouping of horses, but there is a lack of all-over organization.*[42] *Girl, age ten, 1964, spontaneous pencil drawing.*

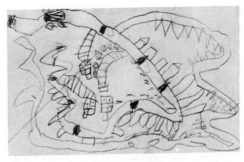

Figure 108. *FREEWAYS. THIS WAY WE WENT ON OUR TRIP. Using closed shapes and scribble, the child attempted to show direction and turns. The motor activated layout is dotted with houses and cars.*[19] *Boy, age six, 1963, spontaneous pencil drawing.*

"How come painters can paint so it looks far away?"[18]

In primitive schema and early schematic representation, most objects are repre-

Figure 109. *RAINY DAY. Space has not been indicated at all, except by including clouds. Humor is shown by the dog with the umbrella at bottom center.*[40] *Girl, age nine, spontaneous pencil drawing.*

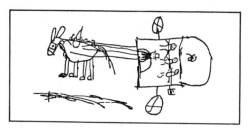

Figure 110. *A combination of views (all clear as separate parts) of the horse, cart, and riders has been used in this drawing.*[28] *Age seven, France, 1900's.*

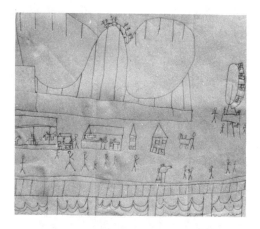

Figure 111. *BOARDWALK. Bottom: board-walk. (with telescope) with waves washing up. Second standline: street with people and vending booths. There is a third standline for the Ferris wheel. A schema in which stick figures are used. Girl, age seven, spontaneous pencil drawing.*

sented as though suspended in a vacuum. However, it has been said that there is no entirely spaceless representation even among the youngest school children, because of the schema's combination of front-view (elevation) and bird's-eye view (groundview).[56] The nature of the schema indicates spatial relations through symbolism. A person familiar with child art is able to interpret it.[32]

Piaget states that during the schematic stage the child can absorb the perspective aspect of an object from one point of view, but cannot reconstruct its appearance from other points of observation.[51] At about five or six, children begin to use a standline and with it relate separate objects to a common plane. From this a simple principle for positioning in space is developed. Now the child lines up people, animals, and objects on the standline. He designates the empty space above as air, and places the remote sky far above where he also draws the sun, and sometimes the moon and stars. Depth is tacitly associated with the arrangement. At seven, the strip of sky is expanded more and more frequently.[17] The child seems to "feel" the perspective although he still makes distant objects the same size as nearby ones.

Children's two-dimensional pictures can be interpreted as providing spatial organization in two ways: upward, earth to sky, and backward, foreground to horizon. The drawing paper serves these two extensions simultaneously. To emphasize these spatial meanings, the schematic child has worked out a number of techniques.[20, 32, 33] The foreground to background relationship can be most clearly observed when the child is working with "paper cutouts." If he is not guided, but provided with appropriate materials, he will start with the furthest background, such as mountains, and will let the "mountain-paper" reach the bottom of the page—the earth; superimpose on it the next plane of the remote landscape—perhaps a lake or forest; and will then tack over it the fields in the middleground. Finally he will add the closest foreground with its roads and cars, fences, and people. Unlike painting technique, this procedure enables the child to visualize and represent spatial depth

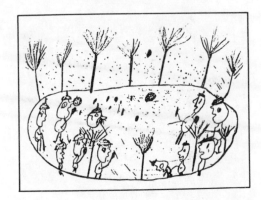

Figure 113. *SNOW BALL FIGHT. Schematic space representation in which dots signify snow. The slight oval shape of the playground indicates perspective. Boy, age ten, ca 1900.*

Figure 112. *VACATION. The space arrangement is particularly schematic; from bottom to top, it is meant to be fairly flat. Note the proportions of the fish (profile), the dragonfly (front view), and boy.[30] Girl, age eleven, color crayons.*

Figure 114. *GARDEN. Bird's-eye view of a garden with side view flowers in a patternized schema.[30] Girl, age twelve, 1936, color crayon drawing.*

successfully when he is not yet able to do so in drawing or painting.

During the schematic stage, children frequently use map-like layouts, or bird's-eye views to suggest space relationships. With numerous schematic details they achieve almost a "picture map," very much like contemporary pictorial maps and those of certain aborigines. Maplike drawings are especially useful in the episodic drawings in which the child seems to place the same characters in the same land area doing different things at different times (see Figure 103).

In the schematic arrangement of larger numbers of objects as in an orchard or flower garden, for instance, the paper on which the picture is made is regarded as if it were a miniature piece of land—the bottom part of the paper is the nearest place, the top the most distant. Thus the land must be interpreted as lying flat, bird's-eye view, although figures and objects are represented as standing up in frontview, and sizes are the same, whether in the foreground or background.[60]

Figure 116. *VIEW FROM WINDOW. "True-to-life" line drawing with perspective overlapping and a tight space arrangement by a talented and very advanced child.*[9] *Boy, age six, Germany, ca 1925, spontaneous drawing.*

The child, in making such a picture, is aware of the actual appearance of what he is portraying. In the case of an orchard, for instance, he knows from his own observation that the trees farther away look smaller than those close by, but he is dominated by his knowledge of their actual size and considers this to be the important reality he wants to express. The adult, on the other hand, is apt to keep in mind the effect of perspective, and is dominated by this in his visualization of the scene.

The transition from the space representation of the schema to the perspective of the true-to-appearance stage may be considered an advance in perception as well as in mental development. "To perceive an object according to a given perspective is identical with seeing it from a certain vantage point of which one does not need, necessarily, to be conscious in order to perceive accurately. To represent in a drawing the same object in the same perspective is . . . to take notice simultaneously of the vantage point from which it is perceived

Figure 115. *BOULEVARD. An entirely schematic space representation. The people on the sidewalk and trees are schematic, but the automobiles are close to true-to-appearance. An extraordinary composition of balance between black and white, and details. A decorative effect has been achieved.*[13] *Boy, age nine, Japan, 1964, woodblock.*

Figure 117. *OLD TRAIN YARD. The arrangement of many tracks is shown in bird's-eye view, on four planes. Diminishing sizes and fainter lines are used to indicate distance.*[40] *Boy, age nine, 1963, spontaneous pencil drawing.*

and of the changes due to the intervention of that vantage point."[51] This is a complicated mental process, and at various ages and stages of development conflicts arise between the perceptive knowledge of perspective and its representation.[52]

Clark's study of the 1890's is an outstanding example of simplicity and clarity in describing how children at various age levels handle the spatial problem of drawing an apple with a pin stuck through it. He fol-

Figure 118. *OLD CITY. A true-to-appearance drawing in which the child avoided using perspective.*[19] *Girl, age twelve, Austria, 1926, free drawing in water color.*

lowed the development from a flat, two-dimensional, plate-like disk to a convincing representation "in the round." He observed all the steps and described the results: from visual impossibilities, such as a pin fully visible inside or across the apple to one accurately foreshortened, entering and emerging from the apple. Clark concluded

Figure 119. *Clark's experiment with the apple shows various steps leading from primitive schema, schematic, and mixed stages to true-to-appearance with shading.*[9]

"that perspective is not a simple subject [but is] acquired slowly through definite stages at each of which the child will stop persistently and stubbornly until ready to develop beyond it."[9] His observations still apply and have been confirmed by other, later experiments.

A recent study by Lewis found that subjects involving spatial depth, such as a landscape, reveal age-related changes in the children's drawings. Elementary school children in their early drawings showed no spatial organization of the objects. Next, they arranged the objects along the lower edge of the paper on a groundline. Later, they used several groundlines for objects of fairly uniform size. Finally they unified the effect by grouping objects on gradually receding planes.[34]

The fact that only an extremely small number of children can work out a realistic perspective representation on their own was noted in Kerschensteiner's early investigation in which he used the total school population of Munich.[24]

Transition from the schematic stage to the true-to-appearance stage spans the last gap between the child's world and that of the young adult. From now on the true-to-life outlook dominates all visual expression. Actual drawing achievement depends on further development of observation, under-

Figure 121. *THE GOLDEN GATE. A neat, detailed perspective drawing in which distance is indicated by softer shading.*[40] *Boy, age thirteen, spontaneous pencil drawing.*

standing, visual memory and drawing skills. In the process the child adds overlapping, shading and color variations to his repertoire and attempts a certain degree of line perspective and foreshortening.

For many children, the first step in transition is very difficult. As a study of 4,500 drawings by six to fourteen year olds of a snowball fight showed, only fourteen children could solve the problem of space and depth.[24] Usually their early observation that distant objects seem smaller than close ones helps them to make the first step by drawing several standlines, then using smaller sizes for distant objects on the upper standlines. Many children stop at this stage and can go no further without specific instruction.

Children usually find the problem of perspective even more difficult in drawing interiors (see Figure 167). A series of drawings of a familiar classroom made clear various steps of development toward perspective and also revealed the kinds of errors that occur in representation. Table X[29] is based on the findings of the classroom study.[43]

Adults who have received no special training, or who have forgotten whatever training they did receive, are as bothered

Figure 120. *In this drawing made during the mixed to true-to-appearance stage, there is a successful attempt to show perspective (even the cast shadows of the telephone poles). Note the "fanning out" of fields as it appears from a moving car.*[40] *Boy, age eleven, 1962, spontaneous pencil drawing.*

Some Characteristics of Art Development

by the problem of perspective as children and make the same kind of "mistakes."[25] One of the most interesting phenomena in children's drawing is that of inverted perspective. The child observes that the apparent convergence of parallel lines helps to make a piece of furniture, for instance, look more real. But in applying this observation, he sometimes turns it around. Then the converging lines of a table are directed to the foreground instead of toward the background. This pictorial oddity can also be noted in some exceedingly sophisticated oriental paintings but here, of course, it is

not a lack of know-how but part of the artist's intention.

Children observe, as do adults, that vertical lines apparently remain vertical whether objects are in the foreground or in the background. This observation clashes with their tendency in the schematic period to lay down vertical lines whenever it serves their purpose. The walls of a room may be shown laid over on the same plane as the floor, or the trees along a road, the houses along a street are drawn as though lying on the ground or leaning halfway over. Even after they have begun to enter the true-to-appear-

Number of Children	Ages	Schematic Space Arrangement			for one or a few objects	throughout	Attempts at Perspective									
		3 or more objects in picture	Standline	2 or more (Standline) Planes			Walls or objects*		Convergence				Sizes			All over Perspective correct or approx. so
							turned down	slanting	2 or more Planes distinguished	No convergence	Reversed convergence	Insufficient or incorrect conv.	Correct or approximate conver.	Not diminished	Insufficiently dimin. or revers.	Correct
83	6	51	78	7	—	—	18*	—	—	1	—	—	—	—	—	—	—
93	7	53	70	4	15	—	24*	—	—	11	—	4	1	15	—	—	—
100	8	47	53	11	16	1	30*	—	—	6	1	13	—	17	—	—	—
100	9	39	46	15	13	3	28*	—	8	6	—	12	—	14	2	—	—
100	10	32	25	31	15	7	33*	3	7	7	2	15	—	21	2	1	—
92	11	26	25	4	9	15	9	—	26	2	8	16	1	17	9	4	—
115	12	30	14	3	15	23	3	3	27	13	17	13	3	31	7	3	—
94	13	18	12	6	15	9	8	6	19	15	10	3	—	20	3	—	—
87	14	38	12	6	17	16	6	1	28	30	11	15	—	41	10	3	—

Table X

Space and Perspective

Based on data of the drawing of a classroom, analyzed in the Cleveland Studies.[29, 45]

Figure 122. *MY SCHOOL. There is no space indication, except for the blackboard. All objects and people are in a "void," and are entirely schematic.*[40] *Girl, age seven, 1963, pencil drawing.*

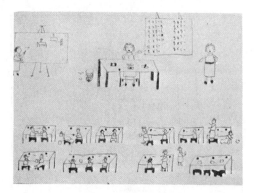

Figure 123. *CLASS. Planes for the rows of desks and the teacher's table are very distinct. Notice the discipline problems, great detail, and very neat lines.*[35] *Girl, age eleven, Spain, 1935.*

ance stage, they sometimes compromise between old practices and new observations and use slanting verticals.

Among the most curious drawings by children are those presenting figures and objects in a circular area. Drawings of such circle games as Ring-around-the-Rosy point up this particular drawing problem. The figures are standing on the same plane dispersed along the circumference of a circle, holding hands and facing the center. Young children, in their early pictures, tend to draw the circle by placing the figures with arms out along the circle (holding hands with their neighbors), feet toward the center, and heads out. Of course, to an adult eye the figures in the drawing appear to be lying down—but to children in the schematic stage this is a quite satisfactory treatment. In another approach, youngsters may not try to show the circle itself but will draw two lines of figures, one on the upper half of the paper, front-face view, and a lower row showing the backs of the figures. They join the ends of the two lines in a variety of ways. In a slightly more advanced approach, the child draws the circle as an oval with same-sized figures all around it, stand-

Figure 124. *CLASSROOM. A true-to-appearance, perspective sketch. Note the different positions of the figures.*[22] *Girl, age fourteen, 1936, crayon drawing.*

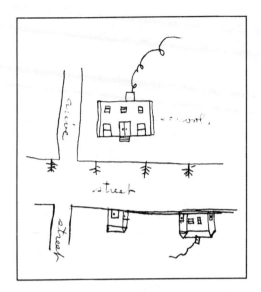

Figure 125. *An adult's drawing of a street; compare with a child's drawing (Figure 18).*[20]

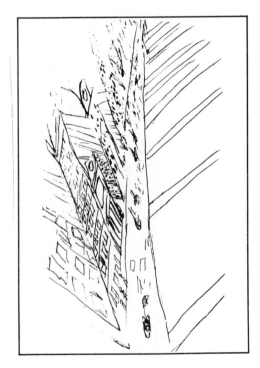

Figure 126. *Perspective drawing of Chicago's Michigan Boulevard by a forty year old mathematician and theorical physicist.*[20]

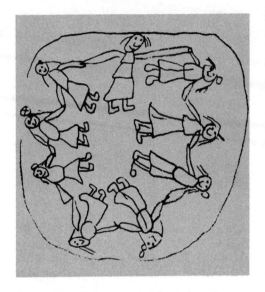

Figure 127. ROUND. *A schematic space arrangement in which the heads of the children follow the periphery of a circle while their feet are directed toward the center of the circle.*[13] *Switzerland, ca 1935.*

Figure 128. *A BIRTHDAY PARTY. A rectangular space arrangement has been used: table edges, plates, and cutlery are seen from above, the chairs are "laid down" tops outward, the children are upright, and the cake and the candles are in a mixed view.*[40] *Boy, age seven, 1963, spontaneous pencil drawing.*

Figure 129. *THANKSGIVING ITSELF. There is a partial solution of space representation of the figures seated around the table. Schematic to mixed stage.*[40] *Girl, age nine, spontaneous color crayon drawing.*

ing up perpendicular to the bottom of the page, front view, side view, and back view, properly disposed but still lacking in the full perspective of true-to-life treatment.

The illusion of distance can be achieved not only by reducing the size of distant objects and placing them on receding standlines, but also by changing the color of the objects. Children, however, find it almost impossible to achieve perspective in their pictures by this method. They observe the faded aspect of colors in the distance in contrast to the brilliance of the same colors nearby. They know what the nearby color is and that they are looking at the same color far away. But the same logical sense of reality that prompts them at an early age to draw the rider's invisible leg on the far side of the horse makes them reluctant even now to show change in color due to distance. They seem to think of color as a constant property of a particular object and their unwillingness to violate what they regard as the "real" color inhibits them from showing true-to-appearance variations related to perspective. Color perspective "ap-

parently presupposes an attitude that is entirely foreign to the child's conception of the world."[49] At most, he compromises: he may make the nearby colors less bold than they actually appear and the more distant colors stronger.

In order to fully create the illusion of three-dimensionality, both foreshortening and shading are necessary. It is a common experience to observe that a nose seen in profile looks longer than a nose viewed front face, just as an arm stretched out sideways looks longer than one stretched toward the viewer. It is important to see and understand this effect of foreshortening, especially in order to draw figures in motion. Children have a constant opportunity to observe foreshortening in life but find it extremely difficult to draw. Again it may be partly because they know the actual size of the nose or arms, and are bothered by the difference between what they *know* and what they *see*. They are apt to compromise by drawing a sideways bend of the arm or the nose turned up slightly as in profile. Until well into the true-to-appearance phase, they treat most foreshortening problems in this manner.

Figure 130. *VACATION. Triangular grouping is achieved by foreshortened, true-to-life figures.*[22] *Talented boy, age fourteen, United States, color crayon drawing.*

LIGHT AND SHADE

Shading is a way of drawing that can make an object look round or thick by showing both light and shadow on it, as well as showing the shadow it casts. It gives a third dimension to a two-dimensional drawing—making a ball appear to bulge out of a flat page. Only after the child has some understanding of light and shade can he draw "in the round" successfully.

It is curious to observe that the young child represents the sun whenever possible. He may even do so in impossible situations, showing the sun inside a house to indicate a sunny day. In fact, young children actually fail to note the relationship of light to shadow. At about five, however, the child may trace shadows to two sources. He sees an apple on the table with its dark shadow on the side away from the lamp. This "internal" shadow, as Piaget points out, appears to the child to come out from inside the object and the connection between object, light and shadow is clearly observable. The external shadow is more difficult to understand. To the child it is essentially the absence of light and is experienced as a mass of darkness around him—in a forest or in a darkened room.[50] In schematic drawings children omit shadows entirely, just as they might do with other details, as if they considered shadows irrelevant to their pictures, and rather as extraneous phenomena. Most probably, they do not associate shadows at all with picturing. When they begin to show an interest in shading, they are seldom successful in using it because it is difficult for them to relate the shadow to the source of light. Once a child has come to the conclusion that "the shadow is a substance that flees from the light [he has] established a relationship between shadow and light."[50] Eventually he discovers that the contrast between them is an important device in drawing. Until then he makes any number

Figure 131. *VACATION. A very rare example of the representation of a cast shadow. A true-to-appearance color crayon drawing with shading, motion, and action.[22] Boy, age thirteen.*

of odd mistakes. Very often children shade opposite parts of objects in a picture even when there is only one source of light; they darken the figure on the side opposite its own shadow, or they may draw a cast shadow on an already shaded area. Even where they show objects in bright sunlight, they may ignore the shadows completely.

MOVEMENT, ACTION, FLEXIBILITY

The seemingly rigid and inflexible approach in many drawings of the schematic stage might lead to the impression that there is not much concern for movement at this time. However, this is not the case. The child at an early age is full of movement

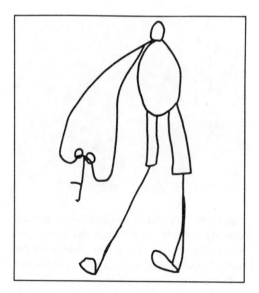

Figure 132. *Schematic drawing showing movement and action.*[30] *Girl, age six.*

Figure 134. *Action and movement are shown in this schematic drawing.*[30] *Boy, age seven.*

Figure 133. *Movement and action in a schematic drawing.*[30] *Boy, age eight.*

and action, and his scribbles reflect this. The scribble may describe the path of moving objects rather than a static situation. Scribble is also frequently used to describe distances that have been traversed or the motions involved in games or play (see Figure 3). It has been aptly described as the "urge of communication and motion." The child thinks of his motion as belonging to the representation itself and clearly experiences great pleasure from it.[1] The experience of

Figure 135. *SURFBOARD. An amazing ability to indicate movement is shown in this early schematic drawing.*[40] *Boy, age six, 1963, spontaneous brush.*

movement is transferred graphically only in these earliest steps. In this period the path of the object covers the object itself.

Figure 136. *Action is indicated by dotted lines and the forward thrust arm. Motion is indicated by water waves in this primitive schematic drawing.*[22] *Boy, age seven.*

Figure 137. *BUCKING BRONCO. Violent motion is shown by the position of the horse, the streaming mane and tail, and the falling hat in this spontaneous, schematic drawing.*[40] *Boy, age six, color crayon drawing.*

In the next stage, "the shape proper becomes discernible, but the rigidity of the schema hinders any vivid characterization of movement (see Figure 96)."[42] Actually, the schema expresses movement and action in a number of ways, which are not always evident in the finished product. Sometimes the child tries to indicate motion by the placement of his figures and objects and their mutual relationships. Sometimes he will draw a bent paw to show action. And at other times he carries on a rambling commentary. He may show movement as on a

Figure 138. *RODEO. Movement and action are strongly brought out although the figure, animals, trees, and space representation are schematic.*[40] *Girl, age nine, 1962, spontaneous drawing.*

stage in which the situation and position of the seemingly rigid figures and objects point to action. Even at kindergarten level one fourth of the figures are meant to be in motion, though the picture offers little evidence of this. By the eighth grade, three-fourths of the figures are intended to be in motion.[62]

A study designed to encourage the depiction of action in a drawing required children first just to draw a man, then to show the same man eating an apple, and finally to show him climbing a tree.[11] It was observed that the action was either disregarded, or simply expressed by placement only, the man holding the apple or merely touching the tree. Children at the schematic stage draw a trajectory course to show action such as the throwing of a ball. After a while, they abandon this method. Later in the schematic phase, some children represent movement by showing many small similar figures row on row, all bent at the same angle. Through repetition they convey a feeling of movement, a mode of picturing action also used by adults of primitive tribes.

Children also show movement and flexibility by using curly, wavy or repeated

Figure 139. *COMBAT. Action, in this schema, is shown by position, attributes, and scribbles of smoke in the sky.*[40] *Boy, age seven, 1963, spontaneous drawing.*

Figure 140. *HURON INDIANS ATTACKING FORT WILLIAM HENRY. The small figures—same schemata—accentuate the height of the fort. Distance is indicated by size.*[40] *Boy, age nine, 1963, spontaneous drawing.*

rhythmic lines. Their little train will sport a stream of curling smoke, a stiff little boat will have a busy wake, or they may use "trembling" lines all through the motion-filled situation they wish to convey.

For children "objects *are* the action they induce." Thus a ladder is a "climbing" thing, and an animal's snout is a "snouter," etc.[42] A three year old, for instance, explained an oddly shaped contour as "a hand that is scolding."[18] Despite the importance of action, the schema appears rigid and inflexible because the child lacks the graphic skill to portray the motion he experiences. To deal with the problem, he ingeniously devises various ways to suggest motion in schematic drawings. For example, apple picking is shown by a drawing of two children, the lower one standing on his head and the apple picker standing on the feet of his helper. Though the picker does not even touch the apples, the positioning alone suggests the frantic and daring activity. (Graphs 6 and 7)

When the true-to-appearance stage is approached, the desire to convincingly represent movement becomes stronger than before, and the child is no longer satisfied with his earlier methods. He tries to capture the fleeting appearance of movement in its many aspects. He seldom tries to indicate

Figure 141. *Motion is indicated by the scribbly treatment of lines. A schematic drawing in which the pilot "rides" the plane.*[41] *Boy, age nine, pen and ink drawing.*

movement by suggestion, such as the whirling of arms or the swirling of skirts. He is more apt to attempt to portray the bent limbs, the proper angle—the "real" appearance. This is difficult for the average child and beyond the ability of most children. Those who want to express motion, and are dissatisfied with the earlier way of doing it, usually are unable to sufficiently master the new technique. As a result, they experience frustration, are slow in developing, and sometimes progress only if they have effective instruction.

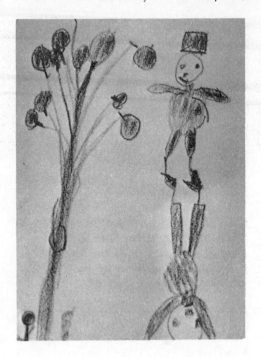

Figure 142. *Though entirely rigid, situation and position indicate intended action in this schematic drawing.*[30] *Boy, age seven, color crayon drawing.*

Figure 143. *Sailing. Movement is shown by the angle of the boat, and line and color variation.*[30] *Talented boy, age nine, color crayon drawing.*

Figure 144. *POLICE FOILED IN ARREST. There is remarkable, organized group action in contrast to the policeman.*[38] *Boy, age nine, Austria, 1918-1919, linoleum cut.*

Figure 145. *THE CIRCUS IS HERE. A predominately true-to-appearance drawing with no space indication except for the placement of animals and people. There is an attempt to show strong movement.*[40] *Girl, age eleven, spontaneous pencil drawing.*

USE OF MEDIUM

Certain media are more suited than others to various stages of children's drawing. There are, of course, a number of media, such as drawing tools like pencils or crayons, paints, clay and other related materials, each lending itself to certain kinds of manipulation.

During the scribble stage, when a child covers a surface with lines, he will find pencil, crayon, chalk or ball-point pen well

7. *THE HOUSE. Delicately multicolored schema. Crayons, spontaneous. Girl, age 8, 1963.*[40]

8. *BEETLES. Decorative use of true local colors, direct use of brush, schema. Opaque paints, made in school. Boy, age 7.*[44]

10. *PORTRAIT. Stylized color, expressionistic, crayons. Talented girl, age 14.*[30]

9. *PORTRAIT. Subtle colors and contrasts, bluish shadows, red lines for hands. Crayons. Talented girl, age 13.*[30]

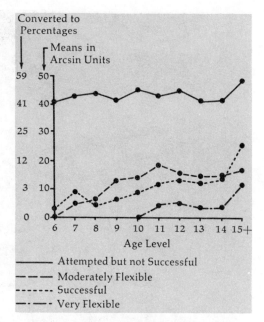

Graph 6: *Developmental trends in terms of chronological age: Motion—flexibility*

Adapted from Lark-Horovitz and Norton.[30]

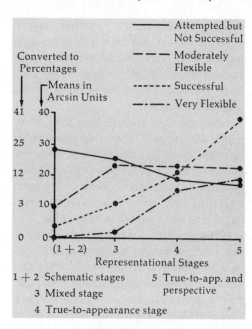

Graph 7: *Developmental trends in terms of representational stage: Motion—flexibility*

Adapted from Lark-Horovitz and Norton.[30]

Figure 146. *There is an attempt to indicate motion by showing bent limbs and a tilted position. Note the hesitant lines.*[30] *Girl, age fourteen, pencil drawing.*

suited for his needs. The nature of the schema and the technique of its execution are also best served by pointed markers which permit definite outlines. Consequently, if a young child who can only shape objects by outlining them is given big brushes and paint, he may be unable to actually produce an outlined form (see Figure 96). He surely cannot be expected to realize fully the potential of the paint-and-brush approach and may even be hampered in the development that pencil drawing permits. On the other hand, he may greatly enjoy the "play" aspects of using brush and paints (see Figure 212), deriving satisfaction from the big muscle movements and taking pleasure in the color. During the last thirty years there has been considerable emphasis on art as an outlet for emotions. Materials that lend themselves to spontaneity of stroke, crude color effects and quick results are favored. The big brush method used with the youngest children will discourage precision of form at a time when pencil drawing encourages it. Teaching which pushes the child into the use of techniques beyond his level of development may hamper his ability to produce at his own level and discourage the growth of his graphic vocabulary.

When children apply colors, they do so within the outlined forms that characterize the object and separate its parts. They use colored chalks, color crayons, opaque paint mixtures, or water colors in much the same way: first they draw outlines with pencil or crayon, and then fill in with colors.

When children make papercuts, the scissors establish the outline (see Figure 30). As in their modeling at this period, they frequently cut out the parts first and then paste them together to compose the entire object. Thus, the child proceeds in a like manner in drawing, painting, and modeling.

At the schematic stage children are eager to try many media (see Figure 193). During the mixed and true-to-appearance stages, they exhibit greater hesitation in such ventures and are apt to remain with a medium with which they are familiar and which they believe they can handle successfully. This was shown in one study[27] which offered a choice between a new medium and one used constantly. Nearly half of the younger children aged six to eleven tried the new medium, while less than one fourth of the older children did so. Similarly, younger children showed more venturesomeness and curiosity in their choice of paper sizes than did the older group. The younger child apparently lacks understanding of the relationship between medium and tool, and paper size. In another study, younger children tended to select small pieces of paper and an inappropriate blunt pencil or crayon, while older children chose large sheets of paper for paints and brushes.[40]

Most children, when left to their own devices, try to transfer a familiar technique to a new medium regardless of its suitability.

Figure 147. *Ship battling a storm. A painterly treatment with a pencil to achieve a dramatic concept.*[41] *Talented boy, age twelve.*

Some children are slow in discovering how to use the new medium and experience a setback by attempting it. Gifted children, on the other hand, like to try a new medium. They show insight into its possibilities, soon discover its limitations, and are often successful at their first try in using it.[27]

About half of all elementary school age children use their medium consistently, that is according to its character and the material to which it is applied, and according to the amount of lines and areas, details and configurations which the nature of the medium can bring into agreement. Up to the age of thirteen, children use any medium with steadily increasing effectiveness. Only ten percent remain inconsistent in their use of media. Very few children achieve a totally effective use of various media before age thirteen, and these are usually the more gifted children. The average child makes his greatest improvement after thirteen.

Consistency in the use of the medium has been found to be related to developmental level in drawing (see Figure 92). Unusual ability in the use of media tends to be found in "early developers" and gifted children (see Figure 94). This is not surprising since those children are apt to progress through all stages to the true-to-appearance representation, and handling media is essential to their competence (see Figure 215). Proper use of media and materials shows less relationship to chronological age than to the level of drawing development. At fifteen, a third of all children are merely consistent in media usage and never go beyond this. Generally, there is a fairly wide range in the skillful use and individual development of various media (Table I).

It is interesting to note that young children, despite their immature coordination, typically outline parts of the entire figure or the object decisively and with competence. Most children retain a certain firmness in line throughout all the grades, while others in the higher grades experiment with shorter strokes. In consequence, their drawings seem weaker and ragged. Weak lines and hesitation reflect the problems of transition to the true-to-appearance stage, trying to draw "life-like." The child's broadening experience in the world and his increasing self-criticism upset his earlier assurance in drawing. His increasing hesitation in technique is an outward sign of inward uncertainty (see Figure 33). Sometimes weakness and hesitancy of line also reflect inability to proceed any further and indicate a break with art as self-expression.[43]

Children show progressive improvement with treatment of areas, from ragged or careless to a smooth, careful handling. The six- to ten-year-olds are about evenly divided between ragged and smooth area

treatment. From age nine on, treatment is mostly smooth, though many children show meagerness in effect.[14] At age eleven some children blend and grade areas, and a small number achieve a remarkably bold appearance[43] (Table I).

DECORATION AND ORNAMENTATION

Children's pictures, always appealing in their sincerity and unpretentiousness, and sometimes in their story-telling quality, often have high decorative appeal as well. Some have extraordinary charm arising from the rhythmic repetition and placement of basic shapes.

The single leaf is used ten or a hundred times in the same form—a device used in folk art, in Persian miniatures, and in some

Figure 148. *Decorative treatment of a cloud in a schema drawing. There is an indication of action.*[30] *Girl, age ten, color crayons.*

Figure 149. *IVY GROWING AROUND WINDOW. Very young children appreciate the decorative effect of a plant and try to express it.*[36] *Boy, age five, Germany, ca 1906.*

Figure 150. *By decorating THE INDIAN'S HORSE and making the Indian very small, the child has shown the importance of the horse.*[40] *Boy, age eight, 1963, spontaneous pencil drawing.*

of the pre-Renaissance art of the Western world. A woman's hair is shown as one curl repeated again and again until the entire coiffure is completed, in this way producing a decorative effect (see Figure 100). This repetitive device enables the child to achieve his pictorial and narrative objectives, and enhance the aesthetic appeal of his picture. The same principle applies to the repetition of figures and animals and to larger scale compositions with an ordered all-over pattern (see Figure 218). Children

employ this approach to depict both a peaceful scene and one of violent action as in a war scene.

The child artist also employs symmetry to achieve a decorative effect. He uses a mirror image on both sides of a central axis and creates complex compositions with many repetitions. Often he uses the standline as a decorative ribbon to create a unifying effect. By treating the same objects or figures with uniformity of style, some children give a most pleasing ornamental character to their schematic drawings.

If the child adds brilliant colors to his combination of symmetrical arrangement, patternlike repetitions, and ribbonlike compositional bases, his work is greatly enlivened. And if vivid colors are also used repetitiously, the total effect is often wonderfully successful.

It might be helpful to review the use of the terms decorate, design, and ornament. All three terms are used almost interchangeably in the literature, so that to make absolute distinctions is both difficult and perhaps

Figure 151. *Nothing impresses a little girl like a wedding and the bride, but to this child, the decorated cake seems more important, and thus it is centered and very large.*[40] *Girl, age five, 1963, spontaneous pencil drawing.*

arbitrary. However, it can be said, that the term to *decorate* implies the existence of an object or space to be embellished. Decorations, for example, may be designs to beautify an object; free-standing ornaments to bedeck a room or honorific adornments to be worn, etc. To *design* implies the act of arranging elements in some pattern in which the design itself may be a single unit (a spiral, leaf, or star). A design can be an over-all pattern composed of designed units. The term can also mean a project plan, a visualization of an idea, not just an element. To *ornament* is to decorate, but an ornament can be more than a unit in ornamentation; it can also be an independent entity used for the adornment of a person or a separate object serving as an art object.

When one asks a child why he is making decorations, he says "to make it pretty." Children in English-speaking countries almost always use these very words. Ideas of prettiness may vary, but the child's motivation seems to be the same the world over. The urge to decorate has been interpreted as being rooted in a rhythmic feeling of the body (see Figure 214), and it always seems to develop along with the urge to represent things and the urge to establish order. School children speak of ornamentation as "a design" and sometimes there is enough of a design quality even in their early scribbles to make an aesthetic appeal to adults. The young child's pleasure, however, seems to arise as much from the action itself as from the resulting effect. Later, when the child begins to develop his graphic vocabulary, he may decorate figures and objects. He also creates "designs" that are quite apart from the representation of objects.

The development of ornamental drawing over the school years has not been studied as extensively as the development of representation, and findings of studies that have

Figure 152. *Experiment in decoration and ornamentation. Dresses were decorated by girls who were supplied with a figure outline; shields (papercut outline) were ornamented by boys.*[31] *Boys and girls, ages six to eight, Germany, ca 1910.*

been carried out are not always in agreement.

One interpretation regards ornament as being at first a geometric patternization; its rhythmic structure continues until it is disturbed by the introduction of object representation.[2] Karl Bühler asserted, however, that there is no genuine ornamentation to be found in the early drawings of children. He contended that, later, schematic forms undergo changes for aesthetic considerations, until they lose all likeness and become decorative shapes. Thus, he viewed ornamentation as growing out of schematic

Figure 153. *Decorating an "actual object" may lead to both realism and ornamentation. A. Rug design as visualized in its surroundings. B. Realistic rug design.*[30] *A. Talented boy, age fourteen, 1936. B. Talented boy, age fourteen, 1933, color crayons.*

representation rather than preceding it or developing parallel to it.[7]

Maitland, in her pioneering study of 1895, reported that entirely decorative designs make up only three percent of children's output up to the age of nine, increasing to eight percent of the art of fourteen- to seventeen-year-olds. She suggested that children's art is representation rather than an aesthetic expression, and questioned whether "children find any need for the expression of the abstract beauty in drawing until a comparatively late stage in their development has been reached."[38]

In the 1890's, M. V. O'Shea was concerned with children's drawings of an ornamented chair. He reported that the five-year-olds did not even try to indicate ornamentation, although it had been requested. Fifty percent of the eight-year-olds showed some ornamentation, and eighty-seven percent of the sixteen-year-olds used ornamentation to some extent.[47]

Some children seem to delight in adding decorative details, especially to women's clothing. In the past, the trimming of ladies' hats received an ever-growing attention, beginning as early as at the age of four and increasing steadily up to eleven and twelve, after which it diminished.[48]

Kerschensteiner, in his far-reaching and comprehensive exploration of the drawing activities of Munich school children, asked them to decorate a plate. The children made either inscriptions or signs such as clocks, garlands or bouquets of flowers, and arranged their motifs in series, rhythmically spaced and repeated. The center and border were treated in a similar manner. Another of his experiments with the decoration of book covers brought poor results. However, decoration of boxes and eggs were outstanding. Girls exceeded boys in the number of rhythmical patterns created, excelled at an earlier age and, in general, were superior in decorative abilities to the boys.[24]

Other studies involving decorating, such as drawing a woman and decorating her dress, or decorating a shield of a given shape, reported that "scribbled schematic figures without any order" were used, and that "only a few showed a decoration of ornamental character." In these studies, contrary to the findings of the Munich study, boys seemed to abandon the schema before girls and to achieve aesthetic organization of space at an earlier phase.[44] The same author, in a similar study, found that children still used "peculiar lines" that were a pervasive decoration for age levels three to four; that, at the first grade level, the lines became regular, wavy and zig-zag, and that not until the middle grades did these lines gain any significance as part of the pictured object.[45] A later study was based on a request to decorate a tea box shown in perspective. The children used a great variety of decorative effects: all-over line patterns, picture-type representations and even compositional designs. Some children proceeded from the center to the border, others in the opposite direction. Some were guided by the shape of the object, the tea box, while others disregarded it.[46]

In one of the Cleveland studies, children were asked to make a rug design, thus testing their ability to make any kind of design element and develop it into a decorative whole within the familiar framework of a rug. The younger children leaned toward simple, symmetrical design, while the older children used more complex, non-symmetrical arrangements. There were other marked age-related differences also, such as an increase in the number of units used and increasingly careful treatment of color and color areas among older children.[43]

Another Cleveland study was undertaken to investigate children's expression of what they consider beautiful. They chose a variety of subjects—representative, decorative, or abstract. They exercised exceptional care for ornamental values and gave far more attention to neatness and to technical execution than they usually gave with other subjects.[43]

FUNCTION OF COLOR

Children's use of color goes through three stages that only roughly coincide with the developmental stages of drawing. Investigators generally agree that the child uses color first just for the sake of color, then for a simple realistic purpose, and finally in a more sophisticated manner (see Table I).

Color as Decoration

The child's first use of colors seems to be for the pleasure of looking at them and trying them out. These first attempts are experiences of delight in the discovery of the different kinds of colors. At this age color is used for its own sake, and the actual color of the scribble or of the object being depicted is of little importance. The color is used because it is "pretty," "my favorite," out of curiosity, easily available, and for the sake of comparison. This stage extends into the early schematic period of representation, and in a few instances, into the schematic stage.

Color Used Realistically

At the next level, beginning at about six, color is used to represent the actual color of an object.[18] The role of color is secondary in the sense that the shaping of the object comes first; then the color is added to fill in the outlined object. Color, in fact, becomes the object's substance. Whatever may be the choice, it relates to reality.

92 CHAPTER 4
Some Characteristics of Art Development

Certain animals and objects are always shown in the same color, as if the color were a consistent attribute of the object; for instance, an apple is always red. Somehow, in the child's mind, the color becomes as essential a characteristic as the shape of the object. One can make a distinction between the aesthetic value (which appears late), and the use of color as an attribute of objects.[60] At the stage when every object is colored in its actual color, distant trees and hills will be colored as green as the trees close at hand. Their apparent color, modified by the atmospheric effects of distance, is not taken into account. Color continues to be used in this way throughout the schematic and mixed stages, that is, as true local color.

An "active use of color" is effected by different factors such as hue, saturation, and brightness. There are periods when children draw large numbers of colored pictures, and periods when little or no color is used. A truly "painterly" picture emerges only at the adult level.[13]

Color as It Appears

The true-to-appearance stage is characterized by a variation of the true local color. There is discrimination in colors, selection and modification of hues and values indicating a more accurate conception of the particular color under various conditions. As in other aspects of true-to-appearance pictures, color variation is not generally achieved in the elementary school years.

Local true color is characteristic of children's drawings and remains fairly constant from the age of six to fifteen, while the variation of local color increases moderately from the age of nine on. Rubbing color in order to soften the contour starts at about the age of eight. Combining of colors be-

gins around age nine.[17] The use of color is more closely related to development in drawing than to chronological age.[30]

Color as a means of expression and as a source of enjoyment takes on a number of aspects that are interesting, complex in interaction, and that can be linked only tentatively to other developmental aspects of expression. A study of the interrelation of ten vital characteristics of children's pictorial output shows color as a most important factor, closely related to shape and style but only slightly related, if at all, to representational development as a whole.[31]

Variety and intensity of colors appear to be related to age. Younger children favor multicoloredness, four or more colors. Gradually, children tend to restrict their use of many colors to two or three in some pictures until, around fourteen, many of them confine themselves to monochromes.[30, 43]

Vivid colors are preferred by younger children and more subdued colors by older children.[57] Use of brilliant color effects, giving an impression of lustre or sparkle, subtle blending of colors, or strikingly bold combinations and contrasts, are found in the work of artistically talented children (see Table I).

There have been inquiries into the relative importance of color and form. Some observers conclude that form is more important than color up to the age of three, then color dominates until after the age of six, at which point form again takes priority over color.[6, 12, 22] Special attention may be paid to either color or form, depending on which of the two dominates the object, if it serves the child's purpose for emphasis.[58]

Studies of color preferences point to red as the favorite color, particularly at younger age levels. Blue comes next. Red was preferred to other colors in studies of different national backgrounds.[15, 16] On the whole, there seems no doubt that red and blue are at the top of color preferences. Even sex differences merely shift red and blue between first and second place in that girls do not prefer red as much as boys do.[26]

Preferences are transitory and change with maturity and education. For example, "red as a favorite color falls precipitately with education;"[15] development of taste and sophistication tend to modify favorite colors, while social status also affects color preferences.[23] Emotional states, too, seem to influence the choice of colors: red reflecting a feeling of happy excitement, and blue a feeling of serenity, dignity, or sadness.[21] Children associate certain feelings with particular colors. Red may be "jolly," but violet "sad," red may stand for action, while blue suggests rest.[41] However, it is not likely that children as a rule perceive colors as advancing-retreating, expanding-contracting, or exciting-calm.[10] One of the most vivid illustrations of association of color with violent feelings was provided by a young child who in recounting a story said: "Then the wolf got a quite yellow voice,"[19] thus using visual imagery for an auditory sensation.

CHAPTER FOUR: TEXT REFERENCES

1. Arnheim, R., *Art and Visual Perception: A Psychology of the Creative Eye*, Berkeley: University of California Press, 1960.
2. Bakušinskij, A. B. A. W., "Das Kunstchaffen und die Kunsterziehung," Forschungsversuche über den Tatbestand der Raumkünste, Neu-Moskau, 1925, in: Wulff, O., "Kernfragen der Kinderkunst und des allgemeinen Kunstunterrichts der Schule," *Zeitschrift für Aesthetik und allgemeine Kunstwissenschaft*, XXVI, No. 1 (1932), 46-85.
3. Baumstein-Heissler, N., "A propos du dessin: quelques opinions et traveaux soviétiques," *Enfance*, VIII, No. 4 (1955), 377-399.
4. Boussion-Leroy, A., "Dessins en transparence et niveau de développement," *Enfance*, III, Nos. 3 and 4 (1950), 276-287.
5. Britsch, G., *Theorie der bildenden Kunst*, edited by Egon Kornmann, 2nd ed.; Munich: Bruckmann, 1930.
6. Bryan, C., and F. Goodenough, "The relative potency of color and form perception at various ages," *Journal of Experimental Psychology*, XII (1929), 197-213.
7. Bühler, K., *Die geistige Entwicklung des Kindes*, Jena: Fischer, 1922.
8. Burckhardt, H., "Veränderungen der Raumlage in Kinderzeichnungen," *Zeitschrift für paedagogische Psychologie*, XXVI (1925), 352-371.
9. Clark, A. B., "The child's attitude toward perspective problems," *Studies in Education*, Stanford University (1896-1897), 283-294.
10. Corcoran, A. L., "Children's responses to color stimuli," in: *Research in Art Education*, 7th Yearbook, National Art Education Association (1956), 84-95.
11. Denner, A., "Dessin et rationalisation chez l'enfant," *Enfance*, VI, No. 4 (1953), 291-328; VII, No. 11 (1954), 41-70.

12. Descoeudres, A., "Couleur, position ou nombre?" *Archives de Psychologie*, XVI (1916), 37-69.
13. Eng, H., *The Psychology of Child and Youth Drawing from the Ninth to the Twenty-Fourth Year*, New York: Humanities Press, 1957.
14. Flakowski, H., "Entwicklungsbedingte Stilformen von Kinderaufsatz und Kinderzeichnung," *Psychologische Beitraege*, III, No. 3 (1957), 446-467.
15. Garth, T. R., "A color preference scale for 1,000 white children," *Journal of Experimental Psychology*, VII (1924), 233-241.
16. Garth, T. R. and I. R. Collado, "Color preferences of Filipino children," *Journal of Comparative Psychology*, IX (1929), 397-404.
17. Ghesquière-Dierickx, B., "Comment dessinent les enfants: Evolution du dessin selon l'âge," *Enfance*, XI (1961), 179-182.
18. Grosser, H. and W. Stern, "Das freie Zeichnen und Formen des Kindes," Sammlung in: *Abhandlungen der Zeitschrift für angewandte Psychologie*, Leipzig: Ambrosius Barth, 1913.
19. Grözinger, W., *Scribbling, Drawing, Painting; The Early Forms of the Child's Pictorial Creativeness*, New York: Frederick A. Praeger, Inc., 1955.
20. Harris, D. B., "Intra-individual versus inter-individual consistency in children's drawing of a man," *American Psychologist*, V, No. 7 (1950), 293-294.
21. Hevner, K., "Experimental studies of the affective values of colors and lines," *Journal of Applied Psychology*, XIX (1935), 385-398.
22. Katz, D., "Ein Beitrag zur Kenntnis der Kinderzeichnungen," *Zeitschrift für Psychologie*, XLI (1906), 241-256.
23. Katz, S. E. and F. S. Breed, "The color preference of children," *Journal of Applied Psychology*, VI (1922), 255-266.
24. Kerschensteiner, G., *Die Entwicklung der zeichnerischen Begabung*, Munich: Gerber, 1905.
25. Lark-Horovitz, B., "Interlinkage of sensory memories in relation to training in draw-

ing," *Journal of Genetic Psychology*, XLIX (1936), 69-89.

26. Lark-Horovitz, B., "On art appreciation of children: III. Textile pattern preference study," *Journal of Educational Research*, XXXIII, No. 1 (1939), 7-35.

27. Lark-Horovitz, B., "On learning abilities of children as recorded in a drawing experiment. I. Subject matter, II. Aesthetic and representational qualities," *Journal of Experimental Education*, IX, No. 4 (1941), 332-360.

28. Lark-Horovitz, B., Unpublished work of "A visual memory experiment," carried out at the Cleveland Museum of Art, Cleveland, Ohio, 1941.

29. Lark-Horovitz, B., E. N. Barnhart, and E. M. Sills, *Graphic Work—Sample Diagnosis. An Analytical Method of Estimating Children's Drawing Ability*, Cleveland: The Cleveland Museum of Art, 1939.

30. Lark-Horovitz, B., and J. Norton, "Children's art abilities: Developmental trends of art characteristics," *Child Development*, XXX (1959), 433-452.

31. Lark-Horovitz, B., and J. Norton, "Children's art abilities: The interrelations and factorial structure of ten characteristics," *Child Development*, XXXI (1960), 453-462.

32. Leroy, A., "Représentation de la perspective dans les dessins d'enfants," *Enfance*, IV, No. 4 (1951), 286-307.

33. Levinstein, S., *Untersuchungen über das Zeichnen des Kindes*, Leipzig: R. Voigtländer, 1905.

34. Lewis, H., "Spatial representation in drawing as a correlate of development and a basis for picture preference," *Journal of Genetic Psychology*, CII (1963), 95-107.

35. Luquet, G.-H., *Les Dessins d'un Enfant*, Paris: Alcan, 1913.

36. Luquet, G.-H., "La narration graphique chez l'enfant," *Journal de Psychologie*, XXI (1924), 183-218.

37. Luquet, G.-H., "Le réalism intellectuel dans l'art primitif. I. Figuration de l'invisible; II. Le rendu du visible," *Journal de psychologie*, XXIV (1927), 765-797; 888-927.

38. Maitland, L. M., "What children draw to please themselves," *The Inland Educator*, I (September 1895), 77-81.

39. Malrieu, P., "Observations sur quelques dessins libres chez l'enfant," *Journal de Psychologie Normale et Pathologique*, XLIII (1950), 239-244.

40. Marshall, S., *An Experiment in Education*, Cambridge, Great Britain: University Press, 1963.

41. Martin, A., "Die Gefühlsbetonung von Farben und Farbenkombinationen bei Kindern," *Zeitschrift für Kinderforschung*, XXVI (1921), 128-156.

42. Mühle, G., *Entwicklungspsychologie des zeichnerischen Gestaltens. Grundlagen, Formen und Wege in der Kinderzeichnung*, Munich: Ambrosius Barth, 1955.

43. Munro, T.; B. Lark-Horovitz; and E. N. Barnhart, "Children's art abilities: Studies at the Cleveland Museum of Art," *Journal of Experimental Education*, XI, No. 2 (1942), 97-155.

44. Muth, G. F., Über Ornamentierungsversuche mit Kindern im Alter von 6-9 Jahren," *Zeitschrift für angewandte Psychologie*, VI (1912), 21-50.

45. Muth, G. F., "Zierversuche mit Kindern, IV: Über eine sehr merkwürdige Linie in den zierkünstlerischen Arbeiten des Kindes," *Zeitschrift für angewandte Psychologie*, XVII (1920), 259-269.

46. Neubauer, V., "Zur Entwicklung der dekorativen Zeichnung," *Zeitschrift für angewandte Psychologie*, XXXIX (1931), 273-325.

47. O'Shea, M. V., "Children's expression through drawing," *Proceedings of the National Education Association* (Asbury Park, N.J., 1894), 1015-1023.

48. Partridge, L., "Children's drawings of men and women," *Studies in Education*, II, No. 5 (1902).

49. Pfleiderer, W., *Die Geburt des Bildes*, Stuttgart: Julius Hoffmann, 1930.

50. Piaget, J., "L'Explication de l'ombre chez l'enfant," *Journal de Psychologie*, XXIV (1927), 230-242.

51. Piaget, J. and B. Inhelder *et al.*, *La Représentation de l'Espace chez l'Enfant*,

Presses Universitaires de France, 1948.

52. Piaget, J. and B. Inhelder, *The Child's Conception of Space*, New York: Humanities Press, 1956.

53. Ricci, C., *L'Arte dei Bambini*, Bologna: N. Zanichelli, 1887.

54. Scupin, E. and G., *Bubi im 4. bis 6. Lebensjahr*. Leipzig: Grieben, 1910.

55. Stern, W., Über verlagerte Raumformen," *Zeitschrift für angewandte Psychologie*, III (1909-1910).

56. Stern, W., Die Entwicklung der Raumwahrnehmung in der ersten Kindheit," *Zeitschrift für angewandte Psychologie*, (1909), 412-423.

57. Subes, J., "Des goûts des enfants pour les couleurs," *Enfance*, XII (1959), 117-142.

58. Tobie, H., "Die Entwicklung teilinhalt-licher Betrachtung von Farbe und Form im vorschulpflichtigen Kindesalter," *Zeitschrift für angewandte Psychologie*, Beiheft 38 (1926).

59. Van der Horst, L., "Affect, expression and symbolic function in the drawings of children," in: *Feelings and Emotion: Mooseheart Symposium*, ed. by L. Reymert, New York: McGraw-Hill Book Co., 1950.

60. Wulff, O., *Die Kunst des Kindes*, Stuttgart: Ferdinand Enke, 1927.

61. Zazzo, R., "Le geste graphique et la structuration de l'espace," *Enfance* (special number on children's drawings), 1951.

62. Zesbaugh, H. A., *Children's Drawings of the Human Figure*, Chicago: University of Chicago Press, 1934.

CHAPTER FIVE

Significance of Various Factors in Children's Art

ACT OF DRAWING

The *act of drawing* is both a play activity and a means of expression. It is also an emotional outlet, different from shouting or jumping. It is play carried out with utter seriousness.[46] The child soliloquizes on paper and is, in a sense, acting. The drawing becomes the visible record of his play. Often the child endows simple objects with all kinds of imagined qualities,[19] and this carries over in his drawing, so that the pic-

ture becomes a realization of the imagined. The child becomes part of the imaginary world he has created in his drawing.

His earliest attempts, his scribbles, seem to originate in unplanned motor activity, deriving from a need to *act*, as distinct from an urge to shape. His scribbles are visible traces of motor action and not the result of definite intent. In scribbling and in drawing, the child seems to be vicariously enjoying an experience in motion and play that goes beyond the mere act of making marks on

Figure 154. *A puppet drawn in pencil to serve as a toy.*[9] *Boy, age three, Germany, 1920's.*

Figure 155. *THE CAT AND THE RAT. The game is made of colored paper cutouts which are glued in position (with help of mother) on green paper (grass) with spots (flowers). The rat is white with pink eyes. The cat is spotted on both sides. The game was used as a "prop" for playing by herself.*[19] *Girl, age seven, 1936.*

paper. *He is* racing across the street as he draws a line across the paper. *He is* flying through the air as he draws a child in a swing.

The urge to scribble and later to draw characterizes a phase of development shared by nearly all children and reflects to some extent the child's mental growth.[66] Once children begin to shape symbols for objects, they have made drawing a constructive act leading to the mastery of their own world.[11] When the child constantly uses the same shapes in his drawings to represent the same concepts, the act of drawing becomes analogous to his use of language in which the same words are used to convey established meanings. Many authorities suggest that early drawings parallel early speech.[13]

When a child has begun to consistently use certain shapes as symbols, he graduates from the scribble to the schematic period. Now he outlines objects. With the outline he seems to establish his concept of what *belongs* in the picture. Then he goes on to define it by using details. Soon he begins to note and convey functions of objects.

Rarely does he desire to erase or otherwise eliminate a "faulty" part of the drawing. Luquet, who systematically observed and recorded his daughter's drawing activities over a period of many years, reports: "After commenting that she was wrong in making a human mouth on the dog because 'a dog has his mouth in the nose', she draws a second mouth but does not erase the first."[46]

The next step occurs when the child colors within the outline. Even when color alone would suffice, he uses an outline. Even when he is aware that it may not be suitable, he may use a black line to delineate water, or to show a cloud in the sky. He may try to lessen the distinctiveness by using a fainter outline or a crayon of the same color, but he needs to make the outline first, to be filled in with color afterwards.

During his schematic or an earlier stage, the child draws from a mental image. He will look at a model if told to do so, but only in order to find out what he is supposed to represent. Then he will proceed as if the model were not there, making his picture without paying further attention to it.[30]

The child follows a mental image which he has developed as the result of various sense perceptions and experiences. This image may not always be a correct reflection of the object, and the child may attach parts at the wrong ends, use incorrect proportions, and add parts not visible from his vantage point. Why the child does these things is not clear. Various explanations have been proposed: that he does this because of fleeting associations, fragmentary knowledge of structure; because of the need to weld parts into a visual whole; or because the experiences on which the representation is based come from a variety of non-visual sources. However, even devices enabling observers to see and record each step the child made in a drawing failed to obtain conclusive answers on this point.[4]

The image in a child's eye may be more complex ("far more beautiful" to quote one child) than his drawing. It may contain elements that he cannot handle with his limited graphic skill. He reacts by making a picture that is descriptive, enumerating the objects, sketching the arrangement but failing to convey the characteristics which made it remarkable.[36] Thus a drawing in many instances is purely a record of what moved the child but not why or how.

Handedness appears to be a significant factor in some representations. The average right-handed child, for instance, will draw a profile facing left. Even if a model, whether human or animal, is placed before children so that its profile faces to the right, the right-handed child will show it facing left, the direction he is accustomed to drawing. He acknowledges the profile position but not its direction.[55]

Before the fifth year, the product has no lasting value for either the child himself or for other children. At about the age of seven, when drawing becomes an intentional act and the product becomes more representational in character, then the drawings begin to acquire an independent existence in the child's eyes. This new appreciation reaches its zenith at about age ten.[74]

Once the child has fully developed his schemata and reached the peak of his individual achievement (when he feels no more can be added or improved), then the act of drawing becomes automatic. The pictorial symbols are drawn without hesitation and often with incredible rapidity. Automatism has set in. After a while the symbols begin to degenerate; they are drawn more and more carelessly; they lose form, accuracy and character. Pictures become dull and uninteresting.

The state of automatism must be overcome within a relatively short time or stagnation may lead to a permanent regression. At best, the individual may continue schematic drawing into adulthood.[35] The charm of the childhood style is lost in adults because they no longer have the child's fresh outlook.

The act of drawing and the act of modeling proceed in similar fashion. In modeling, the child first models the head with eyes, nose, mouth. Then he shapes the trunk which he joins to the head to form the central part of the body. Then he adds legs and feet, arms and hands. In-between parts are wedged or pushed in. Children like to talk while modeling just as they like to talk while drawing.[53] After experiencing enjoyment and a sense of achievement in modeling schematic forms, the average child reaches the same point of disenchantment and resistance to further development as in drawing.

It is disappointing that an activity which has been so promising in early years should wane in adolescence. While some regard this development as an inevitable outcome of the child's turning to language and other means of self-expression and communication, Henry Schaefer-Simmern does not consider this valid. He maintains that organic growth of visual artistic configuration is a process distinct from independent rational thinking, language development or mere emotions. He sees this growth as indispensable to the integration of personality and as continuing regardless of age.[69] This puts the blame, as it were, on art education rather than on natural development.

Others, however, hold that just as "the need to draw during an early period can be taken as a sign of development, its later repudiation often represents growth."[66] The child's change of mental attitude prompts the search for other creative channels in which self-criticism can operate more fruitfully and give more satisfaction. At this point drawing begin to serve different needs and objectives.

VISUAL MEMORY

The child's ability to express himself graphically is dependent, in a very direct manner, upon a widely developed and strongly selective visual memory. It is significant that "the main difference between visual and verbal accounts of what has been seen becomes apparent when an individual attempts to draw."[28] Even when verbal accounts of what they have seen, given by average and artistically gifted children, are much alike, their choice of picture subjects and the drawings themselves are very different. The process of drawing demonstrates clearly the difference both in their awareness and in the quality of visual recall.[70] Children, especially in the pre-school period, normally think in visual images. This pre-verbal way of thinking is also characteristic of pre-literate groups. With a mastery of language, pre-literate groups, like older children, come to rely less on visual images. In our society, visual thinking usually diminishes substantially after adolescence and tends to be replaced by verbal thinking. However, painters, sculptors, choreographers, and often poets and script-writers as well, "visualize" their thoughts and ideas before they can execute them.[45]

In the visual arts, the role of the senses and their specific influence on memory is of great significance, since pictorial memory is largely dependent on sense impressions. Although sight and hearing dominate the adult's recollections, it is evident that smell, taste, touch and muscle sensations are of equal and sometimes even more importance in the child's memory. For example, a child can pick out, without a moment's hesitation, her brother's pajamas though they may be identical with her own, merely by smelling them.

There is sometimes a fascinating interchange of sense impressions in children. One four-year-old wanted to picture the flight of partridges which he had often heard take off at his approach but never actually seen. He drew the surroundings in which partridges live—woods, clearing and river—and represented the partridges themselves by a number of parallel, zigzagging lines to picture the whirring noise these birds make when they fly up. He said he wanted to show the sound only, since the partridges always managed to hide from him. The child had undertaken to visually represent sense impressions that were not visual. Another four-year-old, upon coming home from her father's laboratory announced: "I saw a nasty smell."

At one time it seemed to be taken for granted that the visual appearance of things was all that counted in visual representation. It was believed that "what an individual can reproduce represents his highest memory performance."[20] Allport, for example, investigated the change in visual memory by observing changes in drawings and their decay over a period of time.[1] Osterrieth allowed children to study the model, then removed it. A large number of children, particularly from age seven or eight on, made better drawings more quickly than when they referred to the model. Most children continued to copy the type of drawing they had devised for their own use. Children between four and seven had difficulty in recalling details and often drew from memory at a lower level than they had achieved when the model was in view. From the ages of nine to fifteen, children made progress in improving recall and representation. Most adults were unable to progress much; some regressed.[64]

Certain tests suggest that the visual memory of the deaf is superior to that of hearing children, perhaps as a result of a compensatory psychological phenomenon.[10]

It is difficult to judge the duration of the child's memory in connection with his drawing. Duration and vividness of recall seem to be affected by the child's interest in the subject as well as by its emotional significance for him.[45]

The direction of change in memory seems to be toward a more integrated whole.[16] This was shown by studies[37] of children, aged six to fifteen, in which they drew the same objects over a period of three years. To analyze the changes in these drawings made from memory, all the drawings were superimposed over one another, the later ones over those made directly after viewing the model and after an interval of months between drawing it from memory. Most children retained many characteristics of their first drawing: size, direction and individual characteristics. All the drawings combined gave a unified pictorial effect in spite of many differences of detail. This curious phenomenon suggests the influence both of the primary image of the original model and of the individual's first drawing, even after a lapse of three years (see Figures 188 and 189). The older children, eleven to fifteen, whether still in the schematic stage or already in phases leading to the true-to-appearance level, show this tendency, namely to be true to their own visual memory, as do also gifted children. The talented children have exceedingly ready and detailed visual recall. Most of their visual impressions show better comprehension of the visual components of objects and their significance for representation. As a result, their drawings from memory are often astonishing in their completeness.

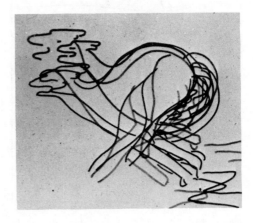

Figure 156. *Superimposition of four drawings, the fourth made one year after the first. The model shown to the children, ages eleven to fifteen, was a sketch of a leaping dog by the American artist Flannagan. The first and later drawings were made by the children after the artist's sketch had been withdrawn (they never saw it again). The sameness of sizes and positions, as well as other characteristics, are retained to a surprisingly high degree by talented children, to some degree by average children.[31] Girl, age thirteen, 1939-1940.*

HUMOR

Children's drawings show little evidence of intentional humor; few of their pictures are meant to be funny. In about four thousand drawings made by children, many of whom had free choice of subject, there were only a few scattered humorous presentations and fewer than one percent were cartoons. The drawings that showed humorous intent were caricatures or pictures of misbehavior in the classroom—a topic not apt to be considered funny by adults.[59, 38]

Figure 158. *Humor is found in misbehavior in the schoolroom. A mixed to true-to-appearance drawing with alignment, flexible lines, and movement.[22] Boy, age fourteen, color crayon drawing.*

Figure 157. *A series of five drawings from memory done after viewing a ceramic polar bear for about two minutes. The first drawing was made immediately after students saw the model. The last of these drawings was done nearly three years later. The second sketch is an example of a younger average child's efforts to remember the bear with the help of the living habits of bear. The third drawing comes closer to a bear face, while the fourth regresses. The fifth drawing has some bear character that is partially achieved by placing the bear on an ice flow.[21] Boy, age eight (at start of experiment), 1938.*

The child's sense of humor and wit is different from that of the adult, and it is as difficult for the adult to appreciate children's humor as it is for the child to understand adult humor.

The funny situations depicted by younger children are sometimes quite nonsensical, such as a picture of a horde of animals—and people—with two heads, or other improbable situations. One child drew a giant with a head-cold whose huge nose-drips create a pond on which tiny boats are floating, while around it walk people holding umbrellas.[67] A kindergarten child may find humor in what he considers exaggerated emphasis on cleanliness or unreasonable standards of manner and behavior.

Younger children sometimes express their humor by exaggerated proportion and by unexpected color and lines, intending to draw attention to a comic situation. The younger child seldom achieves the comic effect he strives for. On the other hand, he is often aware of the unintended comical effects in some of his serious drawings when he can't draw what he wants to show. In self-criticism, he recognizes and enjoys the unintended humor of the product. He "may explode in laughter, saying: 'Oh, look at my horse, he looks like a pig.' "[48] Many pictures that seem funny to the child artist and to his classmates may not seem so to an adult. Some children, even at ten and twelve, consider that an automobile crashing into a telephone pole or some similar accident is funny[36]—most adults don't.

It is the story that the child offers in conjunction with his picture which stamps it as intentionally humorous. For example, the comic implication became clear when one child chanted the funny—really naughty— ditty which she was illustrating.[47]

In an analysis of subject matter chosen from spontaneous drawings by adolescents,[23] nearly a fourth were caricatures. These caricatures, mostly by boys, showed

Figure 159. *In this example of humor, a farm woman is tearing her hair when she finds that all the creatures in the barnyard are double-headed.[42] Girl, age seven, 1961.*

Figure 160. *FUNNY MAN. He has a cold which makes his immensely big nose run, and soon there is a pond at his feet. The boy finished by putting boats in the pond and people walking around it.[34] Boy, age eleven, French, ca 1912.*

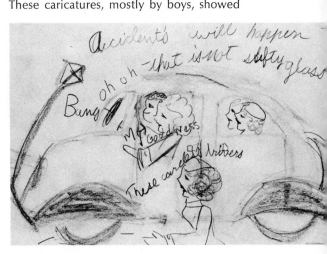

Figure 161. *There is humor because of an accident. This is a true-to-appearance drawing with "pretty girl" faces.[41] Girl, age ten, 1940, pen and ink drawing.*

Figure 162. *The humor in this drawing is based on a ditty, "The Little Merchant of Onions," and the age of the child to whom such a subject appeals; she was singing the ditty while drawing:"There was a little man -ton-ton-derontaine —A little onion merchant—" etc.*
Who climbed the mountain
On his hobby horse.
While climbing the mountain
Off went the cannon, whereupon
He made - - - - on his heels.
All the ladies of the town
Came a-rushing with rags to rub him down."[27]
Girl, age five, French, ca 1900's.

peculiarities of physique, such as long nose, Adam's apple, receding chin, etc., in cartoons of men; and prominent teeth or badly kept hair in cartoons of women.

The humor of older children is quite different and very complex. Some of them depict a combination of the adventurous,

Figure 163. *CARICATURE.*[30] *Boy, age twelve, 1936.*

the strange and the humorous. Others produce drawings that are quite satirical, containing sharp criticism, or implying a social or moral judgment (see Figures 12 and 144). Examples can be seen in certain types of cowboy portraits, drawings of classrooms or street scenes, in which children show their own bad behavior (with the teacher as a target)[59] or the side they take in a fight.

EMOTION

Discussing the role of emotions in child art, Clarapède said a child's drawing is a bit of his soul spread out on paper. This eminent educator and psychologist was convinced that even drawings that appear very matter-of-fact involve some emotion on the part of the child. Children are involved emotionally in their play activities, and play is, in turn, involved in drawing. Their need to communicate has an emotional basis and

Figure 164. *A humorous "type" or tough guy. Note the very decisive lines.*[22] *Boy, age thirteen, 1933.*

Figure 165. MOTHER. *The large detailed feet, the scribbly hands (probably indicating movement), and the baby in the highchair all indicate how the child experiences members of his family. Detail from a spontaneous schematic drawing.*[40] *Girl, age four, 1965.*

Figure 166. *The emotional involvement and pride of going out in the rain with boots and umbrella are clearly expressed by the size of the boots and the details. Girl, age... Boy, age six, 1938, schema.*

their achievement in art offers them an emotional satisfaction. Thus, their emotional involvement in drawing goes beyond just the need to communicate.

Even in the earliest stage of drawing—in the scribble to early schematic period—just making the lines is an important experience in "doing," an early exercise in simple problem solving and the achievement of satisfaction.

Once the awkward stage of manipulation has been overcome, the child may no longer puncture the paper in a burst of emotion and eagerness to express his thoughts, but the strength of strokes, the flow of lines, or a tortured angularity also appear to be projections of his emotions. The specific emotional involvement is articulated, if at all, by words rather than by graphic means.[5]

When the child reaches the transitional schematic and schematic phase, the expression of emotion in his pictures is more perceptible, and therefore more readily interpreted. In characteristic schematic fashion

Figure 167. *OUR TEACHER. Desks with children appear in three planes, one topping the other. Note the enormous size of the teacher's head which indicates her importance.*[13] *Girl, age seven, Japan, 1964, print.*

emotions and feelings are expressed by attributes or situational arrangements rather than by the realism of adult art. Children's drawings are not, therefore, only representative of their perceptual acquaintance with the world around them. On the other hand, it would seem unwise to assume that children's drawings are entirely the result of outbursts of overcharged emotions, as implied by Montessori, who described them as "monstrous expressions of intellectual lawlessness."[74]

Perception, imagination, and emotion all play a part in different proportion. Thus, the fanciful is strong in young children, but after age seven or eight, perception plays a greater role. In drawing, the child relies on remembrance, particularly in the schematic phase, but is selective in what he remembers, depending to an appreciable extent on feeling; "guiding emotion" is important for future "productive work."[58]

To a child, an object drawn is not just an object but the expression of an action, the souvenir of an experience, or the means of re-living an emotion (see Figure 68).[19] When he draws a house, he is not just drawing a building but the place in which he lives or wishes to live—a place of security and coziness where father and mother live. In drawing a house, the child experiences the meaning it has for him, and the emotions connected with it.

Children who had seen their homes destroyed in their war-devastated country depicted later, as refugees, the horror of the experience in their drawing, spreading the terrible disaster all over the page. Yet the children of another country, although they had experienced the same misfortune, drew their houses as they once had been, peaceful, with flowers in the garden and curtains at the windows.[7]

Children are amazing in their responses. One group, for example, when requested to draw the "most important event in their lives," drew such various incidents as being spanked, falling, having an accident.[14]

Adults can easily be misled in trying to interpret the emotions reflected in the art work of children. Configurations that symbolize a particular emotion to an adult may have a quite different meaning for the child. For instance, at the schematic stage, a child may draw upturned lines for the mouth—this being the usual schematic symbol for it. To the adult, the pictured face shows a toothy grin, but the child did not intend to draw a laughing face. The mouth that he did was just the best he could draw. If a drawing is misinterpreted by an adult in the

Figure 168. *SINGING. The large, oval mouth, larger than both feet combined, expresses the feeling of exultation in singing. A spontaneous crayon drawing in which the child used his human schema, which included using transparency.[40] Boy, age six, 1963.*

child's presence, the child will sometimes correct the grownup and inform him that he should keep his, the child's, intention in mind. Most children, however, don't bother with explanations, either because they don't care about adult interpretations of their drawings or because they take understanding for granted. Of course there are occasional drawings showing distorted expressions that are intentional exaggerations,[58] such as the circle to represent the wide open mouth of a singer, though the circle is otherwise rarely used as symbol for the mouth. Some distortions may be deliberate efforts to convey emotions, but in general they are the result of particular forms of children's schemata. As Kerschensteiner put

it: "Whether the child represents a funeral or a snowball fight, the human schema remains the same."[30]

Early research in children's art did not underline the relevancy of emotion. Some important studies interpret distortion as inaccurate visualization or the result of conflict between the child's desire to represent the subject in a particular way he has in mind and his inability to do so.[76] Other investigators, such as Luquet, point to the importance of an "internal model," which is not an artificial abstraction of a perceived object, nor a simple copy of it, but represents some reality in the child's mind. The internal model often distorts the object that it represents in spite of its spontaneity, and the reconstruction the child makes from it is complex and elaborate.[48] Emotions probably affect the internal model and account for the importance of the human figure. In particular, psychologists have not, as yet, agreed on why the humans almost always look like "head-men."[11]

More recent studies make emotions a central point of interest, viewing the drawing of a child as the expression in pictures of inner experience, reflecting the child's individuality. Specifically between the ages of six and seven "the drawing is not a pictorial reproduction, but . . a piece of experience."[74] When a younger child represents a horse, he rarely shows a horse by itself; he nearly always draws the rider too, while the average adult, upon being asked to draw a horse, does just that and no more.[35] The child thinks of the horse as a beloved companion. With similar personal feelings, a younger child draws an airplane or spaceship. He feels himself zooming through the air, speeding through the clouds. In fact, he identifies with the pilot or astronaut, and "rides" the airplane—as he once did the horse (see Figures 69 and 141).

The drawing may not be accurate in proportion or details. It is merely a symbol for the real thing, just as a ragdoll is a symbol for a person. It is a stage prop for the doll's play-acting. Girls tend to make drawings, papercuts, and the like that take the place of actual play activity or game (see Figures 154 and 155). Boys, after ages eight or nine, become particularly interested in machines, showing details of the plane, car, train, or spaceship as carefully as possible.

Differences and distortions in the drawings made by abnormal children have been used to further our understanding of the emotional states of the normal child.

Studies have also been made of the work of the deaf and the blind to learn whether distortion of shape, line, or color reflect the particular anxieties of each group. Some of the distortions recall the aspects of some of the art of primitive peoples and invite comparison of the disturbed child's emotional involvements with the influence of supernatural powers associated with primitive art.

A study of the art work of blind children and blind adults and the art work of non-handicapped children revealed characteristics similar to those observed in the expressionistic art of adults. The expressive (haptic) artist "uses the human figure as the interpreter of his emotions and feelings." The haptic child, as Löwenfeld used the term, is "primarily a subjective type."[43, 44] He deals with muscular sensations, kinesthetic experiences, touch impressions—including "all experiences that place the self in value relationship to the outside world." The proportions in his drawings reflect values. The descriptive (or visual) type, even in his purely schematic representations, is guided by visual perceptions of nature and avoids gross exaggerations, unnatural colors or distorted shapes.

The adult must understand that the child's experience of his own body plays a vital role in his visual expression of experiences and feelings. "Observation of his own body, the investigation of body movements when at work or play" are significant to the child.[32] As Boutonier has shown, "Without any previous learning experience for the representation of man, the child creates a shape no one has taught him, a shape that does not satisfy the graphic demands of the adult, but that satisfies the child's own expressive intention. What is the basic source . . . that inspires those drawings which resemble one another? It is the child himself . . . an expression of his being."[11]

The body is the most intimate point of reference in any activity. Machover avers that "the drawing of a person involving a projection of the body image provides a natural vehicle for the expression of one's body needs and conflicts." The way in which a child draws a figure is tied to his personality, and the characteristics of his drawings are projections of his personality structure.[49]

Differences in personality underlie the marked individuality that distinguishes one child from another and sets him off against all others of the same age level or developmental stage. Within the pattern of developmental changes, there is a stability in the projection of personality.

The form in figure drawings is related to the ego-ideal and body image.[33] However, the way in which these are expressed is not always direct and simple. One group of sixth-to eighth-grade boys, who had made quite accurate estimates of their own height and weight, made drawings quite at variance both with these figures and with what might have been considered their ideal image.[71]

The sophisticated adult today, acquainted with expressionistic art, is able to identify and respect the many corresponding elements in child art: distortion of lines, overemphasis in size of one object or person in relation to the whole, emphatic magnification of a part, or the shriveling or complete omission of other parts. The significance of an object or part of it is shown by size—and this, in a way, communicates a subjective judgment. Lack of importance is pictured by a part omitted, shrunk, or barely indicated.

The choice of color and its vividness, brilliancy, or strangeness are other means of communicating feelings. To emphasize an emotional occurrence, young children may color ordinary objects differently from the way they usually do, or use a strange or unrealistic color. Children in the schematic stage seem frequently to emphasize their feelings through color. Those who have reached the true-to-appearance stage use atypical color for emphasis only occasionally. Artistically talented children use color consciously and effectively. When children in an experiment were asked to "Draw something you liked very much, that you loved greatly," emotion was sometimes expressed by "gaudy, loud colors," useful in accentuating other emotional attitudes expressed by the picture.[51] Troubled and depressed children neglect color and in one study showed preference for brown and purple.[73] Aggressive or impertinent children tend to choose dark colors which may express anxieties masked by aggressiveness. Timid children incline toward light colors.[40]

Arrangement and composition, asymmetry, emphasis on a central figure, or complete absence of human figures are ways of expressing emotions. Drawings of disturbed children were found to be characterized by the absence of human figures, although they pictured objects in use by humans.[73,7] Underprivileged boys did effective and colorful paintings, showing a feeling for composition, but with few exceptions devoid of anything living—human, animal or plant. When they did paint plants, they showed them as withered or dying, while other objects are shown in a state of dilapidation.

It is as though, as Van der Horst expresses it, "only the experience and not the perception is depicted . . . that objects are taken according to their expressive value."[74] In other words, the adult cannot share in this inner life of the child and thus the expression the child gives to it is usually strange to the adult.

LEARNING ABILITY

In trying to ascertain what can and cannot be learned in visual expression, one must first distinguish between progress due to maturation and natural development, and progress due to actual learning. Unfortunately, few attempts have been made to investigate learning ability in visual expression, though this area of research is obviously important because much of the curriculum and teaching in art is based on it.

Exhibits of children's art usually leave one with the impression that works chosen for display are the best examples of the work in the group and of any individual children. The work on display seems to have been done by children who have had considerable guidance and instruction in art. This impression is usually correct. However, the degree of direct instruction by art teachers working with children varies considerably.

In some countries, art educators advocate direct instruction which goes so far as to correct the child's work, so he can "see the mistakes he makes."[9] On the whole, directed correction is not approved by art educators in the United States and may not exist anymore in other countries. An exhibit of child art of the Soviet Union (January, 1966) points to uninhibited development of children's representation. The trend is to adapt teaching to the child's readiness and his stage of development.

It is important to realize that any teaching of drawing is bound to have an influence of some kind on the child. It can encourage or inhibit his development and vitally affect his visual attitude toward the world.[31] The paradox is, of course, that on the one hand the child draws what he knows, and on the other hand he learns to know through drawing.[74] Timing and direction of instruction must be geared to the child's readiness for it.

Such research as has been done in this field suggests that art instruction of children must be undertaken with great caution, since apparent temporary success can often be more than cancelled out by long range impairment of the child's natural development in art. For example, though very young children in their free drawings may omit parts of a human figure, it was found that if a partial form (as a man with a single arm or leg) was given to them, they filled in the part they omitted in their own free drawing. This "suggests that the help of a partial form advances behavior at the earlier ages." However, this apparent gain, it turned out, "actually hinders performance at later ages."[2] In the long run, it seems that attempts at acceleration do not further healthy develop-

ment, for maturation proceeds along a fairly well-defined sequence, both in average and highly talented children. The child pushed beyond his ability may resist change and end up by remaining on the same level of achievement for a longer period than is normal.[15]

In a study made of the improvement in figure drawing with boys of about ten years of age, who were given fourteen hours of instruction over a period of three months, it was found that their drawings became more accurate in terms of limbs and

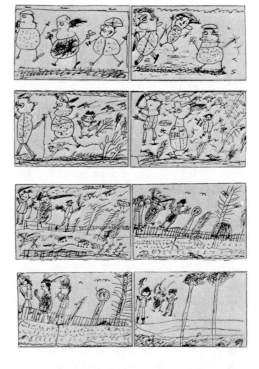

Figure 169. *FATHER, MOTHER AND CHILD GO FOR A WALK. This series of drawings was made over a period of three months, with intermittent instruction regarding figure drawing, composition, and technique of line treatment. Though the figures remained schematic, the schema was better developed, and the arrangement of the pictures became clearer.[14] Boy, age ten, Germany, 1910, pen and ink.*

positions of body parts, proportion and movement, and organization of the parts of the picture. The boys applied what they were taught, and some advanced beyond their level to the next phase. However, some advance might have occurred in this period as a result of other factors, but effect of instruction was easily demonstrable. Moreover, the boys retained their individual style of drawing.[26]

At one time it was thought that stick figures would be helpful in furthering figure-drawing development. Although pre-school and elementary school children seldom use stick figures, older children sometimes use them effectively, even without being shown, in drawing herds of animals, crowds of people, street scenes, and lively, heavily peopled scenes of warfare. Krötzsch, evaluating the usefulness of stick figures in improving children's drawings, observed that not everyone is able to move from stick figure to natural form. In fact, he concluded that stick figures can become more of a hindrance to development than an aid.[32]

In the early part of this century, teachers watched for the effect of specific training on the development of artistic ability. The findings were unsatisfying since they left many questions unanswered. One of these studies was concentrated on girls who were instructed in modeling for two years. They were assigned a topic involving the representation of people in motion and their surroundings. Instruction given to these girls appeared to have had little effect, since they made only a small degree of progress. When the same girls were assigned the same topic but asked to do the modeling while blindfolded, their work was poor, very much poorer than when they could see what their hands were doing.[53] Furthermore, it was poor when compared to that of the blind. The conclusion drawn was that seeing children rely so largely on sight that without

seeing what their hands are doing they cannot produce work that even compares favorably with the modeling of blind children.[54]

Obviously, good visual memory is of vital importance in drawing and in pictorial communication in general. Meumann, one of the great educators of all time, concluded that faulty visual memory is the result of lack of understanding of what one is seeing. In one of his experiments students were asked to draw from memory a decorative pattern that he showed them. The pattern was actually a group of ganglia in the sympathetic nervous system, but the students were not told this. Their drawings of this pattern, depending on visual memory, were poor. Meumann concluded that because the students did not understand the nature and the function of what they were to reproduce, their constructive perception was ineffective.[57]

Cézanne, for example, studied the geological structure and plant life of the landscape he planned to paint so as to gain full understanding of his object. Any person drawing any subject benefits from careful observation of it and a knowledge of its functions.

A good visual memory, however, is only one of the factors needed for pictorial communication. Among others are acquired pictorial schemata, analytical perception, memory for complex pictorial relationships, and the ability to figure out, fit in, and coordinate that which is missing in visual memory. Also important is the ability to empathize, to enter into the nature of the object, feeling an intimate relationship with it, and comprehending its aesthetically relevant features. Sensitive and effective teaching of art can greatly improve the students' ability to observe and apply their observations.

Within the classroom, the teacher can go far in establishing a "climate" for careful observation, where she can guide the children toward appreciation and understanding of the variety and forms of people and things that make up the wonderful world around them.

Cooperative projects, such as the painting of a mural or the design and execution of a textile, are worthwhile endeavors which provide an opportunity for a group of children to work together with the teacher as a moderator, to choose a subject, select a medium and a technique, plan the arrangement, and agree on the task of each individual in carrying out the details.

A child learns to compare his work to that of other children, to develop a certain sensitivity to their talents and respect for their achievements. He gains much from working with others and from learning to adjust to their different personalities and needs. The work of Langevin and Lombard[34] and also of Marshall[52] confirms these observations; the cooperative works of the children in their classes were spectacular. These experiences in social give and take are of particular value in the difficult transition from childhood to adolescence.

Cooperative work is most fruitful if the children are in the same stage of visual development, even if not of the same ages. Schaefer-Simmern, in working with mentally retarded children, found this to be true with his students, also, and stated "cooperative effort is only possible if the persons selected are of the same stage of visual conception [developmental stage] for only this condition guarantees a shared understanding in their work."[69]

Ability in visual expression does not comprise a body of knowledge and does not function in the same way in the child's mind. The various stages must be viewed as steps in maturation which, like baby teeth, are discarded and replaced. Each stage should be encouraged and guided in order to make sure that the next step will develop.

Often school exhibits of children's drawings and paintings show richness in execution, in imagination and in technical achievement. They testify to long hours of work, great patience and love of the subject drawn. Lark-Horovitz, during her years of teaching in Vienna schools and, later, at the Cleveland Museum of Art, in Cleveland public schools, and New York, observed that average European children seemed to draw more in this elaborate, detailed way than American children who seemed to show less patience. She was tempted to interpret this apparent difference as the need of the European children to experience vicariously many things that they could not act out because of crowded conditions or cultural inhibitions; while American children, she felt, had more opportunity to use their energy directly in active play, sports and outdoor life. However, she also felt that the children here were not given enough time to stay with their projects to bring their ideas to fruition. Expenditure of time and patience was obvious in the recently shown drawings and paintings of children of the Soviet Union.

INTELLIGENCE AND DRAWING

Intelligence is positively correlated with drawing ability. Children who draw well are also bright. The reverse does not hold, however, since the drawings of many bright children are quite unremarkable, either developmentally or aesthetically, and are in some cases quite poor.[59] In young children, in particular, the strong relationship between development of drawing and intelligence is revealed by the number and variety of objects that appear in their drawings and the way in which they are organized. Drawing tests therefore derive their scores from the number of details included and from the accuracy of placement and proportion. The value of such tests has been affirmed.[17, 18] It consists in their being nonverbal and thus usable with young children in situations where written questions and replies pose problems. These tests are not concerned with expressive or aesthetic elements but only with developmental factors. The tests are useful with children of different cultures and have yielded data on the number, variety, and organization of objects represented by children tested.[66]

The peak of drawing development is reached at around ten to eleven years of age. After this, graphic techniques become secondary to verbal ones in the expression of ideas, and drawings cease to provide a satisfactory index of intelligence. From this period on, drawing becomes a more or less specialized ability.

There are generally observable relationships between drawing ability, reading ability,[68] over-all school achievement and intelligence. As early as 1894, O'Shea observed that "the children who impress their teachers as being bright and who always show interest in what they are doing usually make drawings that preserve the logical arrangement of events and objects and in which the proportions are fairly good."[63] Good copyists, however, are not likely to be good students.[67] Better students tend to draw fairly well, and those who are especially good in free design, generally have high intelligence, whereas poor students are usually poor in drawing.[24] Children who draw well are better prepared for first grade work.[21]

The mean I.Q. of artistically talented children is higher than that of average children of the same age level, but the difference is neither great nor consistent. As a group, artistically talented children are intelligent, but some higher individual I.Q.'s can be found among the less talented group.[59] In an investigation of a group of prodigies, the conclusion was reached that such children rather than being one-sided are in fact mentally versatile.[6] It seems quite clear that the ability to draw is a significant one, and can be helpful in forecasting the young child's potential. The older child, with a highly developed drawing technique, can obviously use his skill to complement his achievement in other areas.

SEX DIFFERENCES

The most striking difference between boys' and girls' drawing is that, when given a free choice, boys almost never draw women and girls rarely draw men. An early analysis[27] of a large collection of children's drawings[24] showed that in free and spontaneous drawings children pictured mostly adults. Only one percent of the drawings made by boys were of women and one percent of those made by girls were of men. In a more recent study,[8] 94 percent of eight-year-old girls drew only girls, while only three percent drew boys, and three percent drew both.

Adolescent boys liked to make caricatures, 56 percent of which were of men and only 5½ percent of women.[23] Males drawn by boys exaggerate essentially male characteristics, while females drawn by girls glamorize feminine aspects. Girls have difficulties drawing males and often complain that the males in their pictures look like girls.[42] Between the ages of nine and twelve, boys like to draw vehicles, especially ships, tanks, trucks, airplanes, rockets, flying saucers, and space ships. Girls seldom draw vehicles but often draw horses.

From the age of nine on, the differences between the sexes in product and attitude becomes increasingly evident.[74] Girls are more likely to choose still life as a subject than are boys (see Figures 74 and 75).[38] Boys are attracted by machines and start drawing them at an early age. Girls, if they draw machines at all, do so later. In construction—and in some kinds of pictures—girls fashion things that they can use as a toy or make-believe (see Figure 155). Girls are concerned with formal and aesthetic qualities; boys are concerned with technology.[61]

Choices in subject matter are undoubtedly conditioned by the prevailing culture. In the United States, males are interested in machines, transportation and the like, and reveal this interest in their drawings. However, Du Bois reports from Alor, an East Indian island, that in that primitive culture girls drew tools four times as frequently as boys, while boys drew more figures of humans, spirits, and flowers than girls.[12] In his art ability tests, Lewerenz found that girls were more original and better in color recognition but more conservative in other areas than boys. Boys are more analytical and daring; they are willing to take more risks but are more likely to fail in getting the results they hoped for.[41]

As to sex differences in modeling, girls seem to be superior to boys in the use of the medium and technique and more likely to show details; boys are more interested in trying to show movement.[53]

Boys tend to represent actions that are joyful, extraordinary, heroic. They show Man's power, his activities. Girls, on the other hand, draw what is pretty and comment poetically on their pictures: "This is

a water castle, filled with the perfume of spring."[51]

Boys abandon the schema around ten or eleven, while girls cling to it until they are twelve or thirteen. Girls' drawings are more primitive; they seem to avoid perspective representations,[30] and lag behind boys in dealing with spatial representation.[39]

Girls appear more susceptible to suggestions than boys, perhaps because they think they are expected to be compliant rather than independent.[3]

PERSONALITY MANIFESTATIONS IN DRAWING

Child art is being used increasingly as a tool for achieving deeper understanding of the child's personality, because drawing offers an exceptional vehicle for subconscious projection of personality.[72] A child's joys, his fears, his enthusiasm, his conflicts, and his problems may show up in his drawings.

Observation of a child drawing his family can provide insight and even precise knowledge of his emotional state. The way in which he places the members of his family in his drawings shows the place they hold in his feelings. They are ranked by size, by coloring, and by intended imperfections such as omission of an arm or a hand, or other parts.[11] In his picture arrangement, the child gives an account of how well or badly he fits into his family.[65] Indeed, children project their emotional involvements with members of their family into pictures that seem to be "induced from frozen dreams," as Hulse has described them.[22]

The figure the child draws is intimately related to his personality. The projection of his body image provides a means of expressing his personality and his conflicts; details in drawing are interpreted as symbolic of

Figure 170. *GRANDMAMI. Glasses are hooked over the ears, the mouth is a line, the chin a long dividing line, and hair is indicated by scribble.*[24] *Boy, age four, 1961, spontaneous drawing.*

Figure 172. *THIS IS MY FATHER AFTER LIFE. In this portrait, the child tries to show the observed position of arms and hands while talking.*[19] *Girl, age six, 1935, spontaneous pencil drawing.*

Figure 171. *MY DAD is a schematic portrait of a child's father, a physician.*[40] *Boy, age six, 1963, spontaneous pencil drawing.*

character traits.[49] The fullness or sparsity of details, special emphasis, or omissions are all revealing. In the drawing of a person the head seems, rather understandably, to be its important center, the location of the "self." In general, young children draw large heads, making "head-men." The head may stand for the entire person. The trunk, neck, arms or legs by themselves are never used as a symbol for the entire man. The head

Figure 173. *FATHER AND MOTHER. Made in the presence of a psychologist, "the tiny mother on the left, [disappears in contrast to] father [who] has not a human shape, [is] like a formidable divinity." The child is of normal intelligence, and lives with the mother. The parents, in divorce proceedings, quarrel over child.*[3] *Girl, age five, France, 1952.*

looms large because it is the center of awareness in respect to feeding, sensory stimulation and speech activity, the obviously important part of the person.[49]

The way in which a child draws familiar things can also provide a clue to his emotional state. Individuals who are depressed or withdrawn compulsively reduce the size of the head in their drawings.[49] A fence may be symbolic of desired protection or unwanted restriction.[73]

Children who frequently draw the sun are usually free from emotional troubles, yet its absence does not necessarily suggest mental illness. Empty spaces seem to indicate inferiority feelings. If there is a group of figures, one of them, the child himself, is often drawn larger.[73] The house is a symbol of shelter and security. If a child draws repeatedly unusually long and narrow houses, it may indicate emotional disturbance.[29] Certain choices in the act of drawing are suggestive of personality problems. Anxious, depressed and neurotic children select drawing papers of very small sizes; psychotic children very long and narrow ones.[73] The timid child uses color in an entirely different manner from the aggressive child.[40] Depressed children often neglect color or have a marked preference for brown and violet.[73] Symmetry is minimal or absent. Neurotics use much black and little red; withdrawn children use no color at all.

Boys of around eleven years of age in whom resentment has built up may show this by depicting explosive fantasies in their drawings.[50] Defensive children who mix socially seem to be more reticent in their drawings than are children who are socially isolated. Nondefensive children apparently are more voluble in their drawings than the socially isolated children.[75]

In general, the drawings of disturbed children do not differ much from those of normal children, but there are certain recognizable differentiating features. Whatever his mental development, the disturbed child treats areas in a chaotic, scribbled, ragged, and smudged-over fashion. The degree of aggression is indicated by the extent to which lines and areas are scribbled and ragged. The absence of living things also differentiates their drawings from those of normal children. Baumgarten, describing the house drawings of Polish children of war-destroyed areas, mentions the fact that some children did not show a single person.[7]

A disturbed child, under observation in therapy, reveals much in his drawings and in his comments while engaged in art activities. Some of his problems can be more clearly ascertained by this method, and art activity can often help in the improvement of his condition under therapy. Children's drawings before and after psychotherapy at times give dramatic testimony to the sequence of his experience in therapy.[60]

A child's drawing therefore provides clues to many facets of his personality. They can be indications of cognitive and perceptual growth. They offer some hint of his general ability to communicate. Children's drawings have proved to be useful in diagnosis of disturbances and helpful in therapy.[25]

However, only professionals, trained in clinical psychology, should attempt to use children's art for diagnostic or therapeutic purposes. Teachers and parents should have some knowledge of findings in this area so that they can recognize that certain peculiarities in children's drawings cannot and should not be corrected since their origin is deep-seated, a symptom of problems or maladjustment that cannot be helped merely by trying to change the child's manner of self-expression. Not until the reasons for the peculiarities have been removed, can the child be expected to develop in a normal direction.

SH. Two color scribble. Mixture of favorite colors: purple
d green, named after completion. Crayons, spontaneous.
y, age 3.[19]

utdoors. Colors in part at random, in part "true." Primitive
hema (red airplane in right corner). Crayons. Boy, age 7.[30]

14. A SUNNY DAY FOR TAKING PICTURES. Random
colors, not true. Primitive schema, crayons, spontaneous.
Girl, age 4.[40]

13. CABLE CAR. No "true" colors, "beautiful"
colors to express setting sun. Primitive
schema. Crayons, spontaneous. Girl, age 5.[19]

16. *CHRISTMAS TREE. Decorative paper paste-up, spontaneous. Boy, age 6.*[19]

15. *THE GOLDEN GATE. Yellows and blues perhaps symbolic. Tempera, spontaneous. Girl, age 14.*[40]

17. *Abstract Landscape. Bold loud, daring colors. Painted at boys' club. Aggressive, insecure, disturbed child. Boy, age 10.*[47]

18. *PRIZE. Bold color contrast, spot-effect. Watercolor, spontaneous. Talented girl, age 10.*[42]

CHAPTER FIVE: TEXT REFERENCES

1. Allport, G. W., "Change and decay in the visual memory image," *British Journal of Psychology*, XXI (1930), 133-148.

2. Ames, L. B., "Free drawing and completion drawing: a comparative study of pre-school children," *Journal of Genetic Psychology*, LXVI (1945), 161-165.

3. Ausubel, D., et al., "Prestige suggestions in children's art preferences," *Journal of Genetic Psychology*, LXXXIX (1956), 85-93.

4. Barnhart, E. N., "Developmental stages in compositional construction in children's drawings," *Journal of Experimental Education*, XI, No. 2 (1942), 156-184.

5. Baruch, W., and H. Miller, "Developmental needs and conflicts revealed in children's art," *American Journal of Orthopsychiatry*, XXII, No. 1 (1952), 186-203.

6. Baumgarten, F., *Wunderkinder*, Munich: Ambrosius Barth, 1930.

7. Baumgarten, F., "Die Hauszeichnungen von Kindern als Nachwirkung der Massenzerstörungen im Kriege," *Zeitschrift für Kinderpsychiatrie*, XVI (1949), 74-83.

8. Baumgarten, F. and M. Tramer, *Kinderzeichnungen in vergleichend psychologischer Beleuchtung*, 2nd ed.; Bern: Francke, 1952.

9. Baumstein-Heissler, N., "A propos du dessin: quelques opinions et traveaux de psychologues soviétiques," *Enfance*, VIII, No. 4 (1955), 377-399.

10. Blair, F. X., "A study of the visual memory of deaf and hearing children," *American Annals of the Deaf*, CII, No. 2 (1957), 254-263.

11. Boutonier, J., *Les Dessins des Enfants*, Paris: Editions du Scarabée, 1953.

12. Du Bois, C., *The People of Alor, A Social-Psychological Study of an East Indian Island*, Minneapolis: University of Minnesota Press, 1944.

13. Eng, H., *The Psychology of Children's Drawings: From the First Stroke to the Colored Drawing*, London: Kegan Paul, Trench, Trubner & Co., 1931.

14. England, A. O., "A psychological study of children's drawings. Comparison of public school, institutionalized and delinquent children's drawings," *American Journal of Orthopsychiatry*, XIII, No. 3 (1943), 525-530.

15. Ghesquière-Dierickx, B., "Comment dessinent les enfants: Evolution du dessin selon l'âge," *Enfance*, XIV (1961), 179-182.

16. Goldmeier, E., "Progressive changes in memory traces," *American Journal of Psychology*, LIV (1941), 490-503.

17. Goodenough, F. L., *Measurement of Intelligence by Drawing*, New York: World Book Co., 1926.

18. Goodenough, F. L., *Children's Drawings. A Handbook of Child Psychology*, Worcester, Mass.: Clark University Press, 1931.

19. Hartlaub, G. F., *Der Genius im Kinde*, Breslau: Ferdinand Hirt, 1930.

20. Helson, H., "The psychology of Gestalt," *American Journal of Psychology*, XXXVII (1926), 25-62.

21. Hoffman, H., "Children's drawings as an indication of readiness for first grade," *Merrill-Palmer Quarterly*, IV (1958), 165-179.

22. Hulse, W. C., "Childhood conflict expressed through family drawings," *Journal of Projective Techniques*, XVI, No. 1 (1952), 66-79.

23. Hurlock, E. B., "The spontaneous drawings of adolescents," *Journal of Genetic Psychology*, LXIII (1943), 141-156.

24. Ivanoff, E., "Recherches expérimentales sur le dessin des écoliers de la Suisse Romande," *Archives de Psychologie*, VIII (1909), 97-156.

25. Johnson, S. R. and E. E. Gloye, "A critical analysis of psychological treatment of children's drawings and paintings," *Journal of Aesthetics and Art Criticism*, XVII, No. 2 (1958), 242-250.

26. Karrenberg, C., *Der Mensch als Zeichenobjekt, Ein Versuch zur Lösung der Frage: Kann der Mensch Gegenstand des Zeichenunterricts in der Volksschule sein?*

Leipzig: Otto Memnich (Paedagogische Monographien, edited by E. Meumann), 1910.

27. Katzaroff, M. D., "Qu'est-ce que les enfants dessinent?" *Archives de Psychologie*, IX (1910), 125-133.

28. Keiler, M. L., *The Art in Teaching Art*, Lincoln: University of Nebraska Press, 1961.

29. Kerr, M., "Children's drawings of houses," *British Journal of Medical Psychology*, XVI (1937), 206-218.

30. Kerschensteiner, G., *Die Entwicklung der zeichnerischen Begabung*, Munich: Gerber, 1905.

31. Kik, C., "Die übernormale Zeichenbegabung bei Kindern," *Zeitschrift für angewandte Psychologie*, III (1909), 92-149.

32. Krötzsch, W., *Rhythmus und Form in der freien Kinderzeichnung*, Leipzig: Haase, 1917.

33. Lakin, M., "Certain formal characteristics of human figure drawing by institutionalized aged and by normal children," *Journal of Consulting Psychology*, XX, No. 6 (1956), 471-474.

34. Langevin, V., and J. Lombard, *Peintures et Dessins collectifs des Enfants*, Paris: Editions du Scarabée, 1950.

35. Lark-Horovitz, B., "Interlinkage of sensory memories in relation to training in drawing," *Journal of Genetic Psychology*, XLIX (1936), 69-89.

36. Lark-Horovitz, B., "On learning abilities of children as recorded in a drawing experiment. I. Subject matter, II. Aesthetic and representational qualities," *Journal of Experimental Education*, IX, No. 4 (1941), 332-360.

37. Lark-Horovitz, B., Unpublished work of "A visual memory experiment," carried out at The Cleveland Museum of Art, Cleveland, Ohio, 1941.

38. Lark-Horovitz, B., Barnhart, E. N. and E. M. Sills, *Graphic Work—Sample Diagnosis. An Analytical Method of Estimating Children's Drawing Ability*, Cleveland: The Cleveland Museum of Art, 1939.

39. Lassen, H., "Raumauffasung und Raumdarstellung in Kinderzeichnungen," *Archiv*

für die gesamte Psychologie, CXII, Nos. 1 and 2 (1943), 153-195.

40. Lembke, W., "Über Zeichnungen von 'frechen' und 'schüchternen' Schulkindern," *Zeitschrift für paedagogische Psychologie*, XXXI, No. 10 (1930), 459-462.

41. Lewerenz, A. S., "Sex differences on ability tests in art," *Journal of Educational Psychology*, XIX (1928), 629-635.

42. Lindstrom, M., *Children's Art*, Berkeley: University of California Press, 1957.

43. Lowenfeld, V., *The Nature of Creative Activity*, New York: Harcourt, Brace and World, Inc., 1939.

44. Lowenfeld, V., *Creative and Mental Growth*, New York: The MacMillan Co., 1947.

45. Lukianowicz, N., "Visual thinking and similar phenomena," *Journal of Mental Science*, CVI, No. 444 (1960), 979-1001.

46. Luquet, G.-H., *Les Dessins d'un Enfant*, Paris: Alcan, 1913.

47. Luquet, G.-H., "La narration graphique chez l'enfant," *Journal de Psychologie*, XXI (1924), 183-218.

48. Luquet, G.-H., *Le Dessin Enfantin*, Paris: Alcan, 1927.

49. Machover, K., *Personality Projection in the Drawing of the Human Figure*, American Lectures in Psychology, No. 25, Springfield, Ill.: Charles C. Thomas, 1949.

50. Machover, K., "Human figure drawings of children," *Journal of Projective Techniques*, XVII, No. 1 (1953), 85-91.

51. Malrieu, P., "Observations sur quelques dessins libres chez l'enfant," *Journal de Psychologie Normale et Pathologique*, XLIII (1950), 239-244.

52. Marshall, S., *An Experiment in Education*, Cambridge: University Press, 1963.

53. Matz, W., "Eine Untersuchung über das Modellieren sehender Kinder," *Zeitschrift für angewandte Psychologie*, VI (1912), 1-20.

54. Matz, W., "Zeichen-und Modellierversuche an Volksschülern, Hilfsschülern, Taubstummen und Blinden," *Zeitschrift für angewandte Psychologie*, X (1915), 62-135.

55. Maurer, L., "Das umkehrende Zeichnen,"

Zeitschrift für Experimentelle Paedagogik, VI (1908), 65-69.

56. McCarty, S. A., *Children's Drawings. A Study of Interest and Abilities*, Baltimore: Williams & Williams Co., 1924.

57. Meumann, E., *Vorlesungen zur Einführung in die experimentelle Paedagogik*, 2nd ed., vol. 3, Leipzig: W. Engelmann, 1913.

58. Mühle, G., *Entwicklungspsychologie des zeichnerischen Gestaltens.* Grundlage, Formen und Wege in der Kinderzeichnung, Munich: Ambrosius Barth, 1955.

59. Munro, T.; Lark-Horovitz, B.; and E. N. Barnhart, "Children's art abilities: Studies at the Cleveland Museum of Art," *Journal of Experimental Education*, XI, No. 2 (1942), 97-155.

60. Naumburg, M., *Schizophrenic Art: Its Meaning in Psychotherapy*, New York: Grune & Stratton, 1950.

61. Neubauer, V., "Über die Entwicklung der technischen Begabung bei Kindern," *Zeitschrift für angewandte Psychologie*, XXIX (1928), 289-326.

62. Oakley, C. A., "Drawings of a man by adolescents," *British Journal of Psychology*, XXXI, No. 1 (1940), 37-60.

63. O'Shea, M. V., "Children's expression through drawing," *Proceedings of the National Education Association*, (Asbury Park, N.J.), (1894), 1015-1023.

64. Osterrieth, P. A., "Le test de copie d'une figure complexe. Contribution à l'étude de la perception et de la mémoire," *Archives de Psychologie*, XXX, Nos. 119 and 120 (1949), 205-353.

65. Porot, M., "Le dessin de la famille; Exploration par le dessin de la situation affective de l'enfant dans sa famille," *Pédiatrie*, XLI, No. 3 (1952), 359-381.

66. Rey, A., "Epreuves de dessin, témoin du développement mental," *Archives de Psychologie*, XXXI, No. 124 (1946), 369-380.

67. Rouma, G., *Le Language Graphique de l'Enfant*, Brussels: Misch and Thron, 1913.

68. Russell, I. M., "Relationship between certain aspects of creative expression and reading development," *Research in Art Education*, Seventh Yearbook (1956), 103-113.

69. Schaefer-Simmern, H., *The Unfolding of Artistic Activity. Its Basis, Processes, and Implications*, Berkeley: University of California Press, 1960.

70. Sills, E. M., Unpublished work of a "Memory Selection Experiment," carried out at The Cleveland Museum of Art, Cleveland, Ohio, 1939.

71. Silverstein, A. B., and H. A. Robinson, "The representation of physique in children's figure drawings," *Journal of Consulting Psychology*, XXV (1961), 146-148.

72. Stern, E., "Das Zeichnen als diagnostische und therapeutische Methode in der Kinderpsychiatrie," *Kind und Kunst*, X (1951), 110-127.

73. Traube, T., "La valeur diagnotique des dessins des enfants difficiles," *Archives de Psychologie*, XXVI, No. 103 (1937), 285-309.

74. Van der Horst, L., "Affect, expression and symbolic function in the drawings of children," in: *Feelings and Emotions: Mooseheart Symposium*, ed. by Martin Reymert, New York: McGraw Hill Book Co., 1950, 398-417.

75. Wallach, M. A., et al., "Contradictions between overt and projective personality indicators as a function of defensiveness," *Psychological Monographs*, LXXVI, No. 520 (1962), 1-23.

76. Wulff, O., *Die Kunst des Kindes*, Stuttgart: Ferdinand Enke, 1927.

The Exceptional Child

Some children differ from the majority. They are the exceptions to the general expectations, and because of these differences, they are called exceptional. They differ from other children in a variety of ways. They differ from each other.

Some exceptional children excel vastly in one or more ways of achievement. Others, for a number of reasons, are slower than their classmates. A physical handicap bars others from the ordinary activities of their peers.

THE ARTISTICALLY TALENTED CHILD

Some children stand out among others of their age group, and sometimes among children of any age level, for their extraordinary talent in art. However, many children of high intelligence have no talent in painting, or other aspects of art, but may excel in music, the sciences or the language arts. In the following discussion the term *talented*

Figure 174. *The developmental series, showing specialization in horses, was drawn by a talented girl between ages five and eleven. A, B, and C show an advancing development of animals, but people remain schematic. C. The arrangement and grouping (background) indicate distances, and there is a feeling for black and white balance of medium. D. The horses are true-to-appearance, but the riders are not quite as developed. An amazing representation of motion and action is shown. E. Here, the horses are individualized. Note the placement of horses in stalls. F. FARM. There is great*

clarity of arrangement of the farm buildings and animal pens. The center of the composition is accentuated by the sitting child. Clean, very assured lines are used with delicacy. The spirit and outlook of the picture are those of a child, while the artistry is that of an adult. G. FUNNY HORSE. Caricature. H. HORSE AND FOAL. The expression of love in the animal's faces and positions reflects the artist's emotional participation and empathy.[42] Girl, ages five to eleven. (For pictures of horses drawn at other age levels, see Figures 25, 95, 107 and 184).

Figure 175. *WORK. A true-to-appearance woodblock showing a complex position.*[13] *Talented boy, age twelve, Japan, 1964.*

or *gifted* will be applied to children especially gifted in *visual expression*.

Teachers who work with talented children must understand their special gifts and needs in order to help them develop to their highest potential. Understanding talent also provides insight into the average child. Every child has a capacity for creativity or appreciation, although he himself and those around him may not be aware of it. Though he may not realize it, his teachers should assume that with encouragement he could develop it. The obvious difference between the average and the gifted child is that "the gifted not only knows something better than others, but . . . knows it better and also experiences [it] in a manner denied to the nongifted."[32] Because of the possibility of buried faculties that struggle for expression

but do not come to light, the teacher who is able to recognize special abilities will also be better equipped to guide average children toward obtainable goals. She will not push them beyond their ability but will guide them in the fulfillment of an accessible goal.

General Characteristics

Two questions arise repeatedly: How can one recognize outstanding talent? Where is the line to be drawn between the child who is skillful, and the child who is genuinely creative in art?

Ethnological, psychological, and sociological studies have not yet revealed to any tangible extent the root of artistic talent. Although artistic talent is more likely to be found in children of high intelligence, talent is a special quality which is undoubtedly dependent on general intellectual ability, and is specifically channeled in a given direction. Norman Meier attributes artistic ability to six factors: manual skill, energy, aesthetic intelligence, perceptual facility, creative imagination, and aesthetic judgment, relating this set of factors to heredity.[31] Although these six factors certainly are observable in artists and gifted children, and hold for any of the arts—literature, music, or possibly art-related activities—they can also be found in people who are not creative artists, but are persons who have a discriminating taste and enjoy art in an informal and discerning manner. Besides, a large number of artists and gifted children have been known to come from a background devoid of any connection with art and of any interest in it.

Thomas Munro's suggestion and speculation—anticipated nearly two generations earlier by Benedetto Croce writing on the philosophy of art—seems to carry more weight and appears more plausible. Referring to the mode of expression of average and talented children, Munro pointed out that "there appears to be no radical difference in kind between the gifted and the average child in art, but rather a gradual stepping up of a number of related abilities, plus a strong tendency to experience things visually, and even to try to suggest, represent, and symbolize types of experience in visual terms. This itself might be called an ability—to interpret the world in visual images—but it also involves a direction of interest and motivation, each no doubt stimulating the other."[33]

A number of specific explanations have been advanced as the result of observations. Oskar Wulff, from biographical observations of the art development of his son and others, distinguishes between two ways of perceiving. He claims that some individuals tend to perceive "in the round" and retain a visual image with three-dimensional sculptural quality. Others retain flat optical impressions and use them as such, even transforming three-dimensional impressions into a silhouette. The two kinds of perception combine in varying proportions in different individuals. "The problem and objective of all graphic development is reconciliation of both."[42] Accordingly, the ability to synthesize the perceptual data accounts for special visual ability. This explanation, however, seems inappropriate in dealing with the schematic steps in which the drawings are especially flat. Its usefulness also seems limited by the fact that perceptual ability—a pre-condition for creative power in art—must be expressed in appropriate media.

Hartlaub, an art historian and imaginative interpreter of children's art, believed that talent can be explained by the child's motor response to perceptual experiences. He states that the average child's visual concepts are not too precise. They are shot through, in fact often actually dominated, by abstractions. It is more difficult for him to capture a complete visual image than it is for the gifted child who is more able to concentrate on the visual aspect alone.[11] Artists presumably go through the schematic stage at some phase of childhood. Seldom is there any documentation for this. Fortunately, a drawing made by Sargent at the age of four years was preserved, so in his case the schematic stage is on record. Most gifted children seem to free themselves from the various limitations of the schematic stage in two ways: they may retain the schematic "mentality," but develop in their own visions an order, clarity, and richness, often reminiscent of ancient and primitive arts (see Figure 218);[11] or they may grow into an early maturity of art expression by abandoning the schematic viewpoint in favor of a visually dominated and very articulate representation, that of the adult. In doing so, they are able to concentrate the essence of their experiences in the form of visual images.

It is important to realize that a child who shows outstanding ability at an early age is not necessarily destined to become an artist. After years of study and observation,

Figure 176. *A drawing done by the American painter, Sargent, at the age of four, in 1860.*

A

B

C

D

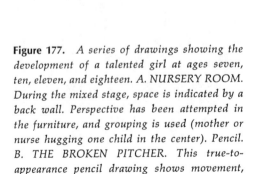

Figure 177. *A series of drawings showing the development of a talented girl at ages seven, ten, eleven, and eighteen. A. NURSERY ROOM. During the mixed stage, space is indicated by a back wall. Perspective has been attempted in the furniture, and grouping is used (mother or nurse hugging one child in the center). Pencil. B. THE BROKEN PITCHER. This true-to-appearance pencil drawing shows movement,* flexibility of lines, and grouping. C. KILLED IN ACTION. In the group around the table, there is gestural expression of grief. The interior space is well developed and shows many details. In this true-to-appearance drawing, freedom and flexibility of line technique are demonstrated.[9] Pencil. D. GOSSIPING NEIGHBORS. This etching is the art of an adult. Girl, ca 1908-1926.*

Cižek concluded that "child art, similar to folk art, is an independent, self-sufficient area that must never be considered as a step to the mature art of the adult."[7] The child does not represent an early phase of a potential artist because art, by its nature, is different from children's or amateur art. The differences are not wholly due to lack of knowledge or practice, though much can be gained from the study of art forms and development of technical skill. Skill alone does not make an artist. As the writer Scheffler suggests: while the dilettante's picture will resemble nature, it is the artist's passionate urge which directs his perception. He sees his surroundings already transformed into art. "He makes use of the rivers and woods, the heavens and trees . . to create harmonies and values, to shape melodies. . . . The truths of nature must become artistic truths. He translates the divine idea of creation into human terms."[36]

Efforts to account for special ability in art, and to penetrate to its roots, have not been successful. Nevertheless, special talent can be identified, and the characteristics that distinguish the gifted from the average child can be pointed out. What we cannot, as yet, explain is why these differences occur.

The child who is outstanding in art is usually beyond the norm of his age group in developmental status, technical skill, and aesthetic judgment; he is *overnormal*. Accelerated development, in itself, is not a reliable indication of genuine and lasting ability, nor of potential adult achievement. The characteristics of the artistic child go beyond mere superiority in general development. The artistic child is one whose work excels in compositional arrangement, enrichment, in decorative and aesthetic qualities. He shows great ease in working with his medium as well as displaying other skills that are independent of developmental status.

The child prodigy is usually characterized by a general level of development far beyond that of children of his age level. He easily masters the expressive means of the adult and shows an understanding of his medium that is quite astounding. But this, too, is no guarantee of future achievement, as Hartlaub pointed out long ago, as the promise of these "over-potential years of childhood" is almost never fulfilled in later life.[11]

Characteristics Shared by Talented and Average Children

Average children are often imaginative in what they attempt to present, but in contrast to artistically gifted children their way of presenting their subject tends to be commonplace.

Apart from their special ability, artistically talented children do not seem to differ much from average children in the general course of development or their ability in areas not associated with their particular gift. No link has been found with other special abilities, such as between visual and musical ability.[33]

Although talented and average children undergo the same sequence of developmental stages, the schematic stage may be briefer and occur at an earlier age in the talented group.[2] The developmental process in the childhood of famous artists must have been extremely accelerated. What little remains of the work of their childhood is on the level of adult art, as for example Dürer's self-portrait, done at the age of thirteen. In the inscription he refers to himself as a child; and indeed, he gave himself the facial expression of a child.

The talented child selects much the same

Figure 178. *SINGLE COMBAT. In this mixed developmental stage drawing, the figures are stiff, and action is indicated by armor and attributes.[47] Boy, age eight, 1963, spontaneous pencil drawing.*

Figure 179. *COMBAT. Violent action and movement are expressed. Notice the use of foreshortening, the great ease in sketching, line treatment, and the remarkable expression of the horse.[2] Boy, age ten, Italy, ca 1910, spontaneous pencil drawing.*

subjects for representation as do his less able peers. Age level seems to be a more influential factor in the choice of subject matter than talent. Interest in the subject matter of works of adult art, paintings in particular, also reflects age level interest, and points to a basic similarity in the attitude of both talented and average children. However, the approach and treatment of chosen topics differ. In the schematic stage all children draw from mental images, or from memory, but for the talented child the storehouse of images is richer.

Characteristics in which the Talented Exceed the Average Children

Talented children's drawings show greater variety within the range of subject choices, especially at the true-to-appearance level. Average children at this stage or at the preceding mixed stage, treat fewer subjects than before because of their difficulty in presenting objects to their satisfaction. Talented children do not experience this difficulty and will attempt a variety of subjects with apparent ease.

The average child develops a graphic vocabulary limited by difficulties he cannot overcome. Because he cannot express his ideas completely through graphic means, he adds to them words and other non-pictorial symbols. Most children at this stage are struggling for accuracy, and they become critical of their own work. If words express their intentions more easily than pictures, they rely more and more on words so that their graphic vocabulary not only fails to progress but may even shrink. In contrast, the child who easily thinks in pictures and symbols increases his graphic vocabulary steadily up to the true-to-appearance stage, sometimes exceeding the average child's pictorial vocabulary to an astonishing degree.[33]

Over sixty years ago, Kerschensteiner pointed to the remarkable degree of accelerated development shown by talented children (see Figure 199).[15] Yet accelerated development in representation may mean no more than precocity and facility and may have little significance from the point of view of mature artistic achievement. Aesthetic merit is not necessarily tied to an advanced developmental level. Some schematic art is unquestionably of high aesthetic value, whereas work on a higher developmental level may not be artistic. Nevertheless, accelerated development is one of the most pervading and significant characteristics of the talented child. There is, however, danger in accelerated development.

In discussing talent, Bauermeister noted that the "leap into the incredibly difficult problem of modern Western art" (from the

Figure 180. *Self-portrait of thirteen year old Dürer, made in 1484 "when I was still a child."*

Comparison of "Averages" and "Talented."

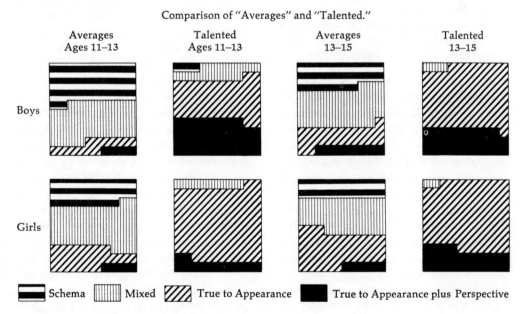

Graph 8: *Representational development: Comparison of average and talented children*
Adapted from the Cleveland Studies.[33]

Figure 181. *This talented boy specialized in pictures of horses which he drew from memory. He could visualize them in all kinds of positions and movements. Notice the use of foreshortening and expression of movement. His pictures of people or objects were not on the same level as his true-to-appearance horses.*[16] *Boy, age eight, Germany, ca 1903, pencil drawing.*

Renaissance into our times), especially the problem of space, is to be deplored since it cuts short and destroys the creative power and growth of the child.[1] These arguments were carried even further when the Chicago educator Jessie Todd declared that accelerated development is harmful and suggested that the period of true child art should be prolonged and that proper instruction should keep the child's development on a child-level so as to keep the creative urge alive.[39] Cižek recognized that child art runs its course, and that the prodigy with his accelerated development in representation should test and develop his talent in the adult world of training.[7] One may take

warning from Franz Liszt's witty remark—that "prodigies have their future in their past."

Imaginative ability is regarded as important to creativeness. It has been described as the child's ability to use his visual concepts for the purpose of representing his own fantasies.[16] Every child possesses some imaginative ability, but the talented child has it to an extraordinary degree. He is often both original and fertile in his fantasies. The shaping of fantasy depends on the richness of visual concepts stored in his mind, and on the extent to which he can manipulate these to express his ideas.

All children delight in portraying action and movement, taking their inspiration from the stories they read and from the history they learn. Accounts of wars and battles seem particularly interesting to them, and as Levinstein observed a long time ago, many children who are themselves peace-loving and quiet in their behavior enjoy depicting violent scenes and terrifying happenings.[27] John Dewey observed that "the realization of an idea in action through the medium of movement is as necessary to the formation of the mental image as is the expression, the technique."[8]

Gifted children are more adept than the average in representing movement (Graph 9), partly because of their more rapid development of skill. At the schematic level, the talented attempt to bring movement into usually rigid schemata. They succeed in doing so by giving all parts strongly accentuated directions, getting the desired effect by multiplication of the same single directionality. They also convey the impression of motion by special effects in line and color. In the true-to-appearance stage, talented children represent movement as it actually seems to occur. Arms and legs bend fluidly at the joints; branches blow in the

Figure 182. *PANTHERS FIGHTING. A schematic drawing showing violent motion and action, indicated mainly in the expression of mouths. The lines in this drawing are clean and decisive.*[40] *Boy, age seven, 1963, spontaneous pencil drawing.*

Figure 183. *The pouncing tiger in this true-to-appearance, foreshortened drawing is in violent motion and expresses its ferocity by its mouth. Note the clean, flowing lines which are like adult art.*[2] *Boy, age seven, Italy, ca 1908, spontaneous pencil drawing.*

wind. They vary the use of their medium to give an impression of flexibility. (Graph 9)

Talented children surpass average children in the conscious and deliberate grouping of objects and people. They are better at organizing and composing their pictures. During the schematic stage, when they line up objects on a groundline—in itself a natural organization—talented children use this kind of grouping with conscious deliberation, while retaining the schematic character of their creations. This understanding and control is also obvious in their manipulation of several groundlines.

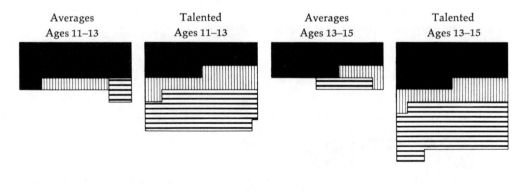

Graph 9: *Motion: Comparison of average and talented children*

From the Cleveland Studies.[33]

Figure 184. *An amazing power and flow of movement are achieved by long swinging strokes. Notice the grouping.*[42] *Talented girl, age five, United States, 1958, spontaneous pencil drawing.*

Figure 185. *An amazing parallel grouping of fast moving horses and riders by an art prodigy.*[2] *Boy, age seven, Italy, early 1900's, spontaneous pencil sketch.*

In the true-to-appearance stage they achieve a remarkably effective composition.[25] At a stage when most children find grouping difficult and avoid it by reducing the number of objects in their pictures, talented children relate people, animals and objects in a manner that describes their relationship and tends to be aesthetically pleasing. Many children who group effectively at the schematic stage lose this ability during the next stages. Some talented children, however, retain this ability through all developmental stages, changing their

concepts of grouping in keeping with the different approaches to representation. During the schematic stage, grouping is usually achieved through bilateral symmetry, with objects distributed along one or more groundlines. Later, near-symmetry is still favored by a large number of average children and also by some of the talented. The latter, however, make a very subtle, almost indirect, use of such equalization, as well as using deliberately planned and balanced asymmetry.[25]

Children in the kindergarten and primary grades strongly favor multicoloredness. This tendency slowly decreases with

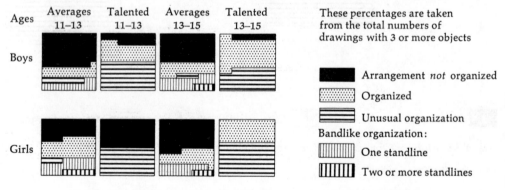

Graph 10: *Grouping: Comparison of average and talented children*
From the Cleveland Studies.[33]

19. *RIDING FLASH. Bold, fresh colors direct brush technique. Watercolor, spontaneous. Girl, age 9.*[40]

20. *STITCHERY. Made in school. Boy, age 12.*[44]

Figure 187. *PORTRAIT. Remarkable individual expression is shown in the face, the turn of head, and the economy in the use of medium (pencil). Lines have been used both boldly and subtly by this talented child.*[30] *Boy, age fourteen, 1936.*

Figure 186. *A talented boy's first use of brush and ink resulted in a quadrangular figure grouping showing pronounced action.*[41] *Boy, age fifteen.*

the age of twelve when fewer colors are preferred and intentionally monochromatic drawings increase. Most children use "true" local color and fairly bright colors at the schematic stage, varying these colors somewhat at the height of the schematic stage and later on. The talented child achieves effects of brilliancy and contrast by well-balanced and integrated coloring. He sometimes blends and tints with subtlety. A few talented youngsters use color for spotlight effect, contrasting a brilliant color with subdued colors all around it. [33, 26]

Talented children are also more aware of the possibilities and limits of media, and adapt technique to the medium they are using. Average children strive for a consistent use of a medium, while the talented child will find original ways of exploring it. For example, while most children try for flat, even color, the talented child will discern ways of achieving texture, and bold and vibrant color effects. While the average child will at best achieve a decisive line, either with short or long strokes, the talented child is capable of attaining subtlety of line and boldness of stroke, sometimes combining both in order to fulfill his vision. (Graphs 11 and 12)

All younger children experiment with a new medium when permitted to do so, but after the age of about ten or eleven, average children hesitate to do so. Talented children, however, remain willing to explore new materials. The average child treats a new medium like one with which he is familiar, even when such use is inappropri-

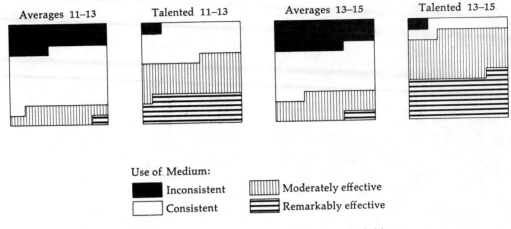

Graph 11: *Use of medium: Comparison of average and talented children*

From the Cleveland Studies.[33]

ate to the nature of the medium. The talented child quickly grasps the difference between the familiar and the new medium (see Figure 198). Even at his first try he gets remarkable results because of his quick insight into the nature of the new medium and his quick understanding of its peculiarities.[23]

Although interest in subject matter at each age level is similar in average and talented children, the gifted children are more willing and able to extend their interest to subjects that are challenging and provocative. They seem ready to break through the barrier set up by emotions and age-conditioned interest patterns. Talented children are willing to go beyond likes and dislikes and to judge a work of art on its aesthetic merit, considering its quality, style, and technical achievement, drawing from

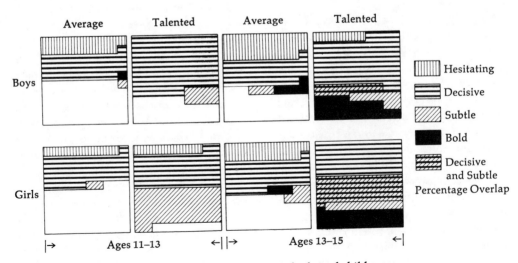

Graph 12: *Use of line: Comparison of average and talented children*

From the Cleveland Studies.[33]

it insights that can be applied to their own work.

Characteristics Distinguishing Talented from Average Children

The artistically talented child brings a strongly visual point of view to the content of his art work. Other children, as well as adults, are less able to isolate the visual from other sense experiences. Their visual images are encumbered by sounds, taste, smell, tactile and muscular sensations which are associated and inextricably enmeshed with their visual experiences.[19]

Artistically talented children, asked to select a subject from something they saw on a walk, chose subjects (and objects representing them) that were more adaptable to pictorial representation than the other children who were asked to do the same. Both groups described similar observations in words, having apparently "seen" the same things. But the total perception of the talented children was visually orientated and more discriminating.[37]

Visual memory in talented children

The first impressions of talented children seem to be complete and exact in form and color (see Figure 181). Later impressions sharpen and reinforce existing visual images. Time and experience strengthen visual memory and sharpen the tendency toward selective visual observation. In talented children, there is an effective interplay between this selective visual observation and a strong visual memory. With a vivid imagination and acute visual memory, the artistically talented child is able to retain impressions of things he saw a long time ago. This phenomenon was confirmed by a "memory experiment" in which a ceramic polar bear, rotating on a base, was shown to children for a few minutes. Shortly afterwards, and

subsequently at time intervals up to three years, these children were asked to draw their model from memory. Average children drew bears—(compare with Table VIII) as "animals" or "bearish" according to their ability, refreshing their memory by the concept "bear," trying to reason out its characteristics, even adding natural surroundings, but almost always unable to maintain their rigid but deteriorating "bear"-memory. On the other hand, most of the talented children retained their fleeting first impression to a remarkable degree, reproducing details of the ceramic, sometimes its texture, the turn of the head and the slightly curving direction of the body. Some of the drawings indeed retained their original shape while others had changed very little. The results of this investigation also raised the question of the extent to which the first drawing had assisted them in retaining the original visual image. It seemed almost as though once they had drawn the bear, their drawing and the actual model fused and thereafter bound them to their first recording of the image.[24]

Average children and adults may remember things over long periods of time and vividly describe them, perhaps saying that they can "see" them as if they were real.[19] Their recollection of the event or object is a combination of impressions, some seen, some heard, some felt or experienced physically. The gifted child, however, recalls clearly, with great completeness, *a detailed visual image* which is obviously far more helpful in representing the subject in some art form.

Learning ability of talented children

Most younger children are satisfied with their work. They do not seek instruction but rely on their inner world of images and work out their own way of expressing themselves. The artistically talented child has a splendid store of such visual images and, being more curious and enterprising than the average child, he is more aware of what he can gather from his surroundings. He has a genuine desire to *learn*, and may show in-

terest in changing and enriching his schema. Unlike the average child who likes to be left alone when picturing, the gifted asks for explanations and instruction. If left to himself, he will learn by looking at pictures

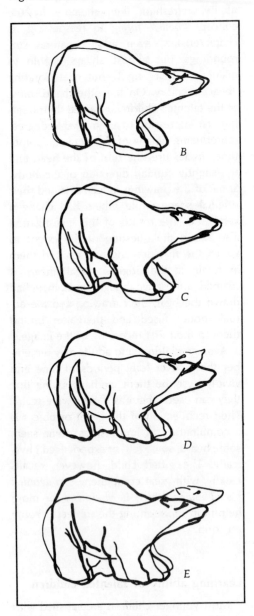

Figure 188. *Superimposed drawings (by a talented child): A on B, A on C, A on D, A on E.*[21] *Boy, age thirteen.*

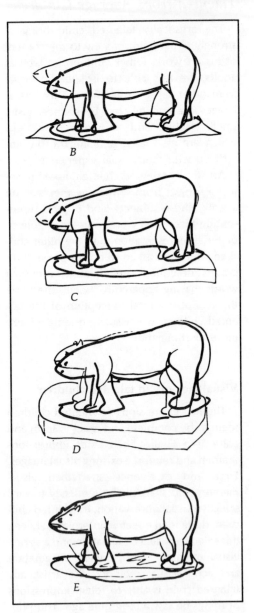

Figure 189. *Superimposed drawings (by average child): A on B, A on C, A on D, A on E.*[21] *Age twelve.*

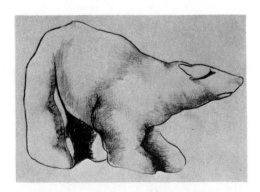

Figure 190. *First memory drawing of a ceramic polar bear. Note the texture that indicates ceramic, the "fused" pair of legs, the downward curve of back and the slight turn of head, the use of shading and shadows in this true-to-appearance pencil drawing.*[21]

and analyze them for what may be useful for him, by watching people and by experimenting constantly.

Older average children also want to learn but in a different sense. It is almost as if they would like to be shown, to imitate and acquire by rote all that they feel they cannot digest on their own. Learning of this kind does not have far-reaching consequences. The talented child, on the other hand, uses all means to fill in gaps in the knowledge he needs for his work. Whereas the average child uses art for his own needs —to communicate, to express himself, or just for the fun and pleasure he gets out of it—the gifted child takes his picturing quite seriously. In his younger years he draws and paints instead of joining in the play activities other children prefer. As he grows older he experiments earnestly and throws himself completely into his art activities. The average child seems content to repeat ways that he has found successful, but the gifted child continuously strives for more adequate ways of expression in subject matter and medium.

Older artistically talented children are far more responsive to unusual subjects in art than are others of their age and are more stimulated and influenced by such work. This was clearly demonstrated by a study of children between the ages of six and fifteen, who were given verbal explanations of various kinds of machines for the benefit of the younger children. All the children were asked to make drawings of the subject. A week later, the same children were shown a large array of works by adult artists, past and present, all of whom had either centered their works around machinery or included it in their pictures. The children were once again asked to draw "machinery." While a large number of the average children repeated their own chosen subject of the week before (some almost exactly), others in their new representations suggested what they had seen or tried to communicate, descriptively, what had impressed them. However, they did this awk-

Figure 191. *This was the preferred picture among a large number shown on the subject of machines and constructions in an experiment to stimulate and suggest subjects for children to draw.*[41]

Figure 192. *Stimulated by Figure 191, a boy in the primitive schematic stage made this pencil drawing. He was influenced by the height of the bridge and an interest in the train.*[41] *Age six.*

Figure 194. *A mixed stage pencil drawing made after viewing Figure 191. Interest in the height of the bridge and the train is expressed. Observation of surroundings in Figure 191 is shown. Boy, age ten.*

Figure 193. *A schematic drawing made after seeing Figure 191. The child was influenced by the bridge and train but had difficulty using the new medium of brush and ink.*[41] *Girl, age six.*

Figure 195. *In response to Figure 191, a girl made this schematic pencil drawing. There is interest in the high bridge and the train.*[41] *Age thirteen.*

Figure 196. *Drawn in response to Figure 191. The influence of the high bridge, train and surroundings are indicated, but all of them lack the contrasting proportions and surroundings of Figure 191. This is rather an enumeration of the content of the impressive picture.[41] Girl, age fourteen, brush and ink drawing.*

Figure 197. *Drawn in response to Figure 191. There is an exaggeration of the features of Figure 191 to achieve a fantastic and adventurous picture. This was the first attempt to use pen and ink and brush by a talented child.[41] Girl, age fourteen.*

wardly, even reverting to an earlier phase of representation. The talented children, on the other hand, seemed highly stimulated by the works shown them. They showed this interest not merely by reference to some particular work but by using it as a point of departure for an original creation of their own. Others responded by accepting certain parts of the works they had seen, and using them in their own drawing, producing essentially new and independent creations. Thus the average child is able, at best, to give a graphic enumeration of content, without stress or emphasis, as though making a list of what he has observed. In contrast to this, the talented child

is able to capture the essence of "the lesson," and to make it his own.[23]

Where the average child may develop excellence in some one direction, the gifted child shows unusual development in several ways. He may combine excellence in form, grouping, movement, and use of color. Although a single outstanding quality is not indicative of real talent, conjunction of several remarkable qualities is.[26]

Gifted specialists

Some children excel only in a particular subject, a curious phenomenon, difficult to explain. No doubt their interest centers on that one chosen subject, the representation of which they have polished until they be-

Figure 198. *Drawn in response to Figure 191. A talented child used the suggestion of the bridge but transformed it into a modern construction scene that is entirely different from Figure 191. This was the first use of brush and ink but unmistakably shows the child's impression of the city in which he lives.[41] Boy, age fifteen.*

lieve it to be perfect. For example, one child will concentrate on drawing horses and will be able to picture them extremely well and in any position (see Figures 181 and 174).[15] Other subjects drawn by these children will usually be far inferior. There are ship and train specialists (see Figure 68),[12] and machine specialists, some very young, who are nevertheless draftsmen in the adult sense, and who produce complicated, though lucid, designs.[16]

There are also children who are extraordinary copyists. Almost every child copies at one time or another. Copying becomes increasingly frequent from the age of ten on. It is particularly common at the stage at which the child begins to look critically

at his drawings, comparing them with the drawings of other children, and admiring those that are more advanced, and which he believes to be within his own reach. Truly able children copy for the purpose of acquiring technique, but they later study and draw from nature and develop their own style. But there are other children who slavishly imitate the work of others and are unable to do anything but copy. Even when they draw from nature, they render everything they see exactly as if projected on paper, without clarification, organization or emphasis. Their work lacks imagination and judgment, but shows an astonishing facility in technique and use of the medium as well as in perception of the superficial qualities of the original which they have copied. Imagination and perceptive penetration are essential for further development, and few longtime copyists show any originality or promise of creative work.

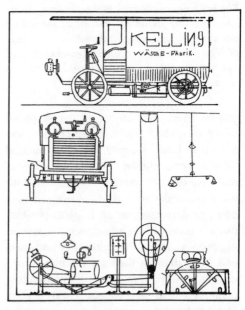

Figure 199. *SHIRT MANUFACTURE by a talented machine-drawing specialist. The child used a ruler and buttons and pennies to achieve clear lines.[17] Boy, age six, Germany, ca 1900.*

Attitude toward the arts

Artistically gifted children show an aesthetic interest in works of art. They are concerned with design and technique, while average children are more interested in the subject or the realism of its representation. Even when the choices of both the average and talented children are alike, the reasons given for their preferences are different. Talented children have less need to identify themselves with the subject of the work of art.[20] For example, the talented child is interested in portraits of older people, because he can study the painter's interpretation of facial expression.[21] Such portraits do not interest most children. Talented children look at a work of art not only as a spectacle that can be enjoyed but as an answer to "how did he do it." They analyze color, composition, texture, and painting technique. Other children may be only dimly aware of the painter's skill. Talented children are far less influenced by associations and personal reasons and judge in terms of technique, originality, shape, line or texture.[22] Their ever-present urge to learn and to use what they learn gives a special flavor to their work and their aesthetic responses.

THE RETARDED CHILD

Retarded children draw like normal children of the same mental age who are chronologically younger.[35] For example, a retarded ten-year-old may draw like a normal child of seven.[14, 9] However, there are likely to be some startling differences.

Retarded children, unlike normal children under the age of six, often place a single object in the entire drawing space, or draw a picture that is quite out of balance.[40]

Figure 200. *Retarded children draw in the manner of normal children in an earlier development stage.*[39] *Upper group, nine-and ten-year-olds, Switzerland, ca 1935. Lower drawing, five year old.*

They also draw in a more stereotyped fashion than normal children, repeating certain forms that have lost their original meaning. These forms become clichés, the drawings become mechanical. They also tend to lack consistency in the relationships of objects in the drawing. Certain proportions are unusually incorrect, arms may be far too long or too short. Such inconsistencies occur more often than in the work of normal children of comparable mental age.[38] A group of retarded boys, ten to fourteen years old, did excellent copying in line but showed a strange preference for an unusual color mixture which they applied most inappropriately to their drawing.[6]

The rate of development is obviously slower in retarded children. Consequently, the successive stages occur at later ages,

Figure 201. *MAN. Subnormal drawing.*[29] *Boy, age fourteen, 1934.*

Figure 203. *HOUSEMOTHER of the institution and himself, by a retarded child.*[16] *Boy, age fifteen, Germany, ca 1904.*

child . . . retains his source of inspiration when the latter dries up because of increasing criticism . . ."[4]

There is a slow but definite increase in drawing ability with advance in mental age, but also a tendency toward fluctuation and regression after the chronological age of ten, regardless of mental age.[38] The retarded child shows no intention of even trying to represent movement.[41]

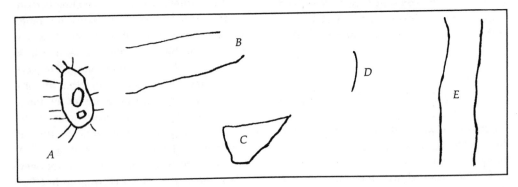

Figure 202. *CLERGYMAN. A dismembered drawing.*[16] *a. head, b. arms, c. mouth, d. nose, e. legs. By a feebleminded girl, age ten, Germany, ca 1904.*

resulting in a more extended period of development. However, "the retarded child who draws at least as willingly as the normal

Unlike normal children, retarded girls tend to draw in smaller sizes than retarded boys, and to draw men smaller than women;

but both boys and girls, as observed at age thirteen, draw their own sex larger.[10]

Juliette Boutonier describes the importance of art work for these children when she says: "Indisputably, drawing provides for the retarded child possibilities to which he can measure up . . . a path of liberation. In terms of humanity, what blossoming! In spite of the definitive weakness that stands in the way of normal development . . . the child who is incapable of assimilating intellectual concepts . . . retains an elementary possibility of unimpaired humanity . . ." through his art work.[4]

THE DEAF CHILD

The deaf child's drawing pattern does not vary too much from that of the hearing child. Lindner, in an early study, claimed that "deaf-mute children like to draw—and draw a good deal—and they are, on the average, better than their hearing contemporaries."[28] This is confirmed by Lark-Horovitz's observations while teaching deaf girls in the 1920's. However, Lampard claims that deaf children stay behind normal children of average drawing ability.[18] It would seem that more data are needed to arrive at definite conclusions on this.

The drawings of deaf children were found to be especially rich in details.[30] More recently, however, it was noted that there are not many people or animals in deaf children's pictures, nor much social interaction shown in their drawings.[18]

The representations of the deaf are dramatic, often showing violence and cruelty. Lindner claims that "these children tend toward representing terrible happenings rather than factual things or contemplative topics; there is more brutality than tenderness."[28] This may be attributed to emotional problems, or fears, related to their inability

to hear. However, as Rouma pointed out in the early 1900's, normal children also make dramatic representations of a cruel or violent nature.[35] In contradiction to this, Lampard found "a feeling . . . of well being in the paintings of the deaf arrived at through a shutting out rather than a working out of anxiety."[18] Again this suggests that more work needs to be done in this area.

Given a choice, the deaf prefer drawing to modeling, although they seem to do better in modeling than in drawing.[30] Deaf children are superior in visual memory, probably due to compensating for their lack of audio faculties.[3] On the whole, "art is an important means of expression for the deaf child, opening a means by which he can express his hostility, anger, doubts and fears."[17]

THE BLIND CHILD

Münz and Löwenfeld claim that touch is the main source of knowledge for the blind, but that awareness of muscle movement is even more important than surface touch.[34] On the other hand Burde, a lifelong teacher of the blind, pointed out that blind people, left to themselves, rely more on hearing than on touch; they do not so much touch objects as sound them out.[5]

Blind children primarily represent things they eat or small objects they can enclose in their hands or handle with their fingers. As might be expected, they are quite expert in modeling fruit.[5] And blind girls copied hats currently in fashion and did so with precision and care.[5]

The psychologist David Katz reported that "whereas living things absolutely dominate" the pictures of seeing, normal children, the blind draw mostly objects. Drawings made by using a special technique of raised lines, a form of braille, resemble those of much younger sighted children. The blind represent humans exclusively frontwise and animals in profile, as do young sighted children, but do not give details such as hair or clothes. Houses are generally drawn as a mixture of floor plan and elevation. In their drawings of houses, the blind tend to show staircases "usually with a banister to hold on." Windows are always represented, and sometimes a chimney which might even have smoke coming out of it. Katz found, surprisingly, that they do not make transparent houses as do normal sighted children.[13]

Blind children tend toward asymmetry in modeling and do better at modeling than sighted children who have been blindfolded.[30] Blind children seem to have some space concepts, though shapes that cannot be explored by touch are usually represented incorrectly. For example, churches are represented without a roof.[30] Mountains are drawn in the shape of cones.[5]

Münz' and Löwenfeld's studies of modeling done by the blind indicated that those born blind create bodiness from experience of their own body, and gain from it an awareness of the relationship of limbs when at rest and when in motion. In their earliest stages, not unlike seeing children, they "model every part separately, as if there were no concept of a whole or totality." At the next stage, up to age ten, the parts are treated as part of the whole. Figures are put together by "combining symbolic forms, gained by successive impressions in the course of time, to a tangible, simultaneously unified entity." Blind children do not show as many parts as normal children. As with sighted children, the eye is represented as a hollow with a ball inserted in it. If there is more than one figure, each is shaped separately, and the space between them is decided upon later. Before the age of ten the blind child develops a concept of totality, though diffuse and incomplete. Around fourteen a change occurs, and blind children who are able to express themselves show a strong molding of certain parts and are strongly realistic and dependent on the concept roused by touch-visualization.[34]

In modeling, blind adults perform the same hand movements they use in fingering objects, which suggests that their manner of thinking is not as abstract as one might suppose.[5] Hardness to touch leads to a definite manner of representation. Certain textures such as hair or the folds of garments are a source of great difficulties.[34]

Löwenfeld, who had many years of experience with the blind, both children and adults, found individuals who strongly expressed their feelings and reactions in art by exaggerations in form and proportion. He also found individuals who tried to keep close to the actual forms and proportions of the subjects they rendered in art. These two different attitudes are shared by sighted persons. Because body experiences such as muscular sensations, kinesthetic experiences, and touch are their main sources of sensation, the blind have a more pronounced natural tendency to subjective (haptic) expression.[29]

Conclusion

Art activity is of great value to all children —the average and the exceptional. It provides opportunity for release and self-expression, for development and self-realization.

The gifted child, blessed with a generous measure of abilities, can find in art an avenue for a rich realization of his potential. The children limited in sight or hearing, in emotional equilibrium or intellectual ability—each can find in art a way for self-fulfillment. The teacher must try to assess the level of readiness, offer encouragement in the appropriate activities, and give guidance toward the ultimate promise of the individual child. In so doing, she not only offers enrichment to their lives but important assistance to their development.

CHAPTER SIX: TEXT REFERENCES

1. Bauermeister, H., "Die Begabungsfrage in der bildenden Kunst," *Internationale Zeitschrift für Individualpsychologie*, VII (1929), 108-111.

2. Beck, W., *Self-Development in Drawing, as Interpreted by the Genius of Romano Dazzi*, New York: Putnam's Sons, Knickerbocker Press, 1928.

3. Blair, F. X., "A study of the visual memory of deaf and hearing children," *American Annals of the Deaf*, CII, No. 2 (1957), 254-263.

4. Boutonier, J., *Les Dessins des Enfants*, Paris: Editions du Scarabée, 1953.

5. Burde, Blindenlehrer, "Die Plastik des Blinden," *Zeitschrift für angewandte Psychologie*, IV (1910), 106-128.

6. Christoffel, H., and E. Grossmann, "Über die expressionistische Komponente in Bildnereien geistig minderwertiger Knaben," *Zeitschrift für die gesamte Neurologie und Psychiatrie*, LXXXVII (1923), 372-376.

7. Cižek, F., "Die Organisation und die kunstpaedagogischen Probleme des Jugendkurses," Spezialvortrag, 4. *Internationaler Kongress für Kunstunterricht, Zeichnen und angewandte Kunst*, Hauptbericht (1912), Dresden, 466-476.

8. Dewey, J., "The psychology of drawing," New York: Teachers College, Columbia University, *Bulletin Series*, No. 10 (March, 1919), 3-5.

9. Goodenough, F. L., *Children's Drawings, A Handbook of Child Psychology*, Worcester, Mass.: Clark University Press, 1931.

10. Günzburg, H. C., "The significance of various aspects in drawings by educationally subnormal children," *Journal of Mental Science*, XCVI, No. 405 (1950), 951-975.

11. Hartlaub, G. F., *Der Genius im Kinde*, Breslau: Ferdinand Hirt, 1930.

12. Hildreth, G., *The Child Mind in Evolution*, New York: King's Crown Press, 1941.

13. Katz, D., *Studien zur experimentellen Psychologie*, Basel: Benno Schwabe, 1953.

14. Kerr, M., "Children's drawings of houses," *British Journal of Medical Psychology*, XVI (1937), 206-218.

15. Kerschensteiner, G., *Die Entwicklung der zeichnerischen Begabung*, Munich: Gerber, 1905.

16. Kik, C., "Die übernormale Zeichenbegabung bei Kindern," *Zeitschrift für angewandte Psychologie* (1909), 92-149.

17. Kitinoja, P., "Creative art and the deaf child," *American Annals of the Deaf*, CXVIII, No. 3 (1953), 312-322.

18. Lampard, T., "Art work of deaf children," *American Annals of the Deaf*, CV, No. 5 (1960), 419-423.

19. Lark-Horovitz, B., "Interlinkage of sensory memories in relation to training in drawing," *Journal of Genetic Psychology*, XLIX (1936), 69-89.

20. Lark-Horovitz, B., "On art appreciation of children: I. Preference of picture subjects in general," *Journal of Educational Research*, XXXI, No. 2 (1937), 118-137.

21. Lark-Horovitz, B., "On art appreciation of children: II. Portrait Preference Study," *Journal of Educational Research*, XXXI, No. 8 (1938), 572-598.

22. Lark-Horovitz, B., "On art appreciation of children: III. Textile pattern preference study," *Journal of Educational Research*, XXXIII, No. 1 (1939), 7-35.

23. Lark-Horovitz, B., "On learning abilities of children as recorded in a drawing experiment. I. Subject matter, II. Aesthetic and representational qualities," *Journal of Experimental Education*, IX, No. 4 (1941), 332-360.

24. Lark-Horovitz, B., Unpublished work of "A visual memory experiment," carried out at The Cleveland Museum of Art, Cleveland, Ohio, 1941.

25. Lark-Horovitz, B., and J. Norton, "Children's art abilities: Developmental trends of art characteristics," *Child Develop-*

ment XXX (1959), 433-452.

26. Lark-Horovitz, B., and J. Norton, "Children's art abilities. The interrelations and factorial structure of ten characteristics," *Child Development*, XXXI (1960), 453-462.

27. Levinstein, S., *Untersuchungen über das Zeichnen des Kindes*, Leipzig: R. Voightländer, 1905.

28. Lindner, R., "Moralpsychologische Auswertung freier Kinderzeichnungen von taubstummen Schülern," *Zeitschrift für paedagogische Psychologie*, XV (1914), 160-177.

29. Lowenfeld, V., "Psycho-aesthetic implications of the art of the blind," *Journal of Aesthetics and Art Criticism*, X, No. 1 (1951), 1-9.

30. Matz, W., "Zeichen-und Modellierversuche an Vokksschülern, Hilfsschülern, Taubstummen und Blinden," *Zeitschrift für angewandte Psychologie*, X (1915), 62-135.

31. Meier, N. "Studies in the Psychology of Art," *Psychological Monographs*, vol. 51, No. 5 (1939).

32. Mühle, G. *Entwicklungspsychologie des zeichnerischen Gestaltens. Grundlagen, formen und Wege der Kinderzeichnung*, Munich: Ambrosius Barth, 1955.

33. Munro, T.; B. Lark-Horovitz, and E. N. Barnhart, "Children's art abilities: Studies at the Cleveland Museum of Art," *Journal of Experimental Education*, XI, No. 2 (1942), 97-155.

34. Münz, L., and V. Löwenfeld, *Plastische Arbeiten Blinder*, Brünn: Rohrer, 1934.

35. Rouma, G., *Le Language Graphique de l'Enfant*, Brussels: Misch and Thron, 1913.

36. Scheffler, K., *Dilettantenerlebnis, Inselalmanach*, 1913, Leipzig: Inselverlag, 1913.

37. Sills, E. M., Unpublished work of a "Memory selection experiment," carried out at The Cleveland Museum of Art, Cleveland, Ohio, 1939.

38. Spoerl, D. T., "The drawing ability of mentally retarded children," *Journal of Genetic Psychology*, LVII (1940), 259-277.

39. Todd, J., *Drawing in the Elementary School*, Chicago: University of Chicago Press, 1931.

40. Traube, T., "La valeur diagnotique des dessins des enfants difficiles," *Archives du Psychologie*, XXVI, No. 103 (1937), 285-309.

41. Wintsch, J., "Le dessin comme temoin de dévelloppement mental," *Zeitschrift für Kinderpsychiatrie*, II, No. 3 (1935), 33-44; 69-83.

42. Wulff, O., *Die Kunst des Kindes*, Stuttgart: Ferdinand Enke, 1927.

Children's Attitudes and Approach to Art

When Dürer asked "What is beauty?" and answered himself "That I do not know, but, in truth, beauty is hidden in nature. Whoever can pluck it out has taken hold of beauty," he was describing the discovery everyone makes in due time, but that should be made, in all its implications, during childhood.

A child's understanding and enjoyment of art is different from his acquired knowledge in other fields. Art appreciation cannot be forced on a child; it must be voluntary and spontaneous. Thus, furthering children's art enjoyment is a different goal and presents different problems from teaching them a set of skills or a body of knowledge.

Among the problems teachers face in trying to help children derive pleasure from art, many questions remain to be answered. What evokes a child's interest in art? How early is it evident? Does his interest remain the same, or does it change with age? Does it differ from the kind of interest an adult has in art? Can it be influenced by environ-

149

ment, teaching, or simply by exposure to art? Which of these factors is most important in arousing and encouraging his interest in art?

CONCEPT OF THE BEAUTIFUL

The child's concept of what is beautiful often seems to be far removed from that of the adult, especially the adult with some background in art. Yet most adults assume that children find beauty in the same things that they themselves do and will take pains to point out to them qualities and details in a work of art, in the hope that this will help the children to share their view. In fact there is very little reason to suppose that any such end is achieved. Children may show some response to adults' suggestions, and girls, especially, may try to please them, but there is no evidence to suggest that a child's art appreciation of a particular work of art has the same basis as the adult's.

Adults tend to value the outward form of figures highly. This seems to be less important to the child. Children are more sensitive to an inner value which they see or project into the object. For young children, being beautiful and being good are one. Thus they unknowingly adopt the philosophy of Socrates and Plato. Each child's concept of goodness, or his sense of morality, enters strongly into his judgment of the beautiful. Only later, around the age of nine and ten, does a certain amount of differentiation between the beautiful and the good affect children's attitudes and judgments. Even then the moral sense dominates the recognition and acceptance of beauty. One finds a comparable approach in unsophisticated drama and fiction, and quite generally in fairy tales. The villain must be ugly, the heroine beautiful. As in

the myths and legends of ancient cultures, health, strength, and physical prowess are identified with beauty. As in fairy tales all over the world, good people are beautiful people, and the strength of the hero is goodness, therefore beauty. Only when strength becomes monstrosity, a deformity, or an abuse, as in an evil giant, does it lose its positive moral value and become ugly and horrifying. The values are then reversed.

Children react to the good by remembering it as beautiful, and conversely, the beautiful is for them a manifestation of goodness. In a group of children, viewing a portrait on one occasion, one third gave as their reasons for liking it the "goodness and bravery" of the expression. Children are unable to find beauty in works of art where the power emanates from ugliness, horror or disgust.

FINE ARTS

Children find a great variety of things beautiful, or in their words "pretty." Barnes found that children give first place to "natural objects," rather than "man-made things." Spectacles, parades, theatres appeal strongly to them, and pictures come near the bottom of their list of pretty things.[3]

The younger child thinks in terms of single objects, such as a flower, as a thing of beauty, while the older child is more inclined to consider a complex, larger unit, such as a garden, a thing of beauty. Awareness of a picture as a beautiful thing comes as a belated thought and then mainly as a by-product of interest in its content. Barnes' study revealed that "buildings, pictures and other works of art are not strong centers around which to gather artistic feelings at any time in the elementary school period."[3]

Since a child very seldom responds on the basis of aesthetic appeal or appreciation of technical excellence, just what does interest him most in a work of art?

Subject Matter

Content is the primary factor, but the bases for preference are rather complex. Subject matter cannot be interpreted as the entire reason for a choice. It would appear that at given age levels the preference for certain pictures reflects the main interests of the child's life at the time and points up strong differences in interests between girls and boys. Lark-Horovitz says that: "reasons . . . for picture choices all point to . . . dominance of the subject itself as a determining factor."[21] (Graph 13)

The dominant interest in subject matter and its relation to life experiences, came to light in another study[23] in which children chose favorites from thirty-nine patterns. An appreciable percentage of younger children pointed to a single detail of whatever pattern they selected as the reason for their choice. The detail reminded them of some real thing—an animal, a flower, a person, or a religious belief. The first choice of six- to thirteen-year-olds was a pattern of stylized but recognizable elephant heads and branches. This same pattern was the second choice of the older age levels.

Interest in geometrical patterns, on the other hand, is very slight,[23] though there seems to be a curious "stability and preference" in this field. In his studies, Jennings found that children over seven who expressed a preference for a certain geometrical pattern continued to reassert the same preference day after day.[19]

In another study, children aged twelve to fifteen were observed in their responses to an exhibit of ceramic objects. It was noted that the first reaction of junior and senior high school children was one of recognition of the nature of the object; this was followed by a recognition of the emotional and social implications of the object. Only after these aspects had been dealt with did they consider the thing being viewed as an object of art.[32]

Country children show a great preference for landscape.[36] In another study, also with country children, their comments sometimes show admiration for the natural scene itself and at other times indicate that their interpretation of it is linked to human associations.[42] The significance of the content of pictures is further underlined by the preferences for realistic paintings with close resemblances to real objects and a negative attitude toward modern abstract treatment. From age seven to fourteen, children show increasing preference for realism, this being

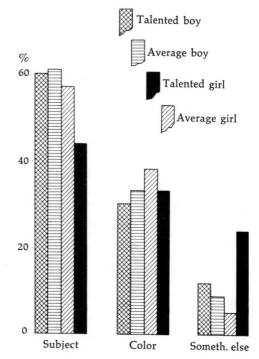

Graph 13: *Most important reasons for picture preferences*

From Lark-Horovitz.[21]

accompanied by a critical interest in content and an improvement in comprehension.[38]

Children value a work of art primarily for its content, not for its artistic form.[16] Preferences in paintings, whether landscape, nature, still life, flowers, or portraiture originate in the association of their subject matter with reality.[15] Thus, works of art stimulate children's imagination, and pictures as well as books sometimes evoke a highly individual response, especially from thoughtful adolescents,[5] yet the appeal which a particular work of art seems to have for children is different from the appeal it has for adults.

The child's mind is drawn to the factual part of the picture. Clarity and a well-defined representation are basic to his interest and are important factors in his preference, as is photographic distinctness because it shows everything. Spontaneous comments of children about a painting of the fifteenth century were "It is just like nature," "It's real."[48]

Children dislike still lifes,[21] especially the kind the French so vividly characterize as "nature morte" in which once vibrantly alive creatures like fish and partridges are shown devoid of life. Unless a child has a particular interest in the objects shown, the most outstanding picture of this kind will bore him, whether it is a realistic one by Courbet, or an expressionistic one by Cézanne. In one investigation, still lifes did not receive a single favorable vote from a group of children of different age levels.[21]

The great interest children have in the content of a work of art does not mean that this is the only element that counts (Graph 14). Art interest is dependent on the dominating interests both of the age levels and the sex of the child. Children's choices of subjects for their own drawings and their expressed preferences of pictures by adult artists confirm this.[32]

However, "preference or liking for a picture is not identical with the impression the picture leaves and its resultant influence," as shown in one study where children viewed slides of works of art and then proceeded to make their own art work. Surprisingly, the pictures they liked best did not influence their art work as much as can be expected.[24] One of the various studies made at the Cleveland Museum of Art concluded "that non-preferred art objects may be as stimulating as preferred ones, or more so."[32]

Artistically talented children share the preferences of their age group but offer different reasons from those given by average children in support of their choice.[21] While no single study has been able to point conclusively to all the factors that determine a child's response to a picture, nor to assess the relative importance of each factor, various studies taken together provide some insight. Obviously, in trying to ascertain the appeal of works of art to children, it is easier to sort out the part played by various factors if children are shown several pictures on the same subject, widely differing as the artists' conceptions of these subjects may be. When this was done, the answers given by children showed that after content, color came next in accounting for their liking or disliking a given picture. (Graph 14)

Color

The evidence suggests that color plays an important part in the attitudes and responses of children. "Children, eleven to thirteen years old, make color and degree of naturalism the criteria of judging."[43] It is often the primary factor in the initial appeal that a picture has for a child, but subject matter may replace it as the chief factor in a considered selection of favorite pictures. Geometric designs eliminate subject matter appeal and narrow the reaction to form and color. Children, making spontaneous selections of textile patterns in a preference study,[23] clearly indicated the appeal of color. They confirmed this in answer to specific and direct questions about the significance of color in their choices. Graph 15 shows the distribution by age level of par-

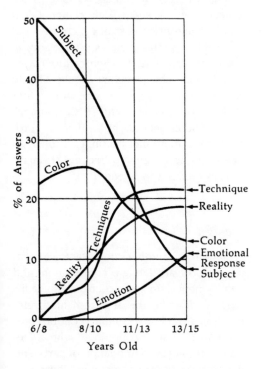

Graph 14: *Increase and decrease of interest in subject, color, reality, technique, and emotion through age levels for both boys and girls*

From Lark-Horovitz.[22]

ticular types of color preferences. In selecting their favorite portrait from a large portrait exhibit,[22] the majority of younger children chose their preferred portrait from color pictures. Fifty percent of the older children chose uncolored pictures despite the fact that two-thirds of the total exhibit was in color. This changing attitude toward color in pictures corresponds to the change in the use of color in their own art work.[25] It does not indicate a growing indifference to color, but rather a greater sophistication in values and combinations of color. Older children lean toward tints and shades and more subtle combinations, while younger children like bright and contrasting color.[43]

The attention children give to color may be strong at one time and then take second place to form at later periods of development.[11] Studies have been made of color preferences of some thirty nationalities.[1] Children of five different cultures show variation in color preferences with red and blue leading. Color preferences seem to be influenced not only by education,[13,14] but also by economic status.[20] No one color is universally and constantly the favorite, but there are general color attitudes. "Loud" colors, for example, tend to be generally rejected by older children.[30]

Color is closely related to emotions. Red is associated with fun and jolliness, and violet or blue with sadness; these same colors do not necessarily depend on pleasant and unpleasant experiences excited by them.[30] Red is associated mostly with things that arouse positive emotions, green with negative emotions. Happy children seem to prefer red.[44]

Subes found that girls from rural environments quite generally have a "real thirst for color".[41] The taste of rural children shows greater variability in reactions to simple geometric areas of juxtaposed color than in connection with pictures; Subes concludes that "the aesthetic sensitivity peculiar to childhood toward works of art is more [due] to age, sex and . . . environment than to color sensitivity." This investigation confirmed the findings of his other studies that five- to ten-year-olds incline toward strong and clear colors, while eleven- to fourteen-year-olds prefer somber colors.

It is difficult to isolate color from other art elements. Color has a close association with some characteristics of works of art, but it is relatively unimportant in others.[46] There is a close relationship between style in painting and the use of color,[25] as for ex-

ample in impressionistic and expressionistic art. Color by itself cannot function without form.

Clarity

Clarity is a significant quality in a work of art and is closely related to the viewer's ability to understand the picture's content. It is therefore an important factor in the preference for realistic presentation.[40] Very young children favor pictures with simple composition even though they may include a large number of objects, as long as the objects are presented with clarity. Older children like more complex pictures.[12] But all children prefer pictures with clarity in spatial relationships.[26] When children were asked what changes they would like to make in certain portraits, one out of four wished for greater clarity.[22] Correspondingly, children seek clarity in their own productions, a trend that continues through all age levels and seems to become strongest at ages fourteen to fifteen.[32]

Design

Design is another important element in works of art. Design, composition, and arrangement are interchangeable terms used to describe the arrangement of elements in a work of art so that it can be comprehended as an "harmonious" whole. Design implies order and relation of parts, and the creation of forms to express ideas.

The average child is seldom conscious of the functions of design in his enjoyment of art. He is not aware that through design, ideas are given a "body."

Design is responsible for "the ability to recognize compositional excellence in . . . art situations or the ability to 'sense' quality in an aesthetic situation."[31]

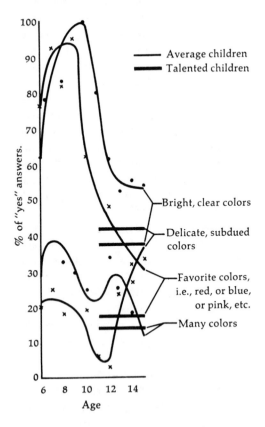

Graph 15: *Variety of color preferences*

From Lark-Horovitz.[23]

Design has meaning for some children but few studies give information about children's attitudes toward design and how much design has to do with total art interest and appreciation. One study enumerates the most popular art qualities that children notice and among them is design.[43] When realistic content is replaced with abstract design, as in most textiles, children become more aware of design and base their preferences on qualities removed from content.[23]

Technique

Technique is related to the nature of the media and the artist's manner of using it. Technique varies within the limits set by the media and within the broad range of approaches used by every artist. The technique of the wood-working sculptor differs from the methods used by the artist working in metal; the fresco painter works in a different way from the painter on canvas. Different techniques produce different effects. In observing a work of art, some knowledge of the methods used is essential to a full appreciation of the work.

One might pause to note the difference between technique and technical skill. Technique is used here to mean the particular combination of media and tools that yield a characteristic type of art—as for instance oil painting, or wood block. Technique is also applied to a particular usage such as for "dry brush" or "montage." The measure of the artist's technical skill is the degree to which he develops the use of his materials. The measure of his effectiveness as an artist is the extent to which his technical skill enables him to combine all the elements of a work of art into a meaningful composition. Technical skill alone is not enough. A good technician may not be necessarily a good artist. But to be a good

artist one must be skilled in technique.

There is another factor that should not be overlooked—the objective of the artist. He may be able to draw and paint in an academic manner with great skill, but he may decide to paint in a startlingly different style, more expressive of his individual outlook. The innovators in art as in any field should be approached with a view to understanding what they are trying to do.

There is little evidence on children's attitude toward technique. One early study done by Bulley used a single portrait by Jean Marchand and asked children to list their reasons for liking or disliking it. One fourth of the reasons given for disliking the picture were directly connected with technique.[7] In another study, children made such comments on a portrait that they had chosen as: "the eyes are well drawn" or "colors are painted smoothly."[21] Such observations are made mostly by talented children, who also are inclined to pay particular attention to technique in abstract art.[23]

Through all age levels, average children have little interest in technique. They are interested in the result but not in the means that lead to it. However, appreciation does increase with age and can be supported by instruction. Gifted children recognize technical skill at an early age and pay close attention to "how it is done." Appreciation of technique is perhaps the largest single factor in their evaluation of art.

Very few art appreciation studies include architecture or sculpture. One that did noted that "architecture and plastic arts are of importance for the boys but seldom mentioned by girls." The reason seems to be that boys are more concerned with realism as some of their comments indicate: "I like sculpture because what one sees is the true thing."[15] In commenting on three-dimensional modeled animals, children's comments, on one occasion, showed that they look upon them as if they were alive. In portraits in sculpture, the interest of the boys far outranks that of the girls until age fourteen or fifteen.[22]

Emotion

Perhaps the most pervasive feature in children's attitudes toward works of art is the general emotional background they bring to art experiences. Sometimes the feelings that are aroused or stimulated by the work of art are the essential factors in the experience. Sometimes emotions enter, indirectly, as an undercurrent. They may be pleasant or unpleasant and may vary in strength. They may be caused by concurrent, immediate events, or they may stem from past happenings of which the child is conscious or of which he becomes aware once more because of the new experience.

One interesting study grouped fourteen-year-old boys according to characteristics regarding emotionality and activeness, and according to normality and retardation. The surprising conclusion was "that emotionality or non-emotionality, as deeply-rooted forms of character, are of little influence concerning choice of pictures of individuals."[29]

Wolff, reporting on his work with preschool children, says: "Young children have color preferences, but they become manifest only if the color experience is within the orbit of a child's emotional experience."[47] The happy look of the people in a picture may bring pleasure to the observer.[43] The facial expression in portraits often stimulates emotional associations.[22]

Lark-Horovitz's comments on the emotional involvement of children in observing art confirm such observations. The importance of facial expression shows that a conscious or unconscious identification of the child with the portrait takes place. The child

"wishes to have a friend like the portrayed person" or the child is reminded of a person he knows. Familiarity, real or imagined, enters into his liking for a work of art. Older children respond more to character traits shown in facial expression. "Older . . . boys are more attracted by [portraits of] men with strong and pensive features." Younger children are more concerned with the action suggested. Boys choose portraits of men, girls of women. Such associations, combined with the child's image of his ideal, may involve moral approval, combined with personal experiences and the need for identification through sympathy or empathy, all of which strongly influence the personal acceptance of art work.[22]

The emotional aspect of choice is evident when reasons for likes and dislikes are given in terms of feelings that pictures evoke. Boys reject works that suggest pain or sadness[7] and like art that amuses them and makes them feel "an inner mounting joy."[15] After their studies on children's "aesthetic sense," Subes and Auzet came to the conclusion that "it is not the reality of the milieu by which the aesthetic sense of children is shaped, but the aspirations which this environment stimulates . . . and which often seems contrary to reality."[42] It seems that, "the child is particularly sensitive to that of which he is deprived." The young city dweller is more stimulated by that from which he is separated and so responds especially to landscapes and animals, while country boys incline toward things that are fantastic and extraordinary.[36]

However, other studies give little support to such conclusions. The generally self-centered bias of most children in their picture preference is also revealed by their lack of interest in portraits of older people with whom they believe they have little in common. They see them outside of life.

Artistically talented children, on the other hand, are interested in old people's looks and find portraits of them worth scrutiny.[22]

The wish to own a work of art that they admire is very strong in most average children. Artistically talented children take a more detached and less proprietary attitude.

Children often express a desire to change something in a work of art they like. This attitude also seems to stem from emotions, since usually the changes would bring the work closer to their ideals. Few suggested changes arise from aesthetic reasons;[22] changes seem to suggest a situation that would be emotionally more satisfactory.

Aesthetic Sense

The child's aesthetic sense is probably of more concern than many other factors. An understanding of how the aesthetic response develops would be invaluable in understanding differences of response at various age levels, and in judging children's readiness for the teacher's suggestions and explanations, thus helping children develop discriminating taste and aesthetic judgment.

Children often respond to pictures with feeling, even exhilaration. They find stimulation and inspiration in them. However, the pleasure and stimulation they derive from works of art are not easily explained. The process is complex. The reaction may spring from many sources and cannot be assumed to arise directly from aesthetic appreciation. An aesthetic attitude apparently arises from an exhilarating state of admiration inspired by a number of things and situations outside the realm of the "arts" as well as by the work of art itself. For the viewer, the aesthetic worth of art depends on the sense of rapport which the work of art elicits from him. It seems to be related

to the degree to which the artist expresses what the beholder feels but is himself unable to articulate. But while this seems to apply to most adults, it does not necessarily apply to children. In the last analysis, an adult's inability to penetrate the child's world and work, to fully sense what the child actually experiences, reduces his understanding of the possibilities and limitations of the child's enjoyment of art. What a child experiences before a work of art remains a mystery to adults.

Sourieau, the great aesthetic philosopher, says that aesthetic appreciation is contained in two combined experiences—the evaluation of the perceived object and the process involved in arriving at an evaluation. He states: "When children, or persons who lack both native taste and an aesthetic background, are used as the subjects of experiment, one can be sure that most of them, in being given works of art to classify preferentially, will be guided in their appreciation for the most part by the . . . degree of affective, intellectual, or practical interest in the whole set of ideas evoked by the subject matter. Then the kind of appreciation is not aesthetic." He proceeds to qualify this statement: "Many children show no genuine aesthetic appreciation in the presence of a work of art. But the same children of whom this is true will manifest vigorous, definite, and even purely aesthetic responses to other sorts of stimuli: a drop of dew . . . an agate marble. . . ." And he concludes: ". . . valid aesthetic appreciation by a child cannot be determined without finding out (1) the sort of stimuli for aesthetic appreciation; (2) to what degree the stimulus offered to him experimentally arouses in him phenomena analogous to those observed in his spontaneous aesthetic appreciation."[37] This accords with Pfleiderer's conclusions that "a child has little feeling for qualities of a formal sensual beauty" and is rarely attracted to those beauties in a landscape that attract a painter.[34]

The aesthetic attitude of children and untutored adults toward a work of art is emotionally conditioned and only loosely affected by demonstrable qualities in the work of art. Older children are sometimes able to point out tangible assets of the work of art they prefer, but usually this is the exception rather than the rule. Through preschool and the early grades, the child's real interest in art and literature is a functional enjoyment of his productive activity. A sense of identification, participation, and achievement enter into it. More exposure to art, improvement in individual understanding and performance may raise the level of appreciation, but even at puberty a full understanding of matters of aesthetic value is rarely achieved. Only during adolescence does a true aesthetic attitude break through.[6] Then the child begins to separate his own egocentric bias from his evaluation of the work. He is able to see the work as the complex expression of the artist's emotions and artistic objectives, his skillful joining of idea and materials to its meaningful entity.

Hegel's definition of a work of art, "the free and adequate embodiment of an idea in a manner peculiarly adapted to the idea itself" is a useful point of departure, but it is extremely difficult to define aesthetic principles and measure art appreciation. The three factors of unity, harmony, and proportion may serve as guides in judging aesthetic awareness. Yet the vagueness of these terms makes it hardly possible to analyze an individual's appreciation of art. There are fundamental difficulties in an experimental situation that endeavors to explore children's aesthetic attitudes and responses. The challenge is to separate the factors which combined to evoke enjoyment as a result of aesthetic sensitivity.

Frequently, exposure to works of art brings forth an aesthetic response, although when analyzed, not a single element seems to be aesthetic. It is as though an intangible "something" permeates the otherwise tangible non-aesthetic characteristics. Design, colors, techniques, and associations, all are involved in producing an aesthetic response. Understanding and evaluation of these factors are necessary for full aesthetic appreciation. Response on an aesthetic level probably should not be expected in early years and, indeed, may not be achieved for some persons at any age. However, there is in each person the potential for appreciation—a dormant "giftedness" that can be released. It is this sleeping sensitivity that art courses, well handled, may awaken.

The results of studies concerned with aesthetic sensibility, sensitivity, and attitudes of children, often reach different and sometimes seemingly contradictory conclusions. There is still much to be learned in this field. Surely a most important factor in achieving an aesthetic attitude is perceptiveness in general. In its widely inclusive meaning, perception involves observation and to a degree all the senses, and a highly complex "sorting mechanism" of great sensitivity. It is more than just seeing. It is an involved balance of the senses with certain discriminatory bridges to conscious thought and subconscious memory.

A person experienced in observing and evaluating art perceives almost at a glance the kind of art he is viewing, the subject, the media and technique, composition and general period of the painting. He need not consciously think about each of these things separately, just as a person riding a bicycle need not remember the separate steps by which he learned to ride or the separate elements of the complicated process of riding. But this almost automatic awareness of many aspects in the complex whole of a work of art does not just happen. It is the result of exposure, conscious learning and developed sensitivity.

Awareness of one's self in relation to the work of art is a factor in aesthetic enjoyment. Indeed, an aesthetic response is, in a way, an experience of the larger self. The degree to which one can experience this is affected by many factors. As cultural exposure and self-knowledge advance, one's ability for full aesthetic experience grows, enabling one to bring to a work of art an awareness of the fundamental differences in the world of art. It will be possible to see a painting as conceived in "Apollonian" or classic style. It will be possible to recognize signs of the "Dionysian," i.e. the contrasting approach—the impetuous, thrusting, highly picturesque. Such background knowledge can and does influence reactions or appreciation and knowledge of self. It makes it possible to understand "contrast of the visually perceptible with what is seen with the inward senses."[28]

It is easy to see that few people can bring full aesthetic appreciation to their observations of art. Children, four to seven years of age, have greater exactitude of memory and more active and mobile associations than adults.[9]

Subes makes some rather sweeping statements on children's art appreciation. "Children, aged five to fourteen, prove their sensibility in an original and definite manner, which it would be difficult to describe as aesthetic sensibility. This aesthetic sense covers formal and pictorial qualities. It manifests itself in regard to techniques, to shapes, to correlative relationships and to values. It is more outspoken than that of artistically cultured adults . . . Children have given proof of the existence of an aesthetic sensibility in childhood; . . . established their aesthetic sense in regard to traditional painting."[41] Subes also considers the flight of imagination as "tending to demonstrate that aesthetic contemplation is for the child

a way of escaping from himself."[39] A bond exists between emotional attitudes and the ability to experience aesthetic enjoyment. Pronounced likes and dislikes of shapes, techniques, or color values indicate this relation and show an emotional quality in some aesthetic responses. However, the child's sensibility may also be a reflection of adult values and therefore one cannot assume that the child's response is not due in part to his environment.[38]

Jean Renoir, in his book on his famous father, relates the following anecdote. As a child he was given a present which touched him deeply. It was a very ugly plate, but as he comments, "I do not believe that children, even those grown in the midst of Renoir canvases, are easily shocked by ugliness.[35]" There is no apparent relationship between standard of living and art appreciation, although a positive relationship can be seen between training in art and art appreciation, and a certain degree of relationship seems to exist between aesthetic judgment and cultural opportunity. A study of fourteen-year-old boys in France indicated that "differences of geographical origin and quantitative differences of intelligence do not influence . . . choices of an aesthetic kind."[29]

Some studies show that children aged ten to fourteen evidence a high degree of aesthetic receptivity. Their responses seemed to be close to those of educated adults and to surpass them in regard to decorative matters. The response was greatest in children who are talented in their own productive work.[18] In another study, only 5 percent of a large number of children explained their reasons for likes and dislikes in terms generally associated with aesthetics.[7]

Another investigator concluded that "the reasons for the choice [of pictures] show that aesthetic elements are only crudely present. . . . The design in the picture, the structure of it, the effect achieved, count apparently only insofar as they accentuate the interesting subject.[21] This also holds true for the average children above the age of ten. Only gifted children offer reasons that can be described as aesthetic.[22] Talented children analyze their preferences and make their choices more in terms of certain aesthetic qualities such as technique, line and shape, texture and material, or originality.[23]

Appreciation of art is deepened by individual activity in art and by exposure to works of art. Informed instruction can lead to more intensified observation and may help to develop "more maturity of aesthetic judgment." Girls progress more rapidly toward this than boys. There seems to be a noticeable relationship to the cultural level or the home background, but also to training in art.

Visits to museums can contribute substantially to developing acute powers of observation, and perceptiveness can be heightened by unhurried schoolroom discussions. For example, one classroom discussed the picture entitled *Garden of Paradise* (1410) by the Master of the Upper Rhine.[48] Spontaneous comments during a first exposure referred to the content of the picture, the activities of the people, and the scenery in which they move. Children made particular note of "its reality, just as in nature," but there were no spontaneous comments on its colors. However, at a later session, a child brought up the question of whether it is night in the picture. The question was approved by the other children because "the entire sky is dark, while in the garden it is surely day," and why isn't the sky as light as in Albert's and Rolf's pictures?" (classmates). This pictorial conflict was noticed only after a thorough analysis and was followed by reflection on "whether the sky is painted dark in order to show up the wall?" This, in itself, is in the nature of an aesthetic consideration.

Though children six to eight were "entirely descriptive in their observational attitude," this decreased by 70 percent when they reach age ten to eleven.[11] Older children move even farther away from the descriptive approach.

Exposure to works of art, sustained by discussion and active participation in creative activity, leads to more critical appraisals of the entire environment. It heightens the enjoyment of life and shows the way to aesthetic living. The experiences of daily life give aesthetic satisfaction. Physical as well as intellectual tasks more easily achieve a balance. Children express appreciations: "a table that is beautiful for having dinner on it," "trees that give shade where it would be cozy." Looking at the painting of Van Gogh's bedroom, for example, one child said he liked it because "there is a bed in which it would be lovely to sleep."[42] The child's imaginative logic combines reasoning with an appreciation of the intimacy conveyed by an artist's presentation.

Taste

Critical appraisal and detailed observation are essential to the development of taste. Taste involves discriminatory judgment. It has been defined as "the power of discerning and appreciating fitness, beauty, order . . whatever constitutes excellence, especially in the fine arts."* The term "fitness" is important in that even a thing of beauty may be in bad taste in some circumstances. In Benedetto Croce's opinion, "the activity of judgment which criticizes and recognizes the beautiful is identical with what produces it. The only difference lies in the diversity of circumstances, since in the one case it is a question of aesthetic production, in the other of reproduction. The activity which judges is called taste; the

* Webster's New International Dictionary, 2nd edition.

productive activity is called genius; genius and taste are therefore substantially identical."[10]

There are relatively few studies that deal with taste, and their results have been difficult to assess. One study found a high degree of uniformity in the taste between grammar school and college,[4] another found that children of all ages showed a startling preference for inferior pictures, possibly because the meaning was clearer and more familiar.[8] When commonplace objects were used to test preferences, a decline in taste from age ten to thirteen was evident, followed by an improvement in judgment thereafter. Undoubtedly, "good art" is more demanding of the viewer. It seems to arouse greater mental activity, to stimulate a larger number of thought changes and require more time.[33] The preference for the familiar, as shown by another study, is quite understandable and not confined to children. Even adults are seldom capable of enjoying new forms of art at a first viewing.[36]

Children's Attitude Toward Child Art

Many educators are convinced that children incline toward works of art done in a style resembling their own; that younger children in the schematic stage, for example, favor pictures somewhat like their own and respond to them because of a non-realistic representation that leans toward the archaic in art. In one study of the 1920's, children were offered the choice of a Swedish artist's illustrations for children's books and pictures made by other children. The pictures made by children, however, included a number from Cižek's class, which were in no sense "primitive" and were mostly at the true-to-appearance level. The children rejected the professional illustrations and chose those made by other children.[45] Subes, however, states that "children from

the age of five years on do not in any way appreciate children's paintings but prefer those of adults. . . ."[39]

It is also worth noting that, when asked to choose the best one of several childlike drawings taken from various developmental levels, children always selected drawings that were more advanced than those they produced themselves.[27] Children tend to judge other children's drawings in relation to their own developmental level. They approve of pictures that are more "advanced" than their own and judge their quality in relation to the age of the author of the pictures. If a child judges a picture by a child of the same age, he will find it good when it far surpasses his own level of accomplishment[40] and will laugh at it and consider it bad art if the picture is on his own level of drawing.

Ability to "Identify" Works of Art

Children become more aware of the styles and characteristics of particular masters and schools of painting as they grow older and have been more exposed to art. They come to recognize the work of individual artists or a group of artists linked by some similarity of style or as belonging to a given period of history. One study of children's recognition of particular works of art reports that 35 percent of eight-year-olds, 43 percent of twelve-year-olds and 52 percent of sixteen-year-olds were able to identify masters by their pictures.[17]

Repeated exposure to art sharpens the perception of children. Although they tend to like the art they know, they gradually enlarge their appreciation as their exposures are widened. With instruction they can learn to broaden the base of their appreciation and can gradually develop an attitude of receptivity and critical judgment.

CHAPTER SEVEN: TEXT REFERENCES

1. Anastasi, A., and J. Foley, Jr., "An analysis of spontaneous drawings by children in different cultures," *Journal of Applied Psychology*, XX (1936), 689-726.

2. Anderson, H., *Creativity and its cultivation*, New York: Harper & Row, Publishers, 1959.

3. Barnes, E., "The prettiest thing," *Studies in Education*, II, No. 5 (1902).

4. Berliner, A., "Aesthetic judgments of school children," *Journal of Applied Psychology*, II (1918), 229-242.

5. Bühler, C., "Kunst und Jugend," *Zeitscrift für Aesthetik und allgemeine Kunstwissenschaft*, XX, Nos. 3 and 4 (1926), 288-306.

6. Bühler, C., *Das Seelenleben des Jugendlichen. Versuch einer Analyse und Theorie der psychischen Pubertät*, Jena: Fischer, 1927.

7. Bulley, M., "An experiment," *The Burlington Magazine*, XXXV, No. 199 (1919), 162-166.

8. Bulley, M., "The child and art; an experiment," *The Burlington Magazine*, XLIII, No. 247 (1923), 179-184.

9. Cramoussel, E., "Ce que voyent les yeux d'enfant," *Journal de Psychologie*, XXI (1924), 161-169.

10. Croce, B., *Aesthetics*, Westminster: Noonday Press, 1958.

11. Engel, P., "Über die teilinhaltliche Betrachtung von Farbe und Form im vorschulpflichtigen Kindesalter," *Zeitschrift für paedagogische Psychologie und Jugendkunde*, XXXVI (1935), 202-214; 241-251.

12. French, J. E., "Children's preferences for pictures of varied complexity of pictorial pattern," *Elementary School Journal*, VIII (1952), 90-94.

13. Garth, T. R., "A color preference scale for 1,000 white children," *Journal of Experimental Psychology*, VII (1924), 233-241.

14. Garth, T. R., and I. R. Collado, "Color preferences of Filipino children," *Journal of Comparative Psychology*, IX (1929), 397-404.

15. Grzegorzewska, M., "Enquête sur les goûts esthétiques de la jeunesse scolaire," *Journal de Psychologie*, XII (1915), 511-524.

16. Hartlaub, G. F., *Der Genius im Kinde*, Breslau: Ferdinand Hirt, 1930.

17. Haubold, M., "Bildbetrachtungen durch Kinder und Jugendliche," *Neue Psychologische Studies*, VII, No. 2 (1933).

18. Heckel, R., "Optische Formen und aesthetisches Erleben," *Untersuchungen über aesthetisches Erleben*, edit. by Oswald Kroh, No. 1, 1927.

19. Jennings, F., "Preliminary investigations to determine the conformity of children to aesthetic principles in graphic art," *Psychological Bulletin*, XXXVII, No. 8 (1940), 555-556.

20. Katz, S. E., and F. S. Breed, "The color preference of children," *Journal of Applied Psychology*, VI (1922), 255-266.

21. Lark-Horovitz, B., "On art appreciation of children: I. Preference of picture subjects in general," *Journal of Educational Research*, XXXI, No. 2 (1937), 118-137.

22. Lark-Horovitz, B., "On art appreciation of children: II. Portrait preference study," *Journal of Educational Research*, XXXI, No. 8 (1938), 572-598.

23. Lark-Horovitz, B., "On art appreciation of children: III. Textile pattern preference study," *Journal of Educational Research*, XXXIII, No. 1 (1939), 7-35.

24. Lark-Horovitz, B., "On learning abilities of children as recorded in a drawing experiment. I. Subject matter, II. Aesthetic and representational qualities," *Journal of Experimental Education*, IX, No. 4 (1941), 332-360.

25. Lark-Horovitz, B., and J. Norton, "Children's art abilities: Developmental trends of art characteristics," *Child Development*, XXX (1959), 433-452.

26. Lewis, H. P., "Spatial representation in drawing as a correlate of development and a basis for picture preference," *Jour-*

nal of Genetic Psychology, CII (1963), 95-107.

27. Lewis, H. P., "The relationship of picture preference to developmental status in drawing," *Journal of Educational Research*, LVII (1963), 43-46.

28. Lowenfeld, V., "Psycho-aesthetic implications of the art of the blind," *Journal of Aesthetic and Art Criticism*, X, No. 1 (1951), 1-9.

29. Marchal, G. L., "Contribution à l'étude du sentiment esthétique," *B.I.N.O.P., Bulletin de l'Institut National d'Etude du Travail et d'Orientation Professionelle*, XV, 2nd series (1959), 219-255.

30. Martin, A., "Die Gefühlsbetonung von Farben und Farbenkombinationen bei Kindern," *Zeitschrift für Kinderforschung*, XXVI (1921), 128-156.

31. Meier, N. C., "A measure of art talent," Psychological Monographs, XXXIX, No. 2 (1928).

32. Munro, T., B. Lark-Horovitz, and E. N. Barnhart, "Children's art abilities: Studies at the Cleveland Museum of Art," *Journal of Experimental Education*, XI, No. 2 (1942), 97-155.

33. Patrick, C., "Different responses produced by good and poor art," *Journal of General Psychology*, XXXIV (1946), 79-96.

34. Pfleiderer, W., *Die Geburt des Bildes*, Stuttgart: Julius Hoffmann, 1930.

35. Renoir, J., *Renoir*, Paris: Librairie Hachette, 1962.

36. Schwarz, L., "Quelques remarques sur l'attitude des enfants de la campagne devant des oeuvres d'art," *Enfance*, VI, No. 3 (1953), 249-261.

37. Sourieau, E., "A general methodology for the scientific study of aesthetic appreciation," *Journal of Aesthetics and Art Criticism*, XIV, No. 1 (1955), 1-18.

38. Subes, J., "La sensibilité de l'enfant à l'art pictural," *Enfance*, VIII, No. 4 (1955), 345-368.

39. Subes, J., "Sensibilité esthétique enfantine et influence du milieu," *Enfance*, X, No. 1 (1957), 43-65.

40. Subes, J., with Pierre and Colas, "L'appréciation esthétique d'oeuvres d'enfants par les enfants," *Enfance*, XI, No. 2 (1958), 115-130.

41. Subes, J., "Des goûts des enfants pour les couleurs," *Enfance*, XII (1959), 117-142.

42. Subes, J. and J. Auzet, "Une tentative d'étude objective du sense esthétique chez l'enfant," *Enfance*, III (1950), 160-167.

43. Todd, J., "Preferences of children for modern and older paintings," *Elementary School Journal*, XLIV (1943), 223-231.

44. Traube, T., "La valeur diagnostique des dessins des enfants difficiles," *Archives de Psychologie*, XXVI, No. 103 (1937), 285-309.

45. Vandermark, P. J., "An experimental study of what types of pictures children are most interested in and why," Columbia University, 1929, in: Morrison, J. G., *Children's Preferences for Pictures Commonly Used in Art Appreciation Courses*, Chicago: University of Chicago Press, 1935.

46. White, R. S. and S. B. Johnson, "Children's choices in modern art," *Child Development*, II (1931), 347-349.

47. Wolff, W., *The Personality of the Preschool Child. The Child's Search for His Self.* New York: Grace and Stratton, 1946.

48. Wommelsdorff, O., *Wandschmuck für Schulen*, Düsseldorf: Paedagogischer Verlag, 1930.

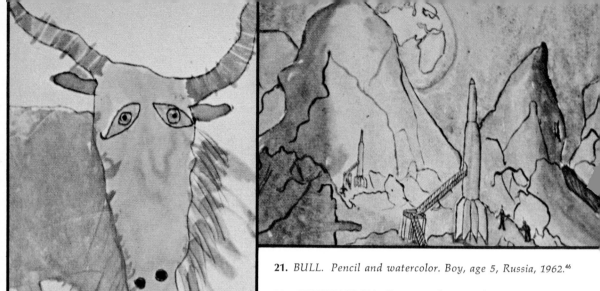

21. BULL. *Pencil and watercolor. Boy, age 5, Russia, 1962.*[46]

22. *AT THE MOON. Crayon and watercolor. Boy, age 11, Russia, 1962.*[46]

23. TOWN. *Startling color contrast. Humor. Pencil and watercolor. Talented girl, age 9.*[42]

24. IN THE COUNTRY. *Balance of colors, ease in use of medium. True-to-appearance, watercolor and pencil, spontaneous. Girl, age 11, 1965.*[42]

25. *Two pages by children, lettering their own story with illustrations. Boys, age 9, Italy, 1963.*[45]

27. THE NEW WASHER. *Paper paste-up. Girl, age 10, England, 1965.*[47]

26. COLLAGE. *Made in school. Girl, age 11.*[44]

28. *A SCENE FROM THE CIVIL WAR. True local colors. Movement Schema, crayons, spontaneous. Boy, age 7.*[40]

29. CRAYONS RESIST FINGERPAINTING. *Crayons and fingerpaint made in school. Teamwork. Boys, age 8.*[44]

CHAPTER EIGHT

Creativity

We are surrounded by the results of human creativity. The art, music, and literature of the world are the products of someone's creativeness. The ideas, theories, and scientific laws we use to understand the workings of the natural and social world are also the results of creativity. All of our lives have been enriched by the efforts of the great creative giants whose names we revere. We have also been affected by the creative work of little known individuals who made their unique contribution in a less spectacular way.

Creativity manifests itself in varying degrees and in different areas of an individual's life. Often creativity is concentrated in a particular sphere of activity—art, music, science. The choice is conditioned by the constellation of the person's abilities, by the avenues of opportunity open to him, and by the demands of the endeavor. In the twentieth century, the creative artist is rarely also a creative scientist. Some people live with "flair," adding a touch of originality to whatever they do, yet are not notably creative in any one area. Others insist that they

165

are not creative. What they usually mean by this is that they are not intensely creative in any particular way and only occasionally exercise their creative powers. Creativity, then, is not a quality which is either wholly present or totally absent in any individual. It exists to some degree in everyone, manifesting itself in a variety of ways.

The elementary school teacher may discern differences in the degree and kind of creativity displayed by the members of the class. Some children will be inclined towards scientific, problem solving creativity while others will demonstrate creativity in artistic expression. Specialization may have already taken place within one mode of expression. Eisner suggests that children who perform creatively in one art medium, such as painting, will not necessarily be creative in using a different medium, such as modeling in clay.[5] To help in the discovery of the direction of a child's creative bent and to help develop it is both the privilege and the obligation of a good teacher.

Only in recent years have educators and psychologists turned their attention to the study of creative behavior. Perhaps this is due in part to the realization that complex contemporary problems demand creative solutions. Perhaps it is also partly due to our high level of productivity which for the first time offers to millions of people the opportunity for fuller development of their potential. Or maybe we seek new ways to express our individuality in reaction to our separation from productive processes and in protest against the growing standardization of our lives. People look hopefully to the schools to nurture creativeness. This responsibility is both a tribute and a challenge to the teacher.

Research workers who study creativity make certain assumptions about its nature

and roots. Some approach it as an aspect of intellectual ability, others as a component of personality, and still others as a function of sensory equipment. Each approach has its own implications for teaching.

We do not yet know with certainty which approaches to the development of creativity are most effective. We *believe* that creativity can be encouraged, but we cannot specify how this can be done, nor indeed guarantee that anything teachers do will have a marked effect on the creativity of their students. All that can be done at present is to acquaint teachers with what various research studies have revealed and suggest procedures we think will work, proceeding on the assumption that creativity rests on many factors, and some intangible catalyst of character puts them all to work.

The three main questions which psychologists and educators have been asking about creativity are: (1) what is the creative process, (2) what are the unique characteristics of highly creative individuals, (3) what factors in the environment facilitate or inhibit creative behavior?

THE CREATIVE PROCESS

First, let us look at the creative process. One way of viewing it, suggested by Wallas[23] in 1926, is as a process with a beginning, a middle, and an end resulting in a new idea. Drawing upon personal accounts of the creative process, he identified four stages which he named: *Preparation, Incubation, Illumination* and *Verification.*

The first stage, *Preparation,* refers to early, deliberate attempts at discovering the answer to a particular problem. While the individual assembles and begins to ponder the ideas that are clearly relevant, the residue of all past experience is brought into play. If a satisfactory solution is not achieved immediately, the problem is set aside while the individual pursues other activities.

The period in which attention is not focused directly on the problem at hand is called *Incubation*. While the individual is working on another problem, engaging in physical activity, or just daydreaming, the answer comes to him as it were, "out of the blue." The explanation for this phenomenon, *Illumination*, is that the subconscious remained at work until the answer was found and then notified the conscious, whose attention had been directed elsewhere. Conscious attention is finally directed at *Verification*, the testing of the solution to insure that it works.

In the comics a light bulb appropriately signals that *Illumination* has taken place. Colloquially we say "it dawned on me." It is as though we cannot force the light to come but can only set the stage and wait. Unhappily, we do not always ultimately achieve a solution to every problem we tackle. Remember that the description of the four stages deals with events surrounding the creative act, an act defined by the occurrence of *Illumination*. We cannot, unfortunately, use the description as a recipe for creativity. Nor can we be certain that the description offered by Wallas applies to all adults. We have even less reason to suppose that it applies in the same way to children.

Wallas's description is useful, however, in cautioning us against expecting creativity on demand. It reminds us that we must allow the child time to prepare and then to put work aside if it is not going well. The

bell that marks the end of recess does not always summon the Muse.

WHAT CREATIVE PEOPLE ARE LIKE

The source of creativity remains a mystery. But in recent years, research workers have looked for clues in the mental abilities, sensory sensitivity, and personality traits of highly creative individuals. Their findings are briefly presented here so that the teacher may explore their usefulness in understanding and guiding children.

The thinking of unusually creative people is characterized by flexibility, fluency, and elaboration.[9] Flexibility is the ability to adapt, redefine, reinterpret, or take a new tack to reach a goal. It is freedom from rigid conceptualization. Flexible thinking is demonstrated in tests of creativity when respondents are asked to suggest unusual uses for bricks and other common objects. Fluency refers to the ease with which ideas are generated. Fluent thinking is demonstrated by the number of ideas suggested in a given period of time. Elaboration refers to the degree of development of the ideas. Elaborate thinking is demonstrated by richness and complexity of detail in performing verbal or visual tasks.

Though creativity is related to intelligence, it is a different kind of mental ability. Highly creative people are always intelligent, but not all intelligent people are highly creative. Barron suggests that I.Q. and creativity correlate at about .40, but that beyond an I.Q. of 120, intelligence is a negligible factor in successful creative performance.[2]

People who were considered by their colleagues to be highly creative were characterized by effective intelligence, openness to experience, freedom from limiting restraints and inhibition, aesthetic sensitivity, cognitive flexibility, independence in thought and action, energy, commitment to the creative endeavor, and a constant striving for solutions to increasingly difficult problems.

MacKinnon found that highly creative people are discerning, curious, receptive, reflective, and eager for experience. They make fine distinctions and seek deeper meanings than less creative individuals. Simple factual statements do not satisfy them. They observe a great deal, collect evidence, but withhold judgment.[14, 15] Creative people are able to tolerate seeming disorder, in which they discover subtle ordering principles. Adult artists prefer drawings that are complex, asymmetrical, and dynamic. Simple, symmetrical drawings do not appeal to them.[2] In this they differ from children who, according to one study, showed creativity in art but shared with other children a preference for symmetry in the drawings they were shown.[12]

The home and family life of creative children seems to differ from that of their less creative peers. One study found that creativity in gifted fourth graders was related to self-awareness and self-acceptance.[24] Often creative children were the oldest, but seldom the favorite child in a family whose members were not particularly close. Parents did not stress conformity to their own values, permitted expression of strong feeling, and accepted the child's regressive behavior. The parents did not over-value the child's abilities. The mother was sometimes ambivalent in her maternal feelings. The father had greater autonomy in his occupation. The parents were not especially well-adjusted in their marriage. This description of the home life of creative children is consistent with the descriptions of childhood

given by highly creative adults in MacKinnon's study, who recalled their childhood as not especially happy.[14, 15] Whether they were, in fact, less happy than other children we can never know. We know only what they remember. But this in itself is significant because it reveals that they do not try to forget or deny what is unpleasant. It may also be that, in some instances, the troubles that marred childhood may also have led to greater sensitivity and thus contributed to the creative development of the individual.

According to Getzels and Jackson, parents of intellectually gifted but not particularly creative adolescents are concerned with visible virtues, such as cleanliness, studiousness, and good manners. The parents of moderately intelligent, highly creative adolescents are concerned with the child's openness to experience, values, interests, and enthusiasm. The parents of the less creative group feel less secure financially and recall financial stress in their own childhood. Adolescents in the less creative group aspire to professions that offer status and security and plan for careers in such fields as medicine, law, and engineering. The more creative adolescents are attracted to less conventional occupations and want to be inventors, writers, adventurers. The more creative group placed a high value on a sense of humor. The less creative group believed that their values, which were like those held by their teachers, were related to success in life. The highly creative group agreed that their teachers' values were related to success in life but found these values to be somewhat opposed to their own.[6]

Creative people trust their own judgment. In an experimental situation in which everyone else present is in a conspiracy to give answers in contradiction to the evidence, creative people resist the pressure to deny their own perceptions, whereas others in the same situation are unable to endure the social conflict and deny their own experience to achieve agreement with the group.[2] Too great a concern for conformity operates against creativity. Fear of making a mistake, worry about what people will say, a need for approval of those in authority, keep people doing the expected, usual, safe. Such people hold their impulses in check and avoid temptation. The individual who tries to adapt his behavior to the expectations of others experiences less outward conflict, but he seems to do so at a price.[18]

Creative people have a considerable amount of psychic turbulence. They are very much aware of these disturbances and are able to live with them. Outwardly they do not appear to be non-conforming, but actually they rely on their own values rather than the values of society in any area they feel is important. They are more highly motivated in situations which call for independent thought and action than in those in which they must go along with the group.[14, 15]

Creative adults are in many ways like secure children. People who bring creativity to their rather ordinary tasks and occupations have a fresh vision of the world, reacting to the world as they see it, free of stereotypes. According to Maslow they are more spontaneous, expressive, natural, and uninhibited. They are able to express ideas and impulses without fear of criticism by others. They are innocent in their freedom of perception and uninhibited expressiveness. The unknown, the mysterious, the puzzling is not very frightening for them. Indeed, they are often attracted to it. They do not try to explain away, run from, or deny, the unknown. They do not cling to the familiar, nor seek certainty, safety, definiteness, and order. When the situation calls for it, they can be disorderly, vague, and anarchic. They can live with indecision.

Uncertainty is, in fact, stimulating for them. They are less afraid of what other people will say and less afraid of their own impulses, thoughts, and feelings than average people. The war between deep inner urges and control that is fought within ordinary people does not incorporate them. Their energies are not dissipated in inner conflict and are available for creative effort. Those who adapt to society by depressing or denying much of the depths of human nature lose the source of creativity.[16]

It must be remembered that the creativity Maslow is talking about is that of people creative in ordinary life and in the little or large things they do.[16] The creativity of a Van Gogh or a Leonardo probably stands on the same psychological foundation, but builds higher. It requires great talent, long training, hard work, perfectionist standards, and a burning desire that cannot be denied.

Creative people are ready to receive the messages of their own perception. They can be described as having greater than average sensitivity to sensory stimulation as well as an unusual capacity for perceiving the relations between various stimuli. Another of their traits is the predisposition to an empathy of wider range and deeper vibration than usual, and sensory motor equipment which allows the building up of projective motor discharges for expressive functions.[8]

Rogers[17] regards such a person as being "open to experience." He is alive to the moment and does not distort experience to make it consistent with predetermined concepts. He can accept a great deal of conflicting information without forcing a reconciliation consistent with previous notions. The experiences he values are those in which he extends himself and realizes his potential.

Creative people do not seek quick and easy solutions. They are able to resist premature closure but have a strong need for ultimate closure. They are persistent and like to think and play with ideas. They like variety and need to do things their own way. They can live with disorder in order to bring about a more profound order. They seek the deeper levels of complexity that lie beyond the simple, generally accepted ideas of those around them.[20]

The picture of the creative person which is derived from numerous separate studies is of someone who is attracted to the baffling, the mysterious and the difficult, who is independent in thought and judgment, questioning, receptive to new ideas, constructive in criticism, energetic, willing to take risks, preoccupied with a problem, persistent, intuitive, sensitive to the external world, and not afraid to regress.[21, 22]

The creative adult bears a resemblance to the small child, whose normal mode of behavior is creative. Children see the world through innocent eyes. They retain the capacity to wonder, the ability to see and respond to the uniqueness in every situation. To little children the world is indeed new. As they explore the world, they respond in their own way because they have not yet learned any other way. As children grow up and become socialized, they learn how others expect them to respond. Past experience begins to govern their response to the experience of the moment.[1] We have no choice, of course, but to teach children how to live in their culture, but we should make every effort to preserve their creativity. There is a suspicion that schooling has a deleterious effect on creativity. Torrance traced an interesting pattern of development and regression of creative imagination in both artistic and problem solving tasks. Creative imagination appeared to reach a peak between four and four-and-one-half years of age followed by a sudden drop at the age of five, the age of entrance to kindergarten. He found a second period of growth in creative imagination from grades one to three declining at the beginning of grade four, rising again in grades five and six, and declining at the end of grade six and the beginning of grade seven. Although we do not know that the increased pressures of entering elementary school, moving into the intermediate grades, and entering junior high are responsible for a decline in creativity, the coincidence suggests an hypothesis well worth further investigation.[22] Another study reports that creative imagination generally increased with age in children between the ages of six and thirteen and decreased with age in individuals from thirteen to fifty-five years of age, but that creative imagination is not closely related to age.[12] It is as though the creative spark struggles against extinction in the elementary school years and finally succumbs in adulthood. Perhaps more careful tending of creativity in childhood would strengthen it sufficiently to preserve it in later years. It is worthwhile to consider how school practices might be modified so as to nuture and preserve the creativity that children bring with them.

NURTURING CREATIVITY IN THE CLASSROOM

Of all the curriculum areas of the elementary school, art offers the greatest opportunity for establishing conditions conducive to the development of creativity.

Rogers points to the conditions both in the individual and in the environment hospitable to creativity. He describes the inner condition as openness to experience, an internal locus of evaluation, and the ability to toy with elements and concepts. The external conditions that encourage creativity are psychological freedom and safety. Psychological freedom is permission to be oneself. Psychological safety is established by accepting the individual as having unconditional worth and establishing empathy.[17]

Through art activities, children can be helped to retain or regain their freshness of vision, their sensitivity to the physical world, or in Roger's terms, their "openness to experience." Art provides occasion to listen to and enjoy the many messages that come through the senses, the shapes, colors, textures, sounds, and scents of nature, which are part of man's world. Perceptual sensitivity is developed as the child observes the wondrous variety of his world. There is dazzling variety even in a single class of objects, such as "trees." The child can be helped to notice that there are gnarled old trees and slender, delicate saplings, trees in leaf and bare trees, flowering trees and fruit trees, leaves of different colors, trees with many trunks or one trunk, and an array of patterns in their branches. In this way, he can also be helped to discover that the single shape and color he had been using for his schema is not as satisfying as finding the right shape and color for each tree. Richness of experience enriches his art.

In an educational system in which great emphasis is placed on external evaluation by tests and report cards, art offers an opportunity to focus on personal satisfaction. In talking about art work the emphasis should be on the child's own feelings of success or lack of success rather than on the opinions of other children or the teacher. In the final analysis only the child himself knows how fully his idea has been expressed, and whether his work was the result of genuine creative involvement or a superficial attempt to impress others by a work that has little personal meaning to him. A piece of art work in itself is not a very good indication of the quality of the experiences out of which it was born.

Winning easy praise by a slick piece of imitation can tempt the child to try to win more praise in the same manner. The child who works in an atmosphere in which success is measured by praise from the teacher or classmate may come to expect it and rely on it. If his sincere labors are not rewarded in this way he may feel disappointed and misunderstood, or he may decide his work was not worthy of praise and seek another, surer route to his reward. Even children are not immune to corruption. Easy praise discourages genuine creative effort, as does arbitrary criticism. Praise must be offered judiciously with sincerity and caution. Instead of passing judgment, teachers need to ask "How do you like it?" "Did you do what you wanted to do?" "Does it look the way you want it to look?" "If you were to do it again, is there anything you would change?" It is important to keep in mind that despite the teacher's judiciousness, children may scoff at the efforts of another child. Children sometimes reject new ideas as "silly." So do adults. The child can be helped to listen to the opinions of others and to consider and judge their merit and usefulness. He can learn to use these opinions and suggestions, but he must also learn that the final judgment should be his own.

Art offers an excellent opportunity for helping children to understand that in some areas of life there is not just one right answer which makes all other answers wrong. It can also help them to realize that it is not necessary to pronounce judgment upon every work. By having their own efforts accepted they can develop tolerance for the fruits of other people's labors.

Creativity is discovering novel and useful ways of relating elements that are not in themselves new. The purpose served may be practical, aesthetic, or both. The tot who has developed sufficient motor control to make lines and circles makes an enormous creative discovery when he puts them together to represent a person. Little children build towers of tin cans and make pies out of mud. As people grow up and grow older, the tendency to think of objects only in terms of their customary uses becomes hardened. Art offers an opportunity to break through this limitation. Children can find unusual uses for common or discarded objects, such as cans, old light bulbs, and egg cartons. These, of course, are commonly used in art programs today. But all too often the creative use of such objects is discovered not by the children themselves, but by a creative adult whose discovery has been published in a magazine and has been taken up by an alert teacher who directs children in duplicating the result of someone else's ingenuity. Such a procedure does have the value of demonstrating to children how someone else has used his creativity. But there is no creativity on the part of the children who slavishly repeat what someone else invented. It is far better to allow children to toy with materials than to remove the possibility of exercising imagination by restricting their use.

The teacher can allow the child to work with freedom and spontaneity, the roots of creativity, and also encourage him to work out his ideas with care, patience, and deliberation, and to evaluate his success in the light of his own goals and standards.

As teachers help a child to a better understanding of the real world, they need to take care not to crush fantasy. Before a teacher pulls a child out of a daydream, it might be well for her to wonder whether the subject matter that the child is escaping is as necessary to him and as rich as the content of his fantasy is likely to be. Encourage children to give expression to their imagination by having them draw fantastic animals, worlds, dreams, wishes, etc. Expression of fantasy through art can discharge potentially destructive wishes in creative ways.

In the tempo of modern life there is little time for children, or adults, to be alone with their thoughts and works. Group activities are, of course, worthwhile and contribute greatly to the development of social skill, but temporary withdrawal from the group must be allowed and provided for. The sensitive teacher must try to distinguish between aloneness that means being with oneself and a hostile or defensive reaction to a group situation too difficult for the child to handle by himself in another way.

Highly creative people, describing the creative process as they recall it, often relate how the idea they had been striving for appears, unannounced, in periods when they have ceased active work. Inspiration does not always come upon demand. Working within time boundaries set by the class schedule is a handicap. For various reasons, many classes are required to operate on a rather precise time schedule. However, within these limits children can be allowed freedom to work at their own pace. There is no reason to expect them to finish their work when the clock says they should. Some children need to spend several periods on a single product. Others can finish more than one during the art period. If the child feels the work is not going well, there is no need to insist that it be finished and handed in. Teachers need not become alarmed if inspiration does not come to each child every art period, nor do teachers need to impose an idea on a child if one does not come from him. At times, talking with the child about his ideas will help to get him started. But it is too much to expect every child to be creative every art period.

Stereotyped notions of what is appropriate for each sex acts as a barrier to creative behavior. Henrickson and Torrance[11] point out that artistic creativity requires both sensitivity and independence. Sensitivity in our culture is associated with femininity and independence with masculinity. Pressure from peers or parents, or the child's own fear of deviating from approved sex-roles may act as a barrier to creativity for both sexes.

There is a widespread notion that children need to be protected from failure. In some instances this idea is translated into a program which is so carefully fractionated that success is virtually assured. Certainly children need to be protected from failure under devastating conditions over which they have little control. But children should not be given the feeling that success must follow all effort, and that failure is to be avoided at all costs. They need to be willing to undertake tasks sufficiently difficult to make success problematical. They need to learn to face the possibility of failure in undertaking tasks that are significantly challenging.

The teacher, on the other hand, needs to insure that the child does not fail because the environment does not offer the resources needed for success. She needs to see that necessary materials and techniques are available to the child. The alert teacher remains in the background while the child is succeeding but senses when he is in trouble and is ready to help him analyze his difficulties, to offer new stimulation, to expose him to the ideas and solutions of others, or to suggest that he let the problem rest for a while and return to it later.

Both teachers and pupils need to understand the distinction between artistic facility and creativity. The upper grade child who can draw a man that looks like a man is not necessarily creative. He probably has good motor control and good powers of observation, but these assets should not be

mistaken for creativity. Teachers need to guard against the easy success of facile children who do not need to struggle. Their greater capacity must be challenged by more demanding tasks. Creativity need not be anticipated only in those instances in which skill has already been developed. It can characterize the work of any age, any developmental stage, and any level of skill. The child who says he cannot draw does not necessarily lack a capacity for creativity. He lacks skill or confidence or has set his goals too high. He needs to be helped to understand that he can create works of merit in art by using the abilities he possesses.

History provides many examples of inventions resulting from a happy accident. Do the individuals who first saw the usefulness of an accidental effect deserve the recognition they are accorded? Many people think they do. They were alert to possibilities which might have, or actually did, escape others. Through art children can learn to make use of accidents. The drip in a kindergarten child's easel painting often provides inspiration for a new form. If left on their own, kindergarten children often incorporate the accidental drips and blots into their painting. The teacher who views accidents as disasters discourages an imaginative reaction by the child. The response to every accident should not be the admonition to start over and be more careful. It can be viewed as an unexpected opportunity to test one's ingenuity by integrating the unplanned effect into the rest of the work.

We must remember that the value of teaching is to facilitate learning. In planning lessons, in carrying them out, and in reflecting on them after they are over, teachers need to focus on what happened within the individuals in the class as a consequence of the teaching performance. It is a mistake to think that the more the teacher "teaches," the more the children learn. Too much direction deprives children of the opportunity to figure things out for themselves, to try out their own ideas, to act on the basis of their own curiosity and desires. The eagerness with which children begin school and their eagerness to learn often disappear. Anderson[1] suggests that the mistrust of children's ability for self-direction leads the schools to establish coercive machinery that compels them to attend and pressures them to compete. He says that lack of respect and confidence in children leads to a use of power over them. This in turn creates anxiety and defensiveness and ultimately results in conformity, submissiveness, or revolt. Domination results in loss of intrinsic motivation and atrophy of the very powers we seek to develop. The teacher, of course, is responsible for maintaining control over pupil behavior. But relying too much on external control prevents the development of internal controls. A situation based on a devaluation of the child is not conducive to optimum development of potentialities, including that of creativity. Creativity thrives in an atmosphere in which the child feels free to be himself and express himself in his own way. In art, his way of drawing, modeling, and the like must be respected. His naive efforts should not be patronized, nor should teachers imply by showing how to do it better that the child's way is not acceptable.

Many teachers wonder just how far they ought to go in teaching art techniques and principles to children. They wonder if such knowledge will facilitate or block creative expression. The answer cannot be stated as an absolute, applying under all conditions.

The selection and pacing of new learning must be governed by the ability of the class to assimilate and put it to use. Too fast a pace with inadequate time to explore new possibilities or the introduction of procedures that are too complex demands all the child's attention. When all energy is directed to carrying out a technical procedure, none is left for using it expressively. The technique must always be the handmaiden of the inspiration. To overwhelm the child with too much stimulation can be as destructive as starving him with too little.

Teachers can encourage children to discover possibilities and invent techniques of their own. The thrill a child experiences when he discovers a new way to use crayons is really not reduced by the fact that, unknown to him, others have used it in the same way before. The teacher need not consider herself a transmission belt passing along a body of knowledge, skills, etc. developed in the past. The child can experience some of the discoveries that have been made before him. The teacher can use her knowledge to help set the stage so that discoveries can be made. For instance, a new box of crayons in the first grade will be used like a pencil if the wrappers are on. A box of unwrapped, broken crayons are much more likely to encourage experimentation.

It is unfortunate that in contemporary American society it is considered a misfortune to be different. The child who is highly creative is different from others in this respect. So is the child who deviates from the average in intelligence, size, personal appearance, athletic skill, and the like. Every child has his own constellation of problems with peers, parents, teachers, and society as a whole. The art teacher can help the creative child and, indeed, all children to accept their own uniqueness and the special problems it creates. She can help them recognize the value of creativity, to nourish it, and gain satisfaction from exercising it.

The art program offers a special opportunity for the development of creativity, because the atmosphere in which creativity flourishes is one in which art also thrives.

But the art period cannot be an isolated island of time within a program that is hostile to the conditions that facilitate creativity. The entire concept of the school must be one which fosters creativity. Only then can we expect to fulfill the hope of society and the demand of our age for a generation of creative human beings.

CHAPTER EIGHT: TEXT REFERENCES

1. Anderson, Harold H., *Creativity and its Cultivation*. New York: Harper & Row, Publishers, 1959.
2. Barron, Frank, "Creative vision and expression in writing and painting," in the proceedings of the conference on *The Creative Person*. Berkeley: Institute of Personality Assessment and Research, University of California, 1961. II, 1-11, 19.
3. Brittain, W. Lambert, and Kenneth R. Beittel, "A study of some tests of creativity in relationship to performance in the visual arts," *Studies in Art Education*, II, No. 2 (1961), 54-65.
4. Crutchfield, Richard S., "The creative process" in the proceedings of the conference on *The Creative Person*. Berkeley: Institute of Personality Assessment and Research, University of California, 1961. VI, 1-VI, 16.
5. Eisner, Elliot W., "A typology of creativity in the visual arts," *Studies in Art Education*, IV, No. 1 (1962), 11-22.
6. Getzels, Jacob W. and Philip W. Jackson, *Creativity and Intelligence*. New York: John Wiley & Sons, Inc., 1962.
7. Ghiselin, Brewster (ed), *The Creative Process*. New York: Mentor, 1955.
8. Greenacre, Phyllis, "The childhood of the artist, libidinal phase developments and giftedness" in *The Psychoanalytic Study of the Child*, Vol. 12, New York: International Universities Press, 1957, 47-72.
9. Guilford, J. Paul, "Creative abilities in the arts," *Psychological Review*, LXIV, (1957) 110-118.
10. Henrickson, Paul R., "Non-verbal manipulation and creativeness in art," *Studies in Art Education*, V, No. 1 (1963), 60-70.
11. Henrickson, Paul R., and E. Paul Torrance, "Some implications for art education from the Minnesota Studies of Creative Thinking," *Studies in Art Education*, II, No. 2 (1961), 36-44.
12. Kincaid, Clarence E., "The determination and description of various creative attributes of children," *Studies in Art Education*, II, No. 2 (1961), 45-53.
13. Lowenfeld, Victor, "Creativity: Education's Stepchild," in *A Sourcebook for Creative Thinking*, eds. Sidney J. Parnes and Harold S. Harding, New York: Charles Scribner's Sons, 1962.
14. MacKinnon, Donald W., "The study of creativity," in proceedings of the conference on *The Creative Person*. Berkeley: Institute of Personality Assessment and Research, University of California, 1961. I, 1-I, 17.
15. MacKinnon, Donald W., "What makes a person creative," *Saturday Review*, XLV, No. 6 (1962), 15-17, 69.
16. Maslow, Abraham H., "Creativity in self-actualizing people," in *Creativity and its Cultivation*, ed. Harold H. Anderson, New York: Harper & Row, Publishers, 1959.
17. Rogers, Carl R., *On Becoming a Person*, Boston: Houghton Mifflin Co., 1961.
18. Sanford, Nevitt, "Creativity and conformity," in the proceedings of the conference on *The Creative Person*. Berkeley: Institute of Personality Assessment and Research, University of California, 1961, VII, 1-VII, 10.
19. Stein, Morris I., *Survey of the Psychological Literature in the Area of Creativity with a View Toward Needed Research*. New York: Research Center for Human Relations, New York University, 1962.
20. Taylor, Calvin W., "Research findings on creative characteristics," *Studies in Art Education*, III, No. 1 (1961), 9-17.
21. Torrance, E. Paul, "Developing creative thinking through school experiences," in *A Sourcebook for Creative Thinking*, eds. Sidney J. Parnes and Harold S. Harding. New York: Charles Scribner's Sons, 1962.
22. Torrance, E. Paul, *Guiding Creative Talent*.

Englewood Cliffs, N.J.: Prentice-Hall, Inc., 1962.

23. Wallas, Graham, *The Art of Thought*. New York: Harcourt, Brace & World, Inc., 1926.

24. Weisberg, P. S., and Kayla J. Springer, *Environmental Factors Influencing Creative Function in Gifted Children*. Cincinnati: Department of Psychiatry, Cincinnati General Hospital, 1961.

CHAPTER NINE

Teaching Art in the Elementary School

Creative development in art stems from the interaction of maturation and learning experiences. The teacher's responsibility is to select learning experiences that are attuned to the developmental process. Resource materials for planning such experiences take up the final part of this volume. Some of the material will be familiar, especially to experienced teachers. Beginning teachers may find many new ideas. It is the authors' hope that teachers will be judicious in selecting experiences for their pupils, evaluating the appropriateness of the various suggestions in the light of the needs of a particular class, and adapting, modifying, or rejecting procedures as their judgment dictates.

It is important to keep in mind that what is gained and assimilated out of experience varies according to the individuality of the learner. What is absorbed at each step along the way influences the next step and the entire course of development.

SKILL AND CREATIVITY

All teaching must be based on the child's natural mode of expression, which is determined by the interplay of his developmental status and his unique personality. Creativity, manifested by the imprint of each child's personality on his work, is preserved by teaching which is responsive to individual needs. The teaching of skill and technical competence must be directed towards extending the means through which the self may find expression. But it must be stressed that self-expression does not imply the encouragement of an unquestioning acceptance of whatever the child does, an attitude of "anything goes." It requires guiding the child to a disciplined and discriminating approach to his work.

The teacher is there to maximize possibilities for creative growth. She must insure that learning in art serves this end. The acquisition of information and the refinement of skill neither assures nor prevents creative behavior. However, a wide range of information and a large repertoire of techniques permit greater flexibility in the expressive use of materials. The teacher must make sure that all that is taught serves creative ends.

Ease in drawing, skill in handling materials, and familiarity with various technical procedures are, of course, desirable. However, facility in art like the facile use of words, does not of itself guarantee creative expression. Symbols, whether they be visual or verbal, are instrumental in creative expression. A large graphic vocabulary makes it easier for creative ideas to find expression but does not affect the quality of the ideas expressed. An accurate literal picture may be devoid of aesthetic merit. A good copy

of nature is not necessarily art. Accuracy in drawing is much less important than the sensitive use of art materials in expressing a personal interpretation.

Time must be provided for children to experiment with new techniques and ideas and to explore their possibilities. The availability of a large array of techniques poses the temptation to savor more than can be assimilated. The result can be indigestion. Seeking after novelty for its own sake must be avoided if mastery and expressive use of art media is to be achieved. Some materials provide immediate stimulation to the imagination; others make more demands, and children must be allowed the opportunity to become comfortable with them before they can put them to creative use.

It is important to let the child discover solutions to problems for himself. Although few teachers these days say, "This is how to draw a horse," some are unable to resist ending the child's frustration by telling him what to do, or even worse, doing it for him. Creativity is the quest for the elusive but fitting solution. The quick and easy answer, the premature termination of search, kills creativity. When a child says he "can't make it look right," he needs encouragement to try again. He needs guidance to help him discover what he thinks is wrong and how it can be changed. Familiarity with developmental characteristics may be useful in helping the teacher understand whether the child needs to elaborate and enrich the schema he has been using or to move ahead to a new developmental stage.

TEACHING AND NATURAL GROWTH

If teaching is not geared to developmental needs it is wasted. The child must be ready to use what he is taught. A child of six is simply not ready to take advantage of teaching concerning perspective, not even of the diminution of sizes in the distance; nor can he understand the use of subtle lines or mixing colors to achieve shades and tints. Perspective drawing is foreign to his way of looking at his surroundings. He is unable to conceive of a representation from a single vantage point. He cannot use subtle lines because he does not think of lines as such but only of outlines that define a figure against a background.

The child develops in two directions: forward toward a more mature representational form; and outward to enrichment through details and variation within a given level of maturity. The teacher must assess the needs of each child and guide the course of his development. For example: an eight-year-old who has worked out a number of schemata for humans, animals, plants and other objects, but with few details, or with hasty contours and rough coloring, must be given time and opportunity to imagine and execute a visual representation that is satisfying to him because it corresponds to his inner idea, and to the feelings connected with it. Another child of the same age may be accelerated in his development and may have reached the point where little can be gained by elaboration of the old schema. He is ready to move toward different modes of representation. His first attempts may seem inferior to his previous work and appear regressive. The teacher who understands what is occurring will be able to encourage and guide the child in moving ahead.

Developmental stages in art are part of the growth process. It is not appropriate to judge stages in terms of adult bias. To overvalue later stages because of a preference for realism is as erroneous as to consider schematic drawing the more desirable because of a predilection for the grotesqueness of primitive art, the naivete of folk-art, or the emotional distortions of expressionist art. Adults who may regret the pass-

ing of the schematic stage must resist the temptation to prolong it. Natural development must not be impeded. Like the snake who sheds his skin so he can grow, the child gives up an early mode of representation to make way for a later one.

OVERCOMING OBSTACLES TO GROWTH

Not every child develops past the schematic stage (see Figures 10, 33, and 85). In many young people graphic art loses its place as a favored means of self-expression and in the teens is replaced by words, music, dance, or other forms of creative activity. It is to be expected that each child will gravitate to the form of expression he is best equipped to use. Good teaching, however, can help keep interest in art actively alive. The teacher can help the child or young person deal with the frustration that comes when he is unable to approximate objects in nature to his own satisfaction. The child can learn that art is not making accurate copies of nature. He can be shown pictures that make no attempt at photographic likeness, such as those of the early Renaissance, primitive art of contemporary and ancient cultures, or modern art. He can be led to recognize that naturalistic representation is but one of many possibilities. If he chooses to work naturalistically, the teacher can help him find ways to make his work more acceptable to him. For example, the child who is concerned about proportion can be shown simple ways of relating the size of one part to the others. If he is dissatisfied because his drawings of people or animals don't look "right," he can be encouraged to draw subjects that are easier until his confidence is restored, and he is willing to try people or animals again.

The child who complains that he can't make his picture look right is likely to be an older child. Ordinarily, younger children nonchalantly adapt their schema to the most difficult tasks. But at times a young child is not able to picture what he has in mind because his notion of what he wants to represent is not clear. In such cases the teacher can help him to clarify his mental image. If, for example, he cannot recall all the components of an object, she can help him enumerate its parts, or show him a picture of it so that he can gain a clearer impression. Having done so, he can resume his work at a later time with a greater chance of success. If a child is having difficulty drawing human limbs, the teacher can help him to observe and experience the muscular activity relevant to the particular part of the body so that he has a clearer understanding of what he is trying to depict.

Sometimes a child loses confidence in his ability, perhaps in reaction to adverse comments or attempts to impose adult standards. He needs to be encouraged to try again.

Lack of confidence may be expressed by copying other children's drawings or by trying to repeat a work that was once gratifying. A number of children copy, at least for a while, chiefly in order to master details that they find too difficult to do on their own. Repetition of their own creations, either in their entirety or in part, of a specific compositional arrangement, or of the schema of humans and animals, houses and other objects, is a usual and normal occurrence, founded in the desire to perfect and master a mode of expression (see Figure 11). But there comes a time when repetition no longer serves a useful purpose, and it then becomes an indication that the child is unable to move ahead on his own.

Those who are reluctant to try something new can be guided toward using a portion of one of their old pictures as a starting point for a new and different one. For ex-

ample, a child who always draws the same house can be encouraged to try a street, or a town, or to make it the scene of some activity by populating it. The child who copies another's work needs to be convinced that his own creativity has more value than the most expert imitation.

Aesthetic elements may also be the source of dissatisfaction. The child may experience uneasiness over a lack of balance, rhythm, and the like, without being able to verbalize it. Looking at the picture freshly, from a distance or even upside down, may help him to identify the disturbing element. If it is not seen immediately, discussion about what pleases and displeases him can be useful in defining the problem and in showing the way to a solution.

One cannot caution strongly enough against the destructive effects of requiring children to color in stereotyped outlines such as those found in reading or arithmetic workbooks. The integrity of a child's art work must be preserved and cared for vigilantly during the entire day, not only in the art period. The prestige attached to drawings in the workbook can and does persuade many children to abandon their own schemata and to draw the workbook way. In so doing they may end the search for more satisfactory symbolization and be cut off from further creative development.

HELPING CHILDREN MOVE AHEAD

The teacher must be aware of the next step, of what it is that children are striving for. Children are not always articulate about what it is they are seeking, nor do their pictures always give evidence of it. For example, the pictures of primary grade children often appear to be static. An adult might conclude from this that they are not concerned with movement. This is not the case. Children think in terms of action and motion and are eager to say so through their pictures (see Figures 96, 136, and 142). They do so in the primary grades by positioning and attributes—a baseball game by a boy holding a bat—and if that does not succeed, by using symbols such as lines or arrows to connect the relevant objects. When visual symbols fail to convey their meaning, they resort to verbal explanations. At this stage, the teacher can help them find adequate visual means within their natural mode of expression to depict action. The child who is approaching his teens often shows by experimentation in drawing as well as by discussion that he is ready to move forward. His own attempts at showing motion provide cues for additional steps. For example, if a man is shown walking by a representation of his legs as partly bent (see Figure 146) or —scissorlike—apart, the teacher can suggest that the arms or other parts of the body also participate in the motion. She can have the child walk and observe his own muscular action. Experiencing and observing motion for the purpose of translating it into pictorial terms can be most helpful to him. Continuing attention to the way an action feels and the way it looks will lead him to more satisfactory ways of portraying it.

The child experiences his environment through many senses. Through art activity a multi-sensory impression becomes a visual expression. The teacher helps the child to become more sensitive to sensory experience of all kinds. She directs his attention, for example, to the texture of a conch shell, the sound it makes, and its distinctive shape. She helps him to look closely at detail and to find ways to make visible whatever can be expressed by visual means.

The teacher must always remember that the mental image of an object is not identical with what the eyes see. Some visual characteristics are of great importance to the mental image; others are not. To the visible qualities are added non-visual qualities, some pertaining to the other senses such as sound or smell, some pertaining to function, movement, and emotional experiences. Many younger children incorporate non-visual qualities in their visual representation. While some children paint "a walk with Daddy" by showing two figures side by side, others re-enact the walk, carefully recording the turns, twists and meanderings through the motion of their brush or pencil, showing mainly the *walk* rather than the people who took it. Picturing action by the motion that takes place is characteristic of nursery school and kindergarten children and lingers on into the lower grades in various forms such as the use of crayon or brush strokes to depict smoke coming out of a chimney, or waves in motion around a boat.

To guide development, the teacher must understand and respect the logic in child art. For example, in the schematic stage the child draws each part of the body separately (see Figure 29), joining the parts as the drawing proceeds, as if he were constructing a marionette. The head, eyes, nose, mouth, hair, the neck, the torso, the limbs, the clothes, are all taken one at a time. The same is true of whatever the child draws. Attempts to lead him prematurely to sketch the whole before starting on the parts in the hope of achieving a unified conception are futile. Despite patience and perseverance on the part of the teacher and great efforts to follow instructions on the part of the child, he cannot succeed if he is not yet ready for this more advanced stage. Until he can visualize the whole, defined by a flowing line, he must build through each separate part.

Whether children use a pencil, crayons,

or a brush, they will first of all attempt the contouring of their shapes, to define the objects and their parts. Many children up to the age of ten or so, are most satisfied when they can use a pencil for this purpose, because it permits the most accurate contouring and is neutral in color. Coloring is done after shapes are defined. If they have nothing but color crayons or paint, they will still do the contouring first. It is their way of pictorial thinking.

Color to primary grade children is a property of the object being depicted, not a phenomenon of light. Although younger children may observe the way in which color changes with distance, they ignore variation in color in their own pictures. Older children who are concerned with how things appear in nature can be guided to observe that yellow fades first and blue last, and that objects become increasingly grayish with distance. They can also be led to observe the interrelation of light, shade, and cast shadows.

Children in the early grades are usually content with a limited number of colors. One red, one orange, one yellow, and the like is all they need. Variation within each hue is superflous. As they grow older they wish to modulate colors. They are no longer content to color the sky like the water. They want to suggest texture, and they begin to shade to convey surface contours.

Although generalizations about age level characteristics are very useful to the teacher, she must be aware of individual differences. The teacher needs to perceive and provide for temperamental differences that manifest themselves in art expression. She must insure that each child selects materials best suited to his own mode of expression and to the demands of the task. Big brushes are for those whose paintings are big and bold and on large size paper. They frustrate the child who wants to make a delicate, de-tailed, sensitive picture or a little one. On the other hand, using a fine point or a thin brush when a large smooth area is intended taxes his patience and leads to poor results. The teacher can also guide the child in selecting materials appropriate to the content and feeling he intends, discussing it with him in advance, or helping him try out various materials to determine which is best.

The most important factor in successful teaching is the quality of contact between teacher and pupil. Although the advantage of a spacious room and modern equipment is obvious, excellent programs are possible under makeshift conditions if the teacher is ready for her task. She is the vital element in establishing the emotional climate of the classroom, and in guiding learning.

It is crucial that teaching be consistent with developmental needs. Teaching that ignores this is either rejected or forgotten, or still worse, acts as a barrier to genuine artistic growth. The teacher's work must be directed toward enriching the child's expression at the level of whatever stage he is in and to easing his transition to the next stage. She should encourage enrichment through ornamentation, through repetition and variation of schematic shapes, and through whatever other means may seem appropriate (see Figures 59 and 99). Without violating the child's own sense of color she should help him to increase the range of colors he can handle. His sense of design can be nurtured within the limits characteristic of composition at his developmental level.

DEALING WITH THE MATTER OF PERSPECTIVE

The value of teaching perspective has long been debated. Linear perspective, like other means of suggesting spatial depth, is part of the cultural heritage of Western art, but is not found at all in the art of some other cultures.

In the Orient, in Chinese and Japanese art, space has been represented in an imaginative and ordered manner that is entirely convincing, though in general, nonperspective. One of the ways of doing this, especially for hilly or mountainous landscapes with rivers and ravines, is by evolving several planes separated by cloudy or misty atmospheric effects and essentially based on a most subtle differentiation of color values, tints or monochrome hues.

Figure 205. *BASES LOADED. This extremely clear topographical exposé of the situation at the game presents the field from above, the players as if laid down on the ground, but shows where and whom they face, while the spectators are recorded in elevation in the shape of faces (circles).*[40] *Girl, age nine, spontaneous pencil drawing.*

Figure 204. *CITY. A tightly built composition on several planes that indicates fore- to background, despite equalsized objects. In the left foreground behind the pasture is a village, much smaller than the far removed city. A large graphic vocabulary is shown.*[19] *Girl, age seven, Austria, 1925, tempera painting.*

Another mode of treating space, sometimes representing whole communities on lake shores with islands and complex inlets, with hills, trees, boats and people, is by taking the view from a hilltop and by using only slight diminutions of size, overlapping in places, and again introducing mistlike effects, that serve to distinguish between distances, and make one aware of expanses of space and distance.

Medieval landscapes and cityscapes solve the problem of space representation without perspective in a different manner using drawing and line structure in a way that reminds one of the child's approach.

Perspective is rather difficult for elementary school children to handle well. Per-

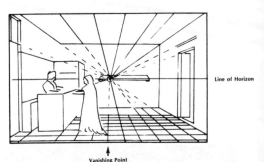

Figure 207. *Paolo Uccello of the 15th century was not only a painter but also a mathematician. He put his knowledge into practice in his perspective paintings. He was supposed to have exclaimed: "How sweet is perspective." He loved its constructive possibilities, its simplicity, and complexity. This picture (a part of a Predella, therefore small) has few objects and peo-* ple, hence shows with utmost clarity its entirely "central" and centered perspective. The vanishing point is in the center of the picture and can be found where the diagonals from the corners intersect. All lines converge to it. The "line of horizon" that goes through it is also at the eye level of the figures. The perspective is of an exact construction.[11]

Figure 206. *This sketch of a potato field by Vincent van Gogh shows the kind of perspective that is easiest to understand and to draw. This scene in Holland has a horizontal band in the foreground. The horizon melts into the innumerable little houses, fences, and garden plots, out of which spires and windmills rise. It is not a geometrically strictly "constructed" perspective; the converging rows of the field reach the vanishing point on the horizon line rather by intuition. Yet it gives the feeling of distance.[7]*

Figure 208. *This perspective picture, by Paolo Uccello, from the same Predella as Figure 207 (picturing the story of the Jew and the Host), also has a precise geometric construction. Here the vanishing point is outside of the picture. Again, the line of horizon is about eyelevel to the figures in the picture, unlike the sketch by Van Gogh. Here, also, all lines meet precisely, those of the ceiling and those of the floor. The perspective shows, in great simplicity, that perpendiculars remain so, as do all horizontals that are horizontal to the observer.*[11]

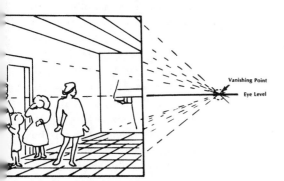

Figure 209. *This sketch by Leonardo da Vinci, one of many made for the background of the Adoration of the Kings (in pen and ink), shows the complexity of geometric construction with* *which he experimented. The vanishing point, slightly off-center, is clearly visible; so are the various smaller but complex line-constructions of other architectural details.*[23]

spective is alien to all but the oldest and most advanced. The principles of perspective when taught as rules are apt to be applied in a mechanical fashion without understanding, and the results are likely to be incorrect. There is also the danger that concern with the proper procedure will interfere with the creative process. Starting at about the fifth grade, some children really feel a need for perspective and at that stage it would be pointless to withhold this knowledge from them. The teacher who is sensitive to the needs and abilities of her pupils is best able to judge whether the possible gains outweigh the potential dangers.

Perspective can be learned either inductively or deductively, that is, children can be led to discover by observation how perspective operates in nature, or they can be taught the rules for perspective drawing. Learning by discovering something for oneself is far better than being taught a mechanical process. Once children have gained insight into the idea of perspective, they are able to apply the rules more intelligently.

Three "rules" can be applied to facilitate understanding of perspective representation. First: the observance of diminution of sizes toward the distant horizon; second: the important observation that verticals remain vertical; third: the apparent slant, in a diagonal fashion toward distance and horizon of what in reality is horizontal. Children can observe differences in size of close and distant objects. They can be shown paintings of the Renaissance which illustrate this principle clearly.

That vertically orientated objects remain so throughout receding distances can be demonstrated by observation of telephone poles, trees, or even bowling pins. From the point of view of reasoning, it may seem obvious. From the point of view of representation it is not. The converging of parallels can be demonstrated by looking at railroad tracks or streets, which seemingly meet at a "vanishing point" in the distance.

How can a child be helped to observe how distance affects what is seen? A simple way is to take a pencil and hold it fairly close to the eye, peer past it toward the closest vertical, then keeping the same position, peer toward the most distant vertical, noticing the descending order of sizes in between. In order to take note of the convergence of horizontals, hold a square, window-like cutout so that two of the sides are vertical and two horizontal. Within this miniature window, the child can observe not only that verticals remain parallel to the vertical window sides, but that the sides of a street on level ground, or the floor of the classroom on which he is standing will appear in upward slant, coming from opposite directions and striving toward the middle whereas the tops of lamp posts along a straight street or the ceiling of the classroom will appear to slant downwards, as if trying to meet at the horizon, or as if the walls, floor, and ceiling lines of the classroom were trying to go through the middle of the wall and continue until they meet at a single point.

The pitfalls of acquiring information about perspective representation at early age levels are obvious. The temptation to use a ruler in a geometrical construction of perspective is great but should be discouraged because it leads the child to a mechanical solution and away from artistic solutions to the problem. It may also involve a number of complications because of the angle from which the perspective is taken or because of sloping streets, hilly or mountainous countrysides, winding rivers, and twisting roads (see Figure 120).

In connection with the perspective of distance and of interiors, the showing of slides or other reproductions of the perspective vistas of the Renaissance and its later emulations are of help, not only in the interests of clarity and simplification, but because of the artistic conception of perspective demonstrated in these works. In them, the perspectives are mostly confined, cut off, or resolved in the distance by a kind of horizontally placed backdrop, such as a group of houses, a cross street, a hill or mountain, barring a further view. Renaissance interiors are especially interesting to young people who want to learn about perspective. The floor tiles and roof beams in a Uccello painting almost appear to be an exercise in the use of perspective.

Children can easily understand perspective phenomena revealed in photographs. Of course, an appropriate photograph must be made or selected and used in conjunction with a line overlay that clarifies what should be observed. If an artist's painting of the same subject can be procured, this would greatly improve the demonstration. And, if the children are asked to sketch and draw either the same site or a similar one, the lesson becomes even more valuable. Photographs taken of the very scenes Van Gogh painted, for example, are exceedingly interesting and useful in illustrating the painter's loose and unconventional artistic freedom in creating a sense of space.

THE TEACHER'S OWN CREATIVITY

The teacher is the one who can help a child develop all his potential, awakening whatever is dormant. She is also the one who may block his progress and reduce his interest in art to indifference. If the teacher is creative in her approach to teaching, to art, and to life, she will project this quality in her teaching and help engender a creative attitude in her pupils.

Ideally, every art teacher should be an active creative artist who has known the struggle, pain, and elation of artistic creation. If she is not an artist, it is important for her to have had some personal art experience and to maintain an intimate contact with art in some form.

Creative work in art deepens the teacher's understanding of her pupils' work. It enables her to experience at first hand both the satisfactions and the frustrations that are part of all creative endeavors. From observation of her own difficulties in creative undertakings she can gain valuable insights into the problems her pupils face. From her ways of overcoming difficulties, she can learn how to help children overcome theirs.

Some teachers may feel that they are not at all creative. They should realize that creativity is not an absolute that is either wholly present or entirely absent. Every teacher as well as every child has a capacity for creativity. The teacher must find ways to develop her own creativity, while she finds ways to stimulate creative efforts on the part of her pupils.

TEACHING CHILDREN WHO ARE DIFFERENT

Most teachers at some time have a pupil who is exceptional in some way. He may be intellectually gifted or retarded, emotionally disturbed, orthopedically handicapped, blind, or deaf. At times such children are placed in regular classes because there is no other provision for them, at least for the moment. In other instances they are placed in regular classrooms, because they are expected to gain more by making their way with a normal group than by being with children who differ as they do. Their ability to participate in the art program or the extent to which it must be modified for them depends upon the nature and extent of their variation. Suggestions below are for teachers of regular classes in which there are some exceptional children. Specialists in teaching exceptional children will need more extensive orientation than is offered here.

The Intellectually Gifted Child

As we already indicated, the child with a high I.Q. is not necessarily either talented or especially creative. In the primary grades gifted children are likely to be at a somewhat higher developmental stage in drawing than their classmates, but this difference fades as they become older. Though gifted children typically have good verbal ability, they do not necessarily have an aptitude for working with art media. As a result they may shy away from using art, expressly preferring to exercise their verbal aptitude. Unless the teacher meets their special needs, art can become their "worst subject."

The teacher can help the talented child enjoy art by finding ways of enlisting his special capabilities in the art program. While continuing to work with art materials, he can also be encouraged to read about art and artists in sources too difficult for the others and to share his information with the class. He can be asked to carry out special projects such as research on costume design for the class play. Special activities and participation in the regular art program can help develop the capacity to appreciate creative effort in the art work of others and to enjoy the rewards of creative involvement.

The Slow Learner

The art work of slow learners reflects both the ways in which they are similar to normal children and the ways in which they differ from them. The content of their art work usually reflects the interests characteristic of their chronological age. Developmentally, however, their art work resembles that of children one or more years younger, though at times their art shows skill and details absent in the drawings of younger children. Although slow learners are not likely to show much inventiveness, they can participate in the regular art program, employing the media used by other children, and doing work of artistic merit. Tasks which call for complex solutions or require complicated procedures are unsuited to them. But their need for repetition makes it desirable for them to be guided and encouraged in the production of art work in which simple motifs and processes are repeated in the development of an extended design.

The Orthopedically Handicapped Child

Unless the disability involves control of the hands and arms, the orthopedically handicapped child who can function in a regular class can enjoy the benefits of the regular art program. If necessary, the pace can be slowed for him and tasks demanding fine coordination avoided. By carefully observing his progress, the teacher can assess his readiness to meet new challenges. As with all children who differ markedly from the average, he must be helped to learn to live with his differences without seeking refuge in them, an aim for which art activities can be useful.

The Emotionally Disturbed Child

Art activity can do much to help the emotionally disturbed child and those around him to deal with his difficulties. His problems are often expressed, directly or symbolically, through drawings, paintings, or other means of art expression. Therefore, his art activities should be encouraged. Psychologists who are trained to interpret art work from the point of view of personality can sometimes find the deeper meanings that are buried in the art work of disturbed children, and the insight obtained can be valuable. Perceptive teachers are frequently in a position to observe and notice recurring characteristics that are indicative of emotional problems, especially if the child is willing to talk about them. However, teachers must not attempt to make interpretations for which special training in psychology is required.

The Deaf Child

The art program can be especially valuable for children with a hearing loss. Children who are unable to hear others or to speak to them can find a way of communicating through art. For deaf children, art experience may reduce the feelings of frustration that accompany their handicap. As with emotionally disturbed children, free drawings and paintings are likely to provide a catharsis for pent-up feelings and provide information which can be interpreted by psychologists and used to contribute to a better understanding of the child.

The Blind Child

Because art is a visual activity, blindness might at first seem an unsurmountable barrier. However, three-dimensional activities and some two-dimensional activities are suitable for blind children. Modeling and carving in a variety of materials in the round or in relief are within their capabilities, as are paper sculpture, papier-mache, making puppets, and tooling of sheet copper,

leather, heavy aluminum foil, or special tooling paper, (Burges). Two-dimensional work is possible with any technique or material that enables the child to be guided by his sense of touch. Among these activities are *collage,* using materials such as buttons, embossed papers, fabrics of contrasting textures; cut-outs; *mosaic* using materials of contrasting size, shape, or texture, such as a variety of seeds; *drawings* made in glue, sprinkled with sand or sawdust while wet, or on a Seul board, a rubber pad on which raised line drawings are made; *painting,* using paint to which textural material, such as sand, sawdust, crushed leaves, and a binder, such as white glue or liquid starch, is added.

The Artistically Talented Child

As noted earlier, talented children go through the same developmental stages in art as do other children but at an accelerated rate (see Figures 116, 144, 174, 177, and 183). Stages are telescoped. "True-to-appearance" representation arrives much earlier, sometimes as early as six or seven years of age. Precocious development, however, does not insure that the child can ultimately succeed as a professional artist. He may simply reach his plateau sooner, and others may overtake him.

The artistically talented child shares the subject matter interests of his classmates. However, his graphic vocabulary grows more rapidly, enabling him to treat his subject in an imaginative and original way. The average child may be equally imaginative but be unable to express himself by graphic means.

The artistically talented child has a more developed feeling for line, color, and composition (see Figures 38, 175, and 187). He has greater awareness of the potential of media. He seems to be able to visualize clearly and in detail. He is able to convey a sense of movement.

Working with such children is gratifying to the teacher. Moreover, the presence of an artistically talented child can be helpful to a class. His way of handling the problems of composition, color, and the like, can help other children find ways to solve the problems presented in their own work. The teacher must insure that others do not copy the more developed symbols of the talented child but continue to evolve their own at their own rate. Above all, the teacher must avoid making the artistically talented child the "star" and by overemphasis of his contribution discourage other children and cause them to lose pride in their own efforts.

At the same time, the teacher must provide an atmosphere in which unusual talent can flourish and grow. Although she may feel that the artistically talented child does not need much help, she must be sensitive to his needs and provide guidance for his individual development, as she does for others in the class.

EVALUATION

Evaluation in art, as well as in other areas of the curriculum, focuses on the goals that are deemed important. In art, the primary concern of teachers must be the quality of the creative experience. Though it cannot be observed directly or measured objectively, this quality does manifest itself in a number of ways. One of the most telling measures is the extent to which the child's individuality of expression in his art work is preserved. This individuality shows itself quite early, and with good teaching it can be nurtured and maintained. Of primary importance in learning in art are the increase of sensitivity to design in the physical world and the growth of the power to objectify experiences and feeling through organized design. Technical skill may facilitate expression through art media; knowledge may heighten awareness of design in art and nature. But skill and knowledge are of value only as they contribute to the growth of responsiveness and creativity.

Observation of a child engaged in art activity provides some evidence of the quality of the inner process. The concentration with which he approaches his task, the perseverance with which he carries it to completion, and the fleeting look of approval he gives his creation as he sets it aside, reveal what is happening within him.

The art work itself shows growth (see Table I). In it the teacher can look for signs of originality, expressiveness, and technical accomplishment. She can judge the way in which the child has grown in his ability to use color, design, balance, and composition in the service of his creative purpose. Art products reveal the extent to which the child recognizes the possibilities in the tools and the medium he is using. It shows the insight he has gained into the way in which the medium can be adapted to express the theme he has chosen. In assessing growth in art as evidenced in art products, the following factors should be considered:

1. Originality of subject matter and concept.
2. Originality in symbolization or form.
3. Expressive power.
4. Interrelation of parts, their cohesiveness and contribution to the dominant theme, and the achievement of overall unity.
5. Arrangement, balance, harmony, and proportion.
6. Color sensitivity.
7. Appropriate use of materials.
8. Technical skill.
9. Suitability of the product for its intended purpose.

Although it is inevitable that teachers and children will compare one child's work to another's, it is important to focus on individual growth rather than status. Comparison of each child's current work with his earlier efforts helps him to note his progress and encourage him to continue to move ahead.

The child must learn to become his own critic. He should be encouraged to be inventive in identifying and in finding solutions to the problems he encounters in his work. He should learn to benefit from suggestions offered to him, but above all he must learn to be the final judge of his own work. Evaluation should never be merely a measure of past performance; it should be the key to future growth.

210. *Diorama. Schoolwork.*[50]

211. *POT. Made in school.*[50]

SUPPLEMENTARY READING

General Works

Alschuler, Rose H., and LaBerta W. Hattwick, *Painting and Personality*. Chicago: University of Chicago Press, 1947.

Barkan, Manuel, *Through Art to Creativity: Art in the Elementary School Program*. Boston: Allyn & Bacon, Inc., 1961.

Bucher, Richard H., *The Teaching of Art*. New York: Philosophical Library, 1963.

Conant, Howard, and Arne Randall, *Art in Education*. Peoria, Ill.: Chas. A. Bennett Co., Inc., 1959.

D'Amico, Victor, *Creative Teaching in Art*. Scranton, Pa.: International Textbook Co., 1953.

D'Amico, Victor, *Experiments in Creative Art Teaching*. New York: The Museum of Modern Art, 1960.

de Francesco, Italo L., *Art Education, Its Means and Ends*. New York: Harper & Row, Publishers, 1958.

Dewey, John, *Art as Experience*. New York: Minton, Balch, and Co., 1934.

Jefferson, Blanche, *Teaching Art to Children*. Boston: Allyn & Bacon, Inc., 1959.

Lewis, Hilda P., *Art Education in the Elementary School*. Washington, D.C.: National Educational Association, 1961.

Lindstrom, Miriam, *Children's Art*. Berkeley: University of California Press, 1957.

Logan, Frederick, *Growth of Art in American Schools*. New York: Harper & Row, Publishers, 1955.

Lowenfeld, Viktor, *Creative and Mental Growth*. New York: The Macmillan Co., 1957.

McFee, June King, *Preparation for Art*. San Francisco: Wadsworth Publishing Co., 1961.

Marshall, Sybil, *An Experiment in Education*. New York: Cambridge University Press, 1963.

Mendelowitz, Daniel M., *Children Are Artists*. Stanford, California: Stanford University Press, 1953.

Mock, Ruth, *Principles of Art Teaching*. London: University of London Press Ltd., 1955.

Munro, Thomas, *Art Education: Its Philosophy and Psychology*. New York: Liberal Arts Press, 1956.

Art for Exceptional Children

Eastern Arts Association. *Art Education for the Exceptional Child*. Kutztown, Pa.: 1955.

Gaitskell, Charles D. and Margaret R. Gaitskell, *Art Education for Slow Learners*. Peoria, Ill. Chas. A. Bennett Co., Inc., 1953.

Gondor, Emery I., *Art and Play Therapy*. Garden City, N.Y.: Doubleday, 1954.

Kramer, Edith, *Art Therapy in a Children's Community*. Springfield, Ill.: Charles T Thomas, 1958.

School Arts, LX, No. 9 (1961), pp. 3-25.

Wiggin, Richard G., "Art Activities for Mentally Handicapped Children," *Studies in Art Education*, III, No. 1, (1961), pp. 88-102.

Kindergarten Art

Bland, Jane Cooper, *Art of the Young Child* New York: The Museum of Modern Art 1957.

Gaitskell, Charles D. and Margaret R. Gaitskell, *Art Education in the Kindergarten*. Peoria, Ill.: Chas. A. Bennett Co., Inc., 1952.

Art Series for the Grades

Ellsworth, M., and M. F. Andrews, *Growing with Art*. Books One through Eight, Syracuse, N.Y.: L. W. Singer Co., Inc., 1960.

Fearing, Kelley; Clyde I. Martin; and Evelyn Beard, *Our Expanding Vision*. Books One through Eight, Austin, Texas: W. S. Benson and Co., 1960.

Jefferson, Blanche, *My World of Art*. Books One through Three, Chicago: Allyn & Bacon, Inc., 1964.

Maxcy, Mabel E.; Flossie Kysar; and Jennie H. Roberson, *Young Artists*. Grade One through Eight. New York: Prang Co., 1959.

Periodicals

Arts and Activities. The Jones Publishing Co., 8150 N. Central Park Ave., Skokie, Ill.

Art Education Today. Bureau of Publications, Teachers College, Columbia University, New York.

Design. Design Publishing Co., 339 S. High Street, Columbus, Ohio.

Everyday Art. The American Crayon Co., P.O. Box 581, Sandusky, Ohio. 4 issues per year.

Junior Arts and Activities. The Jones Publishing Co., 8151 N. Central Park Ave., Skokie, Ill.

School Arts Magazine. Davis Publications, Inc., Printers Building, Worcester 8, Mass.; Monthly, except July and August.

30. *NESTING TIME. Bold colors, dry brush. Watercolors. Spontaneous. Girl, age 10.*[40]

31. *MAN (or HOBO?). Color-spot effect, crayons. Talented boy, age 15.*[30]

33. *GEORGE WASHINGTON ON HIS HORSE. Impulsive color use. Brush outlines, Schema, watercolors, spontaneous. Boy, age 6.*[40]

32. *MIRACULOUS BIRD. Imaginative brilliant colors, watercolor. Talented boy, age 7, Germany, 1920's.*[9]

34. *Water and Boat. Decorative color treatment by streaks of dry brush. Painted at Boy's Club, by highly sensitive boy, age 12, from disadvantaged area.*[47]

35. *JOE, OUR POLICEMAN. Carefully executed colors and composition, made in school. Compare with Nr. 36. A powerful, spontaneous drawing of the same subject. Age 5.*[44]

36. *MY FRIEND, THE POLICEMAN. Bold true local c Policeman image expressed by gigantic hands. Cra spontaneous. Boy, age 5, 1964.*[40]

37. *SAILOR. Two main strong colors. Tough features. Mixed stage. Boy, age 9, from disadvantaged home, at ease at club where he paints.*[47]

38. *FRIENDSHIP. Color contrasts. Mixed stage, crayons, made in school. Girl, age 11.*[44]

39. *IN THE COUNTRY. Varied organized true colors. Adult manner of sketching, water color, spontaneous. Girl, age 13.*[40]

40. *FRIENDS ON THE BEACH. True local c varied. True-to-appearance. Water colors, in school. Girl, age 12.*[44]

CHAPTER TEN

Planning Art Activities

A good art program does not just happen. It is based on a well-thought-out sequence of art activities. In planning each lesson the teacher must bear in mind the goals of the program, the progress children have already made, individual variation, successive steps to be taken, and management of equipment and materials. Preceding sections of this volume have discussed the goals of the program and described the rate, direction, and individual variation in growth characteristics of elementary school children. The sections that follow deal with the kinds of art materials suitable for classroom use at each grade level, and with the ways in which they can be used creatively and with enjoyment.

PLANNING LESSONS

In planning art activities for her class, the teacher should ask herself the following questions:

1. How can the lesson contribute to the development of creative thinking?
2. How can it increase the child's sensitivity to the visual world?
3. How does it contribute to the development of skill?

197

4. What special provisions need to be made for particular children with special needs?

5. Are necessary materials available? Does the budget allow for their extensive use?

6. Is the time available sufficient for an adequate introduction of the activity, a work period, and the necessary clean-up?

7. Will plans need to be made for those who finish early or for the completion of unfinished work?

8. Is the process potentially hazardous? Are safety precautions needed?

9. Are arrangements needed to protect furniture from damage or soiling? Can the children clean up adequately so that additional burdens are not placed on the custodial staff or on the teacher?

A detailed lesson plan is made by many teachers, especially beginners, to remind them of the elements of a well-planned lesson. In preparing for a lesson the following steps are helpful.

I. Purpose of the lesson

Consider the contribution of the lesson to the goals of the art program as a whole and its appropriateness for the specific class for which it is intended.

II. Background for teaching

Gather needed information from books, magazines, curriculum guides, etc.

Experiment with materials to be used.

Discuss plans with experienced teachers, the art consultant, or others.

III. Preparing materials

List all needed materials, including those needed for clean-up.

Order or purchase materials that are not on hand.

Process materials if necessary.

IV. Sequence of the lesson

Plan for the distribution of materials selecting

a) the time of the school day to set out materials: before school, before the art period, before the children start to work.

b) the point of distribution: a single work center, several central desks or tables, each desk or table.

c) people responsible for distributing materials: teacher, monitors, individual children.

If a demonstration is needed, be sure it is clear. Point out the need to handle some parts of the process as shown and stress the opportunity to be inventive in other parts of the process. Prepare any audio-visual materials used in the demonstration. Decide whether children will work along with the demonstration or watch and listen as it is given.

A demonstration often stimulates children to begin to work. A few words of encouragement or a suggestion from the teacher helps them to get started. Inspiration for art activity is often derived from a personal experience in the school or at home. Field trips, stories or poems read to the class, music, holiday celebrations, phenomena in science or social studies can all be used to motivate art experience.

Plan time to work with individual children during the lesson. Help them to move ahead by encouraging them. One way to do this is to help them find the source of their difficulty and to guide them in experimenting with possible solutions.

Plan to tell children that clean-up time is approaching. Allow ample time for clean-up. Arrange supplies for efficient clean-up.

Plan the collection and storage of materials and the storage of finished and unfinished work.

Provide for recognition of progress and outstanding work. Be sure that the work of each child is given attention at some time, not just that of the talented few. Work can be selected for a display, held up for the class to see, with or without discussion, or used in a larger project, such as a mural or puppet show.

Timing: Allot time to each phase of the lesson. If inflexible scheduling makes it necessary to end the lesson at a designated time, plan ways to speed up the lesson, to handle unfinished work, and to provide activities for children who finish early.

V. Teacher evaluation of the lesson

In evaluating the lesson questions such as the following should be considered:

1. Did the activity help the children to become:
   a) More original, independent, and resourceful?
   b) More sensitive to the elements of art—line, color, form, texture, design?
2. Did it help them:
   a) To develop their abilities?
   b) To judge their own work?
   c) To appreciate the work of others?
3. Did the final product:
   a) Directly or indirectly express the topic given to the group?
   b) Reveal the children's attitude towards it?
   c) Reveal something of each child's individuality?
   d) Reveal the children's awareness of the medium they are using?
4. Did the experience present a challenge to them? Were they satisfied with their ability to meet it?
5. Was the work period efficiently organized?

6. What steps need to be taken to improve the quality of future art experiences?

PLANNING ART ACTIVITIES THROUGH THE GRADES

There are no hard and fast rules about the appropriateness of activities for each grade. Children at every grade level vary so much that activities suited to one class may not be suitable for another class at the same grade level. What children are able to master and learn is always dependent on what they have already mastered and learned.

In planning art activities, the teacher must assess the developmental level in drawing and manual dexterity of the group and take into account its interests and attention span. She must also identify children who differ considerably from the average. To do all of this she will need information about previous experience in art in former grades and outside the school. As she gathers the information that will give her a clear picture of the range, variation, and average ability in a particular class, she can turn for guidance to the findings and recommendations based on studies and experiences with other groups, such as those described in this volume.

Below is a listing of possible activities for children in different grades. It is to be interpreted flexibly in the light of the particular needs of each class and of the individuals within it. Certainly, not all activities suggested for any given grade need be undertaken. The list merely suggests the variety of possible experiences without intending to restrict or prescribe what may be done.

THE SCOPE AND SEQUENCE OF ART ACTIVITIES IN THE ELEMENTARY SCHOOL

(Detailed instructions on the variety of projects that may be undertaken and on the different ways in which the materials listed may be used will be found in the second portion of this chapter, Working with Art Media.)

The following media and the techniques associated with them can be used by children from kindergarten through the eighth grade.

In the kindergarten a number of art activities may be introduced. These include:

Block play.

Booklets, made by folding and decorating large sheets of paper.

Chalk, used dry or with water or starch.

Clay modeling. Pottery making use of pinch or other primitive methods.

Construction, using sticks, scrap lumber, screening, plastic, cardboard, foil, Saran, containers, etc.

Costumes, making simple hats or aprons.

Collage using cut or torn paper, fabrics, a variety of discards with interesting color or texture.

Crayon drawing and crayon resist.

Easel painting.

Felt pens.

Finger painting. Ideal for children who still find brushes hard to manage.

Masks made of paper bags.

Modeling in wet sand, or flour and salt mixtures.

Murals of cut paper, tempera or chalk.

Papier maché using a mash or pulp method.

Pencils, plain or colored.

Printing, with sponge, spools, or vegetables.

Stick or paper bag puppets.

Weaving with paper strips.

In the first grade the kindergarten program can be extended to include:

Decorative use of manuscript letters.

Mosaic, using paper or other easily handled inexpensive materials.

Papier maché. using the laminated method.

In the second grade children can participate in activities introduced in the kindergarten and first grade, handling their materials in a more advanced way. They can begin to assume a more important role in arranging materials in the classroom. They can use chalk either wet or dry and work with firing clay. Scoring techniques can be used in paper sculpture. Hand puppets can be introduced. They can make and use simple looms, weaving with yarns, paper or raffia.

In the third grade the following activities may be added:

Carving in plastic or dry unfired clay.

Using crayon in more advanced ways, achieving texture by rubbing or blending colors.

Table-top panoramas, related to social studies or language arts.

Posters, related to health and safety or other activities.

Curling techniques in paper sculpture.

Larger papier maché projects using box or crush methods.

Stencils, spatter printing.

Stitchery.

In grade four, new activities are:

Carving in soft materials, such as wax made of old crayons, soap, styrofoam.

Glazing and firing clay.

Making dioramas and models in connection with social studies and science.

Beginning water color.

In grade five, activities to be added include:

Drawing in ink.

Using slab or coil methods in working with clay.

Making simple mobiles.

Printmaking using wood and linoleum blocks.

The art activities in the sixth grade make use of all media and techniques mentioned for previous levels and may add carving in wood, a material that needs sharper tools, and therefore careful handling.

Activities that may be added in grades seven and eight are:

Bookbinding.

Using a potter's wheel.

Fashion illustration.

Printmaking using silk screen.

Textile printing—batik silk screen.

A listing and description of art materials

Materials and equipment for the art program are listed below in alphabetical order, with brief descriptions, and some suggestions of grade levels at which they can be used. Discards and household supplies, though not listed, can always be used to supplement these materials as indicated in Working with Art Media.

Audio-visual aids (motion pictures, slides, projectors, picture file).

Brilliants (trade name for tempera paint in cake form).

Bristol Board (fine cardboard with textured surface 22 x 28 inches in pastel colors. Upper grades).

Brushes (two inch for varnish, starch, covering large areas).

Brushes, paint, easel (flat bristle brush, size ½ inch and 1 inch. For all grades, but used mainly in K-2).

Brushes (pointed tip with flexible bristles, water color sizes 2 through 12, running from small to large sizes).

Chalk (round and square sticks in assorted colors).

Charcoal (for drawing on white paper. For grades 5 and above).

Chip board (gray in color, 26 x 38 inches, heavy, light, or medium. Can substitute cardboard from cardboard cartons).

Clay cart (to transport clay to different classes and to kiln).

Clay, white burning (moist, very fragile when dry, fire in kiln to give strength. See engobe, glaze, and crayons, underglaze on this list. Clay is available in other textures and colors).

Cloves, oil of (for preventing mold and spoilage in tempera and papier maché. Available in drugstores).

Clayola, colored (4 colors to a box. Oil base clay, like Plasticine).

Cones, pyrometric (#06 used to judge the heat in a clay kiln).

Crayons (8, 16, or 24 colors to a box, square or round, large or small diameter. Smaller assortment, square shape, large size used mostly in kindergarten, early primary).

Crayons, underglaze (for drawing on clay after the first firing, in pencil form).

Cutting tools, linoleum (for cutting linoleum blocks for printing).

Drawing boards (masonite, plywood, pine).

Easels (floor or table type).

Engobe colors (colored slip which gives mat finish to clay when fired. Can be applied to clay before the first or before the second firing. Transparent glaze applied over engobe makes it shine).

Finger paint (ready to use or made by adding tempera powder to liquid starch).

Fasteners (for binding of booklets and for making certain kinds of movable puppets).

Fixative, all purpose (alcohol plus shellac. To protect chalk and other work, spray on with an insecticide spray gun).

Fly sprayers (quart. Can be used for spraying fixative, or for spraying thin tempera paint).

Glue (for binding wood, leather, cloth, rubber, glass, metal).

Glaze (applied to clay and fired for decoration, luster and water tightness).

Glaze, clear, transparent (can be applied to fired, un-glazed clay, or fired glaze or engobe).

Glaze (white opaque, and other colors).

Ink, India, eye dropper top (for drawing and lettering. Can substitute black Alpha color tempera used thin. Mainly for upper grades).

Ink (all colors, black and white, speedball and regular pen points. Mainly for upper grades).

Kiln (for firing clay).

Mica (glitter-sprinkle on glue, paste or wet paint).

Paint, powder extender (used with pigment to make the paint go farther and be more permanent. Can soil clothes).

Paper, chalk (cream, 18 x 24 inches. Mainly for upper grades).

Paper, chart (printed with lines or squares).

Paper, crepe (several colors, flameproof).

Paper, construction (9 x 12, 12 x 18, 18 x 24, 24 x 36 are standard sizes. Heavier and more expensive than poster paper. Packages of single colors and packages of assorted colors).

Paper, finger paint (roll of white, glazed wrapping or shelf paper, 18 inches wide, or special finger paint paper in 16 x 22 and 16 x 11 sizes).

Paper, Manila (9 x 12, 12 x 18, 18 x 24, cream color).

Paper, metallic (silver, gold, and assorted colors).

Paper, mimeograph (8½ x 11. Can be used for drawing and color work).

Paper, newscut (unruled. 9 x 12, 12 x 18, 18 x 24. For tempera painting and chalk).

Paper, newscut (squares. Can be used for cut-out letters).

Paper, poster (about half as expensive as construction paper. 9 x 12, 12 x 18, 18 x 24 sizes. Packages of single colors and packages of assorted colors).

Paper, white drawing (9 x 12, 12 x 18, 18 x 24 sizes. More expensive than Manila paper. Best paper for water color painting).

Paper, wrapping (white or manila, 18 inches or 36 inches wide. For tempera or chalk murals, charts, etc.).

Paste (ready mixed. Mainly for adhering paper to paper or cardboard. Not as strong as glue).

Paste, wheat (comes in powder form and is mixed with water to a consistency of thick cream. Used in papier maché).

Pencils (assorted colors).

Pencils (#2)

Pencils, primary (broader than ordinary pencils).

Pens, ballpoint (for lettering and chart making).

Pens, felt (refillable or disposable, black and assorted colors, for lettering, drawing).

Pens, Speedball (in sizes "0", large, to "5", small, and in four shapes, "A" squares, "B" round, "C" chisel, "D" oval).

Plaster of Paris (a white powder which sets quickly after being mixed with water).

Poster board (for posters and charts. Can substitute construction paper pasted or glued on cardboard from cartons. Mainly for upper grades).

Rubber cement (with applicator. For wood or paper).

Ruler (12 inch).

Scissors (blunt ends, 5 and 9 inch. There are some designed for left-handed pupils).

Shellac (for protecting projects such as papier maché. Use alcohol as thinner. Make fixative by dissolving one part shellac to about 50 parts alcohol).

Sponges (for cleaning or painting).

Starch, liquid (mix with powder paint for finger paint. Use with chalk. A substitute for wheat paste in papier maché).

Stilts, kiln (for stacking a kiln with clay pieces to be fired).

Tag board (oak tag, 24 x 36 inches. For charts and model making. Can substitute construction paper).

Tape, brown paper (1 inch and 2 inch rolls. Use water to adhere. For portfolio making).

Tape, masking (½ and ¾ inch width. Use on wood and glass).

Tape, cellophane (for many surfaces, but not walls or blackboards).

Textile paint, liquid (mix with powdered paint for stenciling and painting on cloth. Mainly for upper grades).

Towels, paper (for papier maché projects, water color, clean-up).

Twine (light and heavy. Use in some papier maché projects and in string printing).

Water color refills (all colors).

Water color sets (8 hole pan with colors and brush).

WORKING WITH ART MEDIA

Drawing

Drawing is the most fundamental art activity. Since time immemorial, children have started to draw on their own initiative. By the time they enter school they have not only been drawing for quite a while but have already progressed beyond the scribbles of early childhood and have developed a variety of symbols with which to represent their environment. The teacher does not have to teach them how to draw, but it is her responsibility to provide them with the materials suitable for the kind of drawing they can and want to do.

The symbols children like to draw at this stage are most easily formed with a pointed tool: a pencil, pen, crayon or chalk stick. The need to outline is so strong at this point that the young child will use whatever implements are at hand to do his outlining. Sharp pointed implements permit him to outline with precision and to add elaborate details; big brushes do not. To provide him only with big brushes is to frustrate his desire and need to gain experience in devising and expanding his pictorial symbols. If he wants to use big brushes to experiment with blobs and splashes of color, well and

Figure 212. *CINDERELLA AFTER SHE MARRIED THE PRINCE.*[40] *Girl, age five, spontaneous brush drawing.*

Figure 213. *The boy is intent on putting down the characteristics of the spray of plants lying next to him. He does not just "copy" as one can see, but is trying to emphasize and clarify certain characteristics. Studies of this kind at these age levels are of educational and expressive value.*[43]

good, but sharp implements must also be available to him because he can more easily control them and use them to make the small intricate lines he uses for his symbols. During the first years of school, it is particularly important for the teacher to help children select media suited to their developmental needs and to their expressive style in art.

Children in the intermediate and upper elementary grades continue to use sharp drawing implements to outline shapes. Indeed, even children who have reached the true-to-appearance stage continue to rely on outlines. Although older children are interested in and capable of using a variety of media and techniques as their artistic expression develops, they still continue to draw.

There are several kinds of implements suitable for drawing: soft and hard pencils, colored pencils, pens, crayons and pastels, chalk and charcoal, brush or stick. Each of these is discussed in detail in the following section.

Chalk

Chalk is versatile and suitable for children in all grades. It requires little or no equipment, is ready to use, easy to store, and does not spoil. Its disadvantages are that it is easily rubbed off, dusts onto clothes, and causes allergic reactions in some children.

There are several types of chalk:

Round sticks of colored chalk in regular sizes.

Large-size lecturer's chalk.

Blackboard chalk, usually limestone, which is harder than colored chalk, but can be used in combination with it.

Pastels, a finer, more expensive chalk, seldom used in the elementary school.

Oil chalk, pigment pressed together with turpentine-soluble material, seldom used in the elementary school because of cost and clean-up problems.

Chalk may be applied to the blackboard and to the following kinds of paper: bogus, poster, colored construction, Manila, and white.

Several techniques can be used with chalk. It can be:

Applied directly with side or tip.

Blended and smoothed with fingers, paper towel, rag, or cotton.

Textured by inserting embossed objects under the paper.

Applied by transfer from a string.

Transferred by drawing with any implement on paper prepared by rubbing the back with chalk and placing under it a second sheet of paper on which the final drawing appears.

Rubbed on a surface to be printed, such as a leaf.

Ground to dust and floated on water through which the paper is dipped to obtain a marbleized effect.

Used with a liquid, such as water, starch, canned milk, buttermilk, liquid soap, paste or glue diluted with water to a milky consistency, and applied to the paper before drawing, brushed on to a completed drawing or rubbed on with a rag; applied to the chalk.

Combined with crayon, tempera, water color, pencil, ink, yarn, collage.

Chalk work may be protected by:

Using liquid with it.

Covering the surface with glass, clear plastic, cellophane, or Saran wrap.

Spraying the surface with commercial fixative (alcohol and shellac), clear lacquer, varnish, clear plastic, glue diluted with water.

Safety precaution: always spray outside of classroom.

Work surfaces may be protected by spreading newspaper or oil cloth over them. Use several thicknesses of newspaper if liquid is being used. Children's clothes can be protected by the use of discarded shirts or smocks.

Dry or wet chalk techniques are simple enough to be used by the youngest children. The introduction of new ways of applying chalk and new combinations of media will be stimulating to older children.

Chalk is especially well suited to:

Lettering—break chalk and use side.

Map making—rub chalk dust for gradation of color.

Murals—use side of chalk to cover large areas quickly.

Crayon

The most frequently used medium in elementary schools is colored wax crayon. Crayon is inexpensive, ready-to-use, easy to store, does not spoil, and is not as "messy" as other media.

Crayon is available in thin and thick sticks and in a wide variety of colors. In the early grades children show little concern for color nuance and are content with the eight standard colors, Older children seek more subtle color relationships and appreciate having a more extensive array of colors to work with. Older children can also be encouraged to extend their palette still further by discovering ways to blend colors. Although the large size sticks are associated with the primary grades, it is wise to make both sizes available for each grade to permit finer contours and to allow for filling-in of large color areas. Crayons may be purchased with or without paper cover and in flat or rounded sticks. Paper covers make for easy identification of dark colors, but paper must be removed to use crayon sides. Flat sticks do not roll off desks and are better suited for work requiring the use of crayon sides.

Crayon may be applied to:

Paper of all kinds, including white, colored, Manila, bogus, wrapping, shelf, typing, wallpaper; cloth, such as old sheets and window shades; wood.

The versatility of crayon makes a variety of effects possible. Familiarity with several techniques allows children to choose the one that best suits the purpose.

Crayon can be applied directly by the following techniques:

With the tip, for fine lines and dots.

With the end for broader lines.

With the side for large areas.

Modulation of color can be achieved by:

Mixing colors directly on the surface.

Applying color to a paper which is then rubbed on the surface.

Pressure differentiation for gradation of color and shading.

Variation in the concentration of dots, variation in the thickness of parallel or cross-hatched lines, variation in the distance between parallel or cross-hatched lines.

Polishing the surface with a piece of paper, a rag, or the finger for a richer color mixture or greater luster.

The surface can be embossed by placing objects such as cardboard, leaves, and coins under it and pressing carefully around the edges with crayon, pushing the paper down around a raised area. Texture can be achieved by placing things such as leaves, sand, or rough wood, under the paper and rubbing the top of the paper with the sides of crayons.

Etching or engraving can be carried out by heavily applying a light color such as yellow, which is then covered with a thick layer of crayon, ink, or poster paint, usually black, and scratching through the top layer with a pin, pen, finger nail, nail, or any pointed object to make a design or picture.

Stencils, cut or torn out of paper, can be used by coloring around them, or coloring inside them. Crayon collected on the edges of the used stencil can be rubbed onto a surface with a paper towel, an eraser, or the fingers.

Transfer techniques can produce fine linear effects by applying crayon to the back of scrap paper and using it like carbon paper. It is possible to remove a line of color by placing a piece of scrap paper over the area and drawing the line on the scrap paper with a sharp implement.

Crayon combines well with other media:

Finger paint over crayon gives a rich texture.

Batik or crayon resist is produced by outlining in crayon and painting over the entire surface with water color or thin tempera.

Crayon can be applied directly or by transfer methods to surfaces containing ink or felt-pen contours.

Crayon and chalk can be combined.

Shoe polish can be rubbed over a crayon surface.

Scrap crayons can be placed between two pieces of wax paper and heated under a cloth with a warm iron for a stained-glass effect.

Ink

Ink is valued for its permanence and intensity (see Figure 198). Used with a pen, it permits sharp delineation of contour and details. Pen and ink demands more motor skill and patience than do other drawing media and is therefore reserved for upper grades. Permanent inks require protection for clothing. Precautions against upsetting ink bottles are needed. Felt pens, however, which produce a broad line and are available in colors as well in black, can be managed by even the youngest elementary school child. Although they are more expensive than other forms of ink, their life can be extended by dipping them into ink after they have run dry.

There are several types of ink applicators:

Drawing pens.

Speed ball pen nibs and holders.

Ball point pens.

Fountain pens.

Old felt pens.

Ink can be applied in other than the usual ways, using, for example:

Figure 214. *Two similar compositions by a child of average ability show the difference between handling a familiar medium (pencil) and trying out a new medium (brush and ink).*[41] *A. Brush and ink drawing. B. Pencil drawing. Girl, age nine.*

String dipped in ink.
A small branch of a tree.
Reeds.
Sponges.

Water color and thin tempera paints may be used as ink. Inks are available in black, in colors, and in washable and permanent varieties.

Any hard-surface paper, colored or white, or poster board can be used with ink.

Ink can be:
 Used to draw sharp lines.
 Applied to a wet surface for a fuzzy line.
 Used to shade areas by cross-hatching, stippling, rubbing.
 Used as a sgraffito technique, applied solidly and scratched through.
 Used as wash by diluting with water.
 Combined with other media, such as paint and crayon.

Ink is of particular value in doing:
 Silhouettes.
 Posters, charts, diagrams, and illustrations in connection with other areas of the curriculum.
 Lettering.
 Cartoons.

Pencil

The value of the commonplace pencil is often overlooked or derogated by those who favor bold line and brilliant color. However, the lowly pencil has unique qualities that earn it a place in well-rounded art programs. Pencil shares many of the desirable qualities of pen and ink, but is free of its disadvantages. Pencil produces a fine line and permits a high level of differentiation in drawing. It is more readily useable than ink, easier to handle, presents no hazard to clothing, and, because it is easily erased, encourages experimentation. Many children like to make a pencil outline to guide work in other media. Although chalk and crayon can also be used to outline, they are regarded as "colors." Most children feel

Figure 215. *An entirely "realistic" true-to-life landscape, so composed as to have a decorative quality, partly because of a centered, balanced near symmetrical arrangement, and partly because of the combination of bold and delicate lines.[30] Talented boy, age fourteen, 1936, pencil drawing.*

more comfortable with the soft neutral pencil outline than the definite color of a crayon or chalk outline. Pencil drawings of younger children usually exhibit characteristics that are more advanced developmentally than those in their crayon drawings, and considerably more advanced than those in their easel paintings. Pencils facilitate developmental progress in drawing, and their use in all grades is to be encouraged.

Pencils are available in hard varieties, such as Nos. 3, 3½, H, 2H, and in soft varieties, Nos. 1, 2, 2B, 3B, 4B. Hard pencils are used for sharp, clear lines, such as in drafting. Soft pencils are used for softer contours, as in sketching. Pencils are available in a wide range of colors. Some types of colored pencils are designed to produce a water color effect when clear water is brushed over a surface colored in pencil.

Any variety of paper, smooth or textured, white or colored can be used with pencil.

Fifth and sixth graders are usually ready to learn to use pencil more extensively than for outlining and ornamentation. They can be shown how to:

Shade by using the side of the pencil.

Shade lightly by penciling in a section of scrap paper and rubbing it on a drawing.

Stipple, cross hatch, vary pressure, or rub to achieve a gradation from light to dark.

Produce a sharp or fuzzy line by using hard or soft pencils and cleaning with an eraser or smudging.

Children can experiment to find ways to suggest the texture of wood, metal, cloth, and other materials.

Pencil is well suited to:

Line drawings.

Preliminary sketches for more elaborate work, such as murals.

Cartoons.

Studies of nature forms.

Shaded letters, produced by tying two or more pencils together and adjusting the pressure.

Stitchery

Stitchery offers a way to extend and enrich drawings and abstract designs. It can be particularly useful for children who have reached a plateau in their drawing development. Interest in drawing and in art generally can be maintained through the difficult transition periods by providing new media for expression that continues to employ the old, familiar schema.

Stitchery includes: applique, the art of arranging and fastening, by thread or by glue, bits of fabric to a backing of burlap or other textiles; embroidery, the addition of colored thread or yarn to a fabric by pulling it through the fabric.

Ordinarily, applique is used to define areas by color, and embroidery is used for linear definition, as in an outline or a line drawing. Applique and embroidery may be used separately, together, or combined with other media, such as textile drawing or printing.

In the primary grades, children can paste brightly colored fabrics in abstract designs. Children in the middle grades who are able to handle a needle and thread can add embroidery to their designs. Yarn or string threaded through large needles demands less skill and patience and is likely to be preferred to thread, especially by boys.

Applique and embroidery may be added to freehand or stenciled designs carried out in the following media:

> Crayon, set by covering fabric with a
>   damp cloth and running a warm iron
>   over it.
> Water color.
> Ink.
> Felt pen.
> Tempera paint.

Printing techniques, discussed in another section of this chapter, can be used with stitchery.

Stitchery can be used to decorate utilitarian objects, such as clothing, handkerchiefs, napkins, or wall hangings.

Weaving

Weaving is an ancient art. It was practiced at the time the first known records of events were made. Some people think the idea of weaving came to Neolithic man as he watched the spider spin his web and the birds build their nests.

Man has woven with whatever was available to him. The earliest weaving was done with grasses. The Egyptians wove sheer linen out of flax in 3000 B.C. Cotton was woven in India, wool in Assyria and Persia, and hemp in the South Sea Islands.

Weaving in the elementary school program should stress inventive use of materials. Colorful paper cut from magazines, nature materials, or discarded yarn can be used in making decorative or useful objects.

A simple loom can be made by inserting pins along the edges of a piece of cardboard, or by making two rows of holes in the cardboard, or by notching the edges; the warp is then stretched over the cardboard, held by the pins, holes, or notches.

Paper-cutting and collage

Paper-cutting and collage (paste-ups), like stitchery, can be used in abstract designs or as a means of utilizing ideas developed in drawings.

In collage, paper is cut or torn and attached to heavier cardboard, glass, wood, or plastic. Any kind of paper available in the school may be used, as well as household papers, such as aluminum foil and

Figure 216. *Decorative color paper cut of realistic fishes and water plants.*[19] *Girl, age eleven, Austria, 1925.*

tissue paper, and discards such as magazines, used greeting cards, and wrapping paper. Other materials, such as yarn, string, cloth, buttons, or any light weight object may be incorporated in a collage.

Scraps of paper, fabric, and odds and ends can be collected, stored, and set out in boxes at all grade levels. In the kindergarten, some children will need to be taught how to use scissors, and some will prefer tearing to cutting.

Paper-cutting and collage can be used in making:

> Murals.
> Paper mosaics.
> Mobiles.

It is useful in activities relating to other areas of the curriculum such as:

> Posters.
> Bulletin board displays and lettering.
> Holiday greetings and decorations.

Print making

Print making is based on duplication. Simple forms may be repeated to develop a more extended design, or drawings, paintings, or designs reproduced one or more times.

Prints can be made in a variety of ways. One way of duplicating a design is by using a stencil as a guide in a free or regular pattern of repetition. Stencils are made by cutting away an area and using what is cut away or what remains to control the application of color. The use of a stencil allows greater control and precision in applying color. Stencils should be made by the children rather than provided for them. Stencils can be made and used at any grade level.

Stencil paper may be purchased or school room supplies, such as drawing paper, construction paper, tagboard, or tape used. The backings of discarded mimeograph stencils

Figure 217. *This print by a six year old Japanese child shows that techniques are attractive and can be mastered at a young age. This child's approach is schematic and in no way different from the drawings of an African child or a child of Western culture.[13] Age six, print.*

are excellent for this purpose. Nature forms, such as leaves, may also be used as stencils.

Stencils may be used singly or in combination. Using a stencil, color in a variety of forms may be applied to surfaces such as paper, glass, wood, cardboard, or cloth. The appropriate media may be tempera, water color, textile paint, finger paint, ink, crayon, chalk or pencil. Color may be applied with a stencil brush, easel brush, sponge, rag, brayer, finger, flit gun, or tooth brush.

A monoprint, one print, is made by painting quickly with thick tempera on a non-absorbent surface, such as glass or shelf paper and blotting it once with an absorbent paper, such as newsprint. The process can be varied by:

> Placing objects, such as string on the painted surface.
> Scraping away areas of the painted sur-

face with the finger or end of the brush.

Stamping methods are used for overall designs in two or more colors. A wide variety of objects can be used. Searching for suitable objects helps to develop an awareness of form and sensitivity to the use of the medium. The method involves inking or painting the object and repeatedly stamping on the surface to be printed. Useful objects, such as wrapping paper, bookplates, and place mats may be decorated. The imprint may be made by the following:

Potatoes or other dry vegetables in which a design is incised or cutaway.

Nature forms.

Discards, such as spools, paper clips, bottle tops, nail heads, cardboard, felt, or a section of an inner tube cut to the desired shape, mounted on wood or cardboard, inked with a roller.

Sponge in its original shape or cut to a desired shape.

String dipped in paint applied directly to the surface of the paper or placed between folded paper and pulled out.

Fingers or hand.

Plasticene, plaster, or clay, flattened and incised, inked with a roller, brush, or sponge.

Roller prints are made by first attaching one or more materials, such as string, tape, rubberbands or leaves, to a brayer (a rubber roller with a handle), bottle, rolling pin, or large dowel, then rolling it on glass covered with printers' ink or thick tempera, and finally rolling on the surface to be printed.

Multiprints are made by wood or linoleum cuts or silk screen. To make a linoleum cut the following materials are needed: linoleum (mounted or unmounted), lino-tools, water soluble printing ink or thick poster paint, a brayer, a sheet of glass or linoleum, paper or fabric. Pictures or designs are drawn directly on linoleum in reverse of the desired print, and the areas not to be printed are cut away with lino-tools. For safety, clamp the linoleum and hold the tool with both hands. The linoleum cut can be tested by placing a piece of paper over the top of the block, rubbing it with crayon or pencil, and holding it up to the light to see how it will print. When the block is ready to print, ink a sheet of glass and roll the brayer over it in all directions until the layer of ink is thin and well-distributed. Roll ink on the block, making sure all surfaces are covered. Print by placing paper or fabric to be printed on top of the block and pressing with the back of a spoon, or place newspaper on the floor, the paper or fabric above it, set the inked block on it and stand on the back of the block.

Figure 218. *ATTACK. The story is told through the patternized use of single units of riding soldiers between trees.*[38] *Boy, age ten, Austria, 1918-1919, linoleum cut.*

Figure 219. *LION EATING HIS PREY. The representation is schematic with human features appearing on the lion's face. The technique and the difficult medium are handled with a fearless know-how that is astonishing.*[13] *Boy, age eight, Japan, 1964, woodblock.*

Wood cuts add the texture of wood to the print. In the process described above, soft, flat wood may be used instead of linoleum.

Silk screen is used for color prints. Materials needed are a piece of silk or organdy, a frame, which can be a lid of a cardboard box or embroidery hoops, thick tempera paint, masking tape, tissue paper, cardboard or rubber squeegee, crayon, and paper. Stretch silk or organdy over the frame. Areas to be printed are cut out of tissue paper and the tissue paper stencil attached to the underside of the screen with tape or paste. The paper to be printed on is placed under the stencil. Paint of the consistency of toothpaste is placed on top of the screen and drawn across it with a squeegee, forcing the paint onto the paper wherever there is an opening in the stencil. Unprinted areas may be filled in with crayon. The design is not reversed in printing.

Block printing, the repetition of a drawing, on paper or fabric may be made using wood or linoleum blocks. Prints on fabric may be combined with applique, embroidery, paint, or crayon. Large wall hangings can be developed in this way in the upper grades.

Painting

During the elementary school years, and especially in the earlier grades, line is of primary importance, and color is used in support of line. Elementary school children, as a rule, do not build up form through color in a painterly way but instead draw outlines even with brushes, and then fill-in. The wise teacher respects the natural mode of expression of the child allowing him the security of the outline for as long as it is necessary.

Paint is a more demanding medium than crayon or colored pencils but produces more brilliant colors.

Painting techniques used in the elementary school include finger paint, water color, and tempera paint. Encaustic, painting with melted wax crayon, may also be used. Oil paints are often prohibited by budgetary considerations, and their use requires greater supervision.

Finger Painting

Finger painting is an ancient Chinese art that has become popular in art programs for young children. The appeal to young children seems to lie in its directness, the immediacy of effect, and the responsiveness of the medium to unlimited manipulation. Many teachers believe the messiness of the process is therapeutic, especially for children who are admonished to keep clean at other times.

Finger paint may be made quickly by adding food color, liquid tempera, or powdered tempera to any of the following:

Liquid starch.

Wheat paste.

Homemade starch.

Commercial finger paint.

Library paste.

Cornstarch.

Buttermilk.

Some teachers prefer a finger paint base made by cooking 1½ cups of starch and ¼ cup of talcum powder with 1 quart of boiling water until glossy and adding 1½ cups of soap flakes and a few drops of oil of cloves when cool. The mixture will keep several weeks if one teaspoon alum is added for each pint of the mixture.

Use liquid coloring agents to thin, or powdered tempera to thicken to desired consistency.

Suitable papers are finger paint paper, butcher paper, white wrapping paper, and shelf paper, used glossy side up.

Before beginning finger painting, cover work surfaces with newspaper or oil cloth; have aprons, smocks, or old shirts that completely cover clothes at hand, set up a place for drying work, such as a section of the floor covered with newspaper, a line and clothespins, or a drying rack; and provide rags, sponges, and water for clean-up. Next, wet paper by sponging both sides of the paper or immerse rolled-up sheets in water and shake off excess. If a wrinkle-free surface is desired, allow water to drain off and smooth surface with one hand, lifting a corner of the paper to allow air to escape.

Colored finger paint may be set out or uncolored base may be provided along with powdered tempera in shakers, such as discarded salt or spice shakers, or jars with perforated tops. Set out colors that mix well together. Children enjoy seeing two primary colors produce a secondary color. If paint becomes too dry, a few drops of water will restore it to the proper consistency. If desired, smooth thoroughly dry paintings by pressing the reverse side with a warm iron.

The feeling of freedom that finger painting offers requires children to stand at a table as they work. They should be encouraged to experiment by using all parts of the hand and forearm, moving in a variety of ways, blending colors, and scraping paint with objects, such as combs, sticks, cardboard, or bottle caps. Texture can be added by sprinkling coarse grained materials, such as sand or salt, over wet paintings. Small objects such as string, buttons, colored paper, may be added, as in collage. Finger paintings may be made on a surface on which wax crayon has been heavily applied. Monoprints may be made by finger painting on a smooth surface, such as glass, linoleum, oil cloth, or masonite and "blotting" with paper.

Finger paintings may be used as pictures or as decorative paper for wrapping packages or for covering surfaces, such as booklet covers, portfolios, waste baskets.

Tempera painting

Tempera is a desirable paint for elementary school use because it is versatile and easy to handle. The powdered form is preferred, because it costs less and stores more compactly.

Powdered tempera is usually mixed with water in the schools but also mixes with liquid starch, shellac, varnish, or linseed oil. The proportions in which water and powder are mixed depend on variations in the pigment and the desired characteristics of the mixed paint. Brilliant opaque colors require about one part water to four parts dry tempera. For a transparent wash, use about four parts water to one part paint. A bit of experimentation will reveal the proper mixture for each color.

The powder can be mixed by stirring, shaking in a tightly sealed jar, or letting it stand for a while. To hasten mixing, especially of red tones, add a drop of alcohol to break down surface tension. Oil of wintergreen or a few drops of liquid starch prevents spoilage.

Tempera paint can be applied to any of the papers commonly found in schools, as well as discards, such as the classified ad section of newspapers, wall paper remnants, wrapping paper, or shelf paper.

Tempera paint can be applied with a brush in various ways such as:

    Spattering.

    Stippling.

    Stroking with a "dry" brush, carrying a minimum of paint, or with a brush "loaded" with paint.

    Overglazing.

It can also be sprayed with a spray gun, wiped on with a sponge or rag, printed, using a brayer or other printing implements, or finger painted.

Children can learn about the medium by mixing and using paint of different consistency and trying out brushes of various sizes and shapes. Color mixing is encouraged by the provision of extra empty paint containers and brushes.

Good work habits are developed by protecting floors and work surfaces with newspaper, showing children how to scrape the brush on the container before lifting it from the can, providing drying areas, and establishing responsibility for cleaning work areas, equipment, and brushes. Children can learn that brushes remain in good condition longer if they are gently cleaned in soap and water immediately after use, rinsed, shaped, dried flat, and stored in a jar with the bristle end up.

Water color

Water color is transparent, unlike tempera which is usually opaque. Colors cannot be covered-over, and mistakes are easier to detect and harder to correct than with tempera. Because of these limitations, preplanning and careful work are required. Usually water color is reserved for older children.

Water color may be applied to any rough grained, light-colored paper that is not too absorbent. Manila paper, white drawing paper, Bogus paper, Alphatone, or water color paper are suitable. Provide a variety of round and flat brushes in soft and hard bristles. Small sponges, rags, and fingers may also be used to apply paint.

Although water color lends itself to a wide range of effects and techniques, it is better to teach children just a few techniques and allow them to master these so that they can use them expressively, rather than to present too many possibilities without sufficient opportunity to handle them comfortably and with assurance.

A water color wash is applied with a

Figure 220. *Outdoor sketching permits older children a close observation of nature and deliberate thought of what happens when a human being tries to express what he sees, and how to give it form.*[43]

brush full of liquid, but not dripping, working quickly down from the top of the paper with horizontal strokes. For a good wash do not rework, mix enough paint and carry the drop from the end of a stroke across to the next stroke, always working on a wet line.

Water color may also be worked using a dry brush technique. Using a semi-dry brush and as much pigment as desired, sweep across the surface. The paint catches on the raised surfaces, leaving the paper partly uncolored.

To use water color in a resist technique, brush over a crayon drawing with one or more colors. The crayoned lines and areas repel the water color and remain exposed.

Experiment in combining water color with ink, finger paint, chalk, opaque paint, pencil sketches.

For a light, textured surface, blot the wet surface with a dry brush or towel.

Paintings on a wet paper set on a damp surface produce a soft-edged, misty effect.

Designs may be scratched into a water color with the wooden end of the brush or any other fairly sharp implement.

A "glaze" can be applied over dry color using little pigment and much water and working as a wash.

Children can try mixing colors directly on the paper and can observe the effects of applying washes over one another.

Clean brushes, water, color cakes, and pans are essential for clear colors. Provide paper towels to wipe brushes and conveniently placed containers for clean and dirty water.

Wax crayon

Melted wax crayon may be used as a paint in an ancient technique known as encaustic. Carefully heat discarded crayons in a double boiler arrangement. Paint on paper, wood or cardboard, using discarded easel brushes.

Mosaic

Pictures or designs in mosaic are traditionally patterns built out of small bits of tile, glass, stone, or other hard materials. Mosaic is especially well suited to the elementary school art program. The material is easy to handle, and little technical skill is demanded. Mosaic lends itself to the use of definite outlines, which is the way of constructing pictures that is natural to most elementary school children. It provides an additional way of maintaining interest in drawing, which is particularly needed during the later elementary school years when many children are not yet ready to step up developmentally. Horizontal enrichment through the execution of drawings in mosaic materials provides opportunity for developing greater awareness of texture. Because materials used are apt to vary in color, mosaic is useful in helping children move away from uniformly filled-in color areas towards increased sensitivity to the subtleties of color nuance. Mosaic murals provide opportunity for group planning and execution.

In the elementary school, inexpensive, readily available, non-hazardous materials can be applied to flat surfaces or used with three dimensional work, such as sculpture or mobiles.

Some materials that may be used are pebbles, marbles, shells, discarded tile, egg shells, colored paper, cloth, seeds, nuts, lentils, and the like. Lightweight materials may be applied to paper or cardboard of various kinds. Heavier materials require a more rigid surface, such as plywood, masonite, or wood. The easiest way of making a mosaic is by gluing on the small pieces, using white glue or any adherent that is safe and works.

Mosaic can be used for individual or group projects. Mosaic is ideal for use on interiors or exteriors of buildings. However, work set on a wall or used out-of-doors requires greater protection than gluing procedures provide. The use of mortar or grout and waterproofing materials requires a great deal of adult participation and is best undertaken under the direction of an adult with some experience in the medium and adequate time to devote to the task.

Modeling

In modeling, the first steps are manipulation and are analogous to scribbling. The schematic approach carried over into modeling produces figures put together out of simple flat or roundish shapes. As children mature, their representational work becomes more consistent with the appearance of real objects.

The choice of modeling materials must be appropriate to the level of development of the child. The youngest need a material that is easily manipulated but not necessarily permanent. Older children need materials that permit finer and more elaborated work.

Clay, the most versatile modeling material, is suitable for all grades. Other materials offer a variety of textural and plastic qualities. Inexpensive modeling materials suitable for younger children are wet sand or shredded asbestos to which wheat paste may be added. A mixture made by kneading together two parts flour, one part salt, and one part water adding, if desired, food coloring, and oil of cloves to retard spoilage, is another modeling material.

Older elementary school children can carry out reliefs or free standing figures in a variety of materials. Reliefs in clay are

particularly valuable, because they permit the child to select content technically too difficult to be handled in the round. Reliefs take advantage of the children's two-dimensional conceptions and at the same time provide opportunity to move towards rounded forms. Reliefs are useful in extending art activities for children who seem unable to move on to the next developmental stage or who seem fixated on a single choice of subject. For example, the child who always draws horses can be offered the suggestion that he try a relief of a horse in clay on a glass base.

Papier maché

Papier maché is an inexpensive modeling material that adapts to a wide variety of classroom uses. It consists of paper, usually newspaper, held together with a binder, usually wheat paste. It has the disadvantages of requiring an extended period of time for completion and storage space for work in progress.

There are several ways of working with papier maché. The choice of method depends upon the nature of the project and the grade level and ability of the group. In general, the pulp and laminated methods are best for kindergarten through second grade.

In the mash or pulp method, paper is torn into pieces an inch or less across and either soaked in water from one to twenty-four hours, or cooked for two or three hours, cooled, and the water squeezed out, if desired. A mixture of wheat paste and water is added. The material is molded, allowed to dry, painted, dried, and varnished.

For larger projects or special uses, a shell is made over a form, such as an inflated balloon, box, stuffed paper bag, tied crushed or rolled newspapers. Strips of newspaper dipped in wheat paste diluted to the consistency of thick cream are applied to the form in several layers until the desired strength is achieved. The final layer is of paper towels. Objects are then allowed to dry, painted, dried and varnished.

The laminated method is used for thin objects, such as a large decorative butterfly. The desired shape is cut or torn out of at least five sheets of newspaper. The paper is wet if desired. Wheat paste the consistency of thick cream is applied between each layer. The object is then shaped as desired, propped up until dry, painted, dried, and varnished.

Papier maché is especially useful in making objects that serve other areas of the curriculum, for example, models, maps, globes, puppets, dioramas, and holiday decorations.

Carving

Carving involves the cutting away of material rather than the shaping of material, as in modeling. Because of the hazards in using carving tools and the expense of tools and materials, this activity is often omitted from the elementary school art program. These difficulties can be overcome by carving soap, dry clay, plaster of Paris, or wax, with dull knives, spoons, paper clips, nails, sticks, or tongue depressors.

Plaster of Paris is prepared by sifting plaster through the fingers into a can containing water until islands appear at the surface. Stir and pour into a form such as a milk carton or paper box. When set, tear off the form and carve. Wax is prepared by melting old crayons in a double boiler and pouring into a cardboard form until hardened.

A bar of soap may be carved with a knife, nail, or orangestick. Pieces can be joined together with tooth picks or by using soap partially melted in hot water. Completed work is allowed to set for a few days and, if desired, painted or polished by rubbing with a paper napkin.

Casting

In casting, the shape is determined by the mold. Sand casting is easiest for children and least expensive. Designs are drawn in wet sand in a box or at the beach, and objects inserted if desired. Plaster of Paris is poured over the design. When set, the cast is removed, providing a mirror image containing the inserted objects. Plaster of Paris can be mixed with other materials, such as sawdust or crayon scrapings. Carved or cast objects can be decorated by painting or by attaching other materials, as in a mosaic.

Construction

Construction is a three-dimensional arrangement of materials, usually abstract or symbolic. Its value for children lies in the opportunity it presents for developing sensitivity to form, color, and texture of materials and for discovering novel uses for ordinary objects.

Discarded objects, such as the following, can be used in construction:

Disposable plates, cups, pans of foil or paper.
Boxes, cartons, and other containers.
Cloth, buttons, thread, spools, string, rope.
Cardboard, cellophane, newspaper, magazines.
Coat hangers, wire, nails.
Corks, shells, rocks, many nature forms.
Wood, mirror, linoleum.

Materials for altering the shapes of materials, such as tin snips, saws, and scissors, and material for joining materials, such as glue, wire, string, tacks, staples, and tape,

Figure 221. *This boy is in a world of his own, oblivious of his surroundings. He is constructing his version of the University of California, Berkeley campus, with variously shaped pieces of wood and is gluing them in place as he thinks they ought to be. Figure 222 shows the result of his work.[19] Boy, age 4.*

Figure 222. *Construction—the University of California, Berkeley campus with the Campanile.[19] Boy, age four, made in school, 1964.*

must be provided. Materials for finishing surfaces, such as sandpaper and paint, should be available for children who wish to use them.

Construction activities are appropriate at all grade levels.

Mobiles

Mobiles, moving forms in space first created in the 1930's, are fascinating to children and adults alike. Mobiles offer the rewards of construction and the added challenge of achieving physical balance and graceful motion.

Mobiles may be supported on dowels, tree branches, coat hangers, cardboard, or any other lightweight, rigid material. Ob-

jects may be suspended on thin wire, string, or nylon. Discards, nature forms, materials from the school supply room can be suspended as they are found or altered by cutting, tearing, sawing, molding, bending, and the like to the desired shape.

Although children of all ages enjoy mobiles, the problem of balancing mobiles is a difficult one for younger children. Therefore, this activity is better suited to children at about grade six.

Paper sculpture

Paper sculpture is the transformation of flat sheets of paper into three-dimensional forms. It can be used decoratively alone or combined with other media. The process is fascinating to children. However, the teacher must guard against the tendency to treat paper sculpture techniques too mechanically. It is wise to teach the basic techniques and to demonstrate their use in one or two projects, encouraging children to be inventive in applying the basic techniques in working out their own idea.

Paper sculpture may be made of a variety of types of paper, suiting the paper to the desired technique and purpose. It is challenging to find ways to achieve the desired shape without fastening, but it is usually easier to use paste, glue, staples, string, or thread.

The basic techniques are as follows:

Folding, cutting if necessary.

Rolling or curling by pulling paper across the edge of a ruler or wrapping paper around a pencil.

Scoring by drawing a straight or curving line with the edge of a scissors or with the finger nail and folding along the line.

Altering an edge by folding, rolling, scalloping.

Pleating.

Slitting to hold two surfaces together.

Paper sculpture is especially suited to abstract sculpture, mobiles, masks, murals, flowers, place cards, and greeting cards.

Ceramic sculpture and pottery

Clay, one of the oldest art materials, was used in the utensils of primitive man and is used today in rockets that explore space. Although children at any age can fashion objects of clay, the teacher must be aware of the properties of firing clay and the procedures the medium demands.

The first step in the process is to provide suitable clay. It is best to order prepared clay, which comes moist in white, buff, or red, packaged in plastic bags. Most clay is sold "pre-wedged." If the available clay is not "pre-wedged," knead the clay or cut it apart and press it together to make it homogeneous. The clay must also be of the proper consistency. If it sticks to the fingers, roll it over newspaper or other absorbent surfaces to dry. If it cracks when bent, work water into it. For work that will

Figure 223. *A three-dimensional set-up, fashioning people and objects and carrying out a space-arrangement, is suitable for younger children and interesting to them because of the techniques they must consider.*[43]

not be fired, add wheat paste to reduce the brittleness of the finished product.

The clay may be worked into the desired shape by a variety of methods. In the pinch, or primitive method, suitable for all grades, clay is rolled into a ball and then worked into the desired shape from the single piece of clay. This method is suitable for modeling animals and other figures and for making utensils.

Clay may be worked by the coil method in grades five and above. The clay is flattened out with the hand or rolled with a rolling pin or cut with a knife or wire. To make a container, a circle of clay is cut with a popsicle stick or other implement to form the base. "Snakes" of clay are rolled and coiled to form the walls of the container. Surfaces to be joined are "scored" by roughening the surface with a stick, and then "welded" by moistening with water or with "slip", a mixture of water and clay, and pressing parts together. Coils may be used in making pottery or modeling figures.

A slab of clay may be used in place of a coil. The shape may be rounded or angular. A paper pattern may be made as a guide to cutting the slab.

The above methods may be combined.

Clay may be molded to reproduce the shape of another object. For example, it may be pressed over the surfaces of a cottage cheese container to make a container of similar proportions.

Texture or design may be added by rubbing, incising, or stamping wet clay pieces with tools or appropriate everyday objects.

After pieces are shaped they are set aside to dry. Slow, even drying reduces the likelihood of cracking. If possible, place pieces in a fairly air-tight cupboard covered with a damp cloth or under an empty inverted tin can. When dry the clay will be "leather hard." If dried for a longer period it will be "bone dry" and very brittle. Pieces may be left in these states as "greenware." If desired, "leather hard" pieces may be smoothed with sandpaper or with sponge and water, and, if desired, may be finished in any of the following ways used alone or in combination:

Incise texture or design.

Apply underglaze and fire pieces that will hold water.

Paint on colored slip, "engobe."

Scratch a pattern through the engobe, "sgraffito."

Cut-out areas.

"Bone dry" pieces may be left as is, painted with tempera, rubbed with shoe polish or wax, sprayed with clear lacquer, or painted with starch or shellac. Engobe can be applied to the moistened surface. If a kiln is available pieces may be fired once, glazed, and then fired again.

When the kiln is loaded, the first firing pieces can touch unless they have been painted with engobe. Gradual heating and cooling is essential. Pyrometric cones that melt at certain temperatures or trip-off switches help control the firing process. The "bisque" or "biscuit" ware that comes out of the first firing may be glazed if desired.

There are a wide variety of glazes producing a variety of effects, transparent or opaque, single or multi-colored, mat or shiny. Engobe always fires dull. The glaze selected should be suited to the kind of clay used. (Dealers will gladly provide the necessary information.) Because the characteristics of fired glazes are not evident before firing, it is a good idea to hang samples of fired glaze on the containers of glaze.

Glaze may be applied by painting on about three coats with a soft brush, or by pouring glaze into and out of a clay container, or by dipping pieces into the glaze. Do not glaze the under-side. Ceramic crayon may be used to draw on clay pieces.

In the second firing, called, "glost" or "glaze" firing, pieces are placed on special ceramic stilts and arranged so that no piece touches another.

Fired clay results in functional or decorative products that can be used in the school or presented to parents or others as gifts. The firing process, however, takes time and is more expensive than other art activities. Furthermore, it can be carried out in a mechanical fashion. But though it does not demand creativity, children can and should be encouraged to creative effort in this activity. The teacher should emphasize the points in the process that offer opportunity for inventiveness and individuality and should urge the children to discover novel and appropriate ways to use modeling, drawing, painting, and stamping in expressing their own ideas through the medium of clay.

224. *Clay figures, painted. Made in school. Age six.*[50]

SOURCES OF ADDITIONAL INFORMATION

BOOKS

Clay

Duncan, Hamlin J., and Victor D'Amico, *How to Make Pottery and Ceramic Sculpture.* New York: The Museum of Modern Art, 1949.

Petrie, Maria, *Modeling.* Peoria, Ill.: Chas. A. Bennett Co., Inc., 1955.

Sanders, Herbert H., *Sunset Ceramics Book.* Menlo Park, Calif.: Lane Publishing Co., 1953.

Snead, Jane, *Potter's Primer.* Jenkintown, Pa.: J. Snead, 1950.

Tyler, Keith, *Pottery Without a Wheel.* London: Dryad Press, 1955.

Crayon

Boylston, Elise Reid, *Creative Expression with Crayons.* Worcester, Mass.: Davis Publications, Inc., 1954.

Cut Paper and Collage

Becker, Edith C., *Adventures with Scissors and Paper.* Scranton, Pa.: International Textbook Co., 1959.

Cox, Christabel, *Cut Paper Work.* Peoria, Ill.: Chas. A. Bennett Co., Inc., 1951.

Lord, Lois, *College and Construction.* Worcester, Mass.: Davis Publications, Inc., 1958.

Drawing

Hull, Joseph W., *Perspective Drawing.* Berke-

ley: University of California Press, 1955.

Nicolaides, Kimon, *The Natural Way to Draw.* Boston: Houghton Mifflin Co., 1941.

Ink

George, Ross F., *Speedball Textbook for Pen and Brush Lettering.* Camden, N.J.: Hunt Pen Co., 1960.

Pitz, Henry C., *Ink Drawing Techniques.* New York: Watson-Guptill Publications, Inc., 1957.

Mobiles

Calder, Alexander, *Mobiles.* New York: The Museum of Modern Art, 1950.

Lynch, John, *How to Make Mobiles.* New York: Studio Publications, Inc., 1953.

Lynch, John, *Mobile Design.* New York: Studio-Crowell, 1955.

Modeling Materials

Foley, Doris E., *Art Recipes.* Dansville, N.Y.: F. A. Owen Publishing Co., 1960.

Mosaic

Argiro, Larry, *Mosaic Art Today.* Scranton, Pa.: International Textbook Co., 1961.

Jenkins, Louisa, and Barbara Mills, *The Art of Making Mosaics.* Princeton, New Jersey: D. Van Nostrand Co., Inc., 1957.

Painting

Kellogg, Rhoda. *The How of Successful Finger Painting.* San Francisco: Fearon Publishers, Inc., 1958.

Kent, Norman, ed., *Watercolor Methods.* New York: Watson-Guptill Publications, Inc., 1955.

Miller, Ray. *The Secret of Finger Painting.* Riverside, Calif.: Bruce Miller, 1961.

Paper Sculpture

Johnston, Mary Grace, *Paper Shapes and Sculpture for School Use.* Worcester, Mass.: Davis Publications, Inc., 1958.

Johnson, Pauline, *Creating with Paper.* Seattle: University of Washington Press, 1958.

Lipski, Tadeusz, *Paper Sculpture.* New York: The Studio, 1954.

Miller, Josephine V., *Paper Sculpture and Construction.* Peoria, Ill.: Chas. A. Bennett Co., Inc., 1957.

Pauli, Anna E., *Paper Figures.* Peoria, Ill.: Chas. A. Bennett Co., Inc., 1957.

Rottger, Ernst, *Creative Paper Design.* New York: Reinhold Publishing Corp., 1959.

Sadler, Arthur, *Paper Sculpture.* New York: Pitman Publishing Corp., 1955.

Shelley, William J., *Simplified Paper Sculpture in the Classroom.* San Francisco: Fearon Publishers, Inc., 1957.

Papier-maché

Betts, Victoria, *Exploring Papier Maché.* Worcester, Mass.: Davis Publications, Inc., 1955.

Johnson, Lillian, *Papier-maché.* New York: David McKay Co., Inc., 1958.

Pencil

Watson, Ernest W., *Gallery of Pencil Techniques.* New York: Reinhold Publishing Corp., 1958.

Print Making

Baranski, Matthew, *Graphic Design.* Scranton, Pa.: International Textbook Co., 1960.

Carlsen, Darvey E., *Graphic Arts.* Peoria, Ill.: Chas. A. Bennett Co., Inc., 1958.

Eisenberg, James, *Silk Screen Printing.* Bloomington: McKnight & McKnight Publishing Co., 1952.

Lewis, Odele, *The Print—An Original Art Form for All.* New York: Odele Lewis, 1959.

Sculpture

Lord, Lois, *Collage and Construction.* Worcester, Mass.: Davis Publications Inc., 1958.

Reed, Carl, and Joseph Orze, *Art from Scrap.* Worcester, Mass.: Davis Publications Inc., 1960.

Rottger, Ernest, *Creative Wood Design.* New York: Reinhold Publishing Corp., 1961.

Stitchery

Krasz, Mariska, *Adventures with Stitches.* New York: Funk & Wagnalls Co., Inc., 1959.

Books for Children

Hawkinson, John, *Collect, Print, and Paint from Nature.* Chicago: Albert Whitman and Co., 1963.

Leeming, Joseph, *Fun with Wire.* Philadelphia: J. B. Lippincott Co., 1956.

Ota, Koshi, *et al.*, *Printing for Fun.* New York: McDowell, Obolensky, 1960.

FILMS FOR THE CLASSROOM

Clay

Let's Play with Clay: Part I, Animals, Part II, Bowls. Young America Films, Inc.

Peter and the Potter. Canadian National Film Board.

Crayons

Crayon Resist. Bailey Films

Painting

Let's Paint with Water Color. Coronet Instructional Films

Papier-maché

Animules. International Film Bureau

Sculpture

Sculpturing is Fun. United World Films

FILMSTRIPS FOR THE CLASSROOM

It's Fun to Combine Art Materials. Society for Visual Education, Inc.

Clay

Art in Our Classroom: We Work with Clay. Encyclopaedia Britannica Films, Inc.
We Like Clay. Society for Visual Education, Inc.

Crayons

Sketching with Crayons. Young America Films, Inc.

There is Magic in Wax Crayon. Society for Visual Education, Inc.
Working with Wax Crayons. Encyclopaedia Britannica Films, Inc.

Cut Paper, Collage, Paper Sculpture

Art in Our Classroom: We Work with Paper & Scissors. Encyclopaedia Britannica Films, Inc.
Cutting and Pasting. Young America Films, Inc.
Working with Paper. Encyclopaedia Britannica Films, Inc.

Painting

Let's Paint. Society for Visual Education, Inc.
Painting with Water Color. Young America Films, Inc.

Papier-maché

Art in Our Classroom: We Work with Papier-mache. Encyclopaedia Britannica Films, Inc.

Print Making

Art in Our Classroom: We Print Designs and Pictures. Encyclopaedia Britannica Films, Inc.
Potato Printing. Young America Films, Inc.

Stitchery

Art in Our Classroom: We Make Designs with Needle and Thread. Encyclopaedia Britannica Films, Inc.

CHAPTER ELEVEN

Helping Children to Enjoy Works of Art

Enjoyment of art begins with the infant's delight in the world of form and color. In its most fully developed form, it is the love of beauty, a capacity to be moved by works of art, an intelligent discrimination of their diverse qualities, and a sensitivity to aesthetic values.

Neither children nor adults learn to appreciate art by being stood in front of a painting in a museum and being told to admire it because it is a great work. A genuine appreciation of art is built on the more general capacity to perceive and enjoy what is visually interesting and satisfying in the world around us—both in nature and in man-made objects and surroundings. The materials useful in developing the capacity to enjoy art are thus not hard to come by. They may be found in the classroom and in the street as well as in the museum. We can nurture the aesthetic sensibility of children by helping them to become aware of form, color and texture, of proportions, of harmonies and interesting disharmonies in a variety of objects and settings.

Teachers with an eye for design can easily find things in nature for children to look at, to touch, and sometimes to hear, smell, or

225

taste. They can point out the design in the veins of a leaf, the scales of a fish, or the magnified wing of a fly. Objects of everyday use which have interesting forms or texture can be brought to class, shown, and discussed.

Younger children can observe the simple, regular patterns around them—pyramids of fruit in the market; furrows in a ploughed field; railroad ties stretching into the distance; TV antennae outlined against the sky. Older children can be shown the more subtle and complex patterns in nature—crystal and rock formations, for example, and the constellation of the stars.

The enjoyment of art is based on the cultivation of the senses. The infant apprehends his world through all of his senses. It is not enough for him to look at an object. He must grasp it, shake it, put it in his mouth. As the child grows up, his eyes and ears become the sensitive receptors of symbolized meaning, through the written and spoken word. Direct sense experience becomes less important in understanding the world. The teacher can give children the opportunity to cultivate their sensory perception by providing them with a whole range of stimulating natural and man-made products from aromatic spices and textured materials to different sounds and music.

There are abundant opportunities for helping children become sensitive to the natural world. A single class experience can lead to many subsequent activities. For example, the class can take a field trip to a park, beach, or even an empty lot to collect natural materials, which can be displayed in various ways or used in the following activities:

Arranging a collection of shells, rocks, weathered wood.

Decorating the cover of a booklet with nature objects.

Using natural clay for modeling, making ceramics.

Using seeds or other natural materials in mosaics, collages, mobiles.

Comparing form in nature with form in drawings, paintings, sculpture.

Arranging seasonal or holiday displays.

Making masks of leaves, bark.

Adding sand, leaves, sawdust to wheat paste to use as modeling material.

Using natural materials in dioramas—adobe, soil, branches, etc.

Using leaves and vegetables in printing or stenciling.

Making wood cuts.

Making puppets of nature objects.

Weaving twigs and branches with string or bark.

USING CHILDREN'S INTERESTS

The art interests and tastes children have already acquired provide a starting point for further development. Because taste evolves through learning and development, it is to be expected that children will not show the preferences of cultivated adults. Even within a class, individual differences in responding to art may be great. Some children may seem more sensitive to beauty than others. Some may have been introduced to the world of art by parents or others outside the school. The emotional component of the response to art is likely to be seen in the intensity of reaction as well as in the kind of experience that evokes it. But despite factors that make for differences, guidelines are useful in selecting styles and content of pictures for children.

Art forms and content that excite the imagination and nourish fantasy—pageants, processions, plays, films and the dance—have an immediate appeal for children. Their imagination is also set in motion by realistic pictures that touch their lives in some way. Younger children are delighted with pictures of animals, fairy tale costumes, and other things they like and admire. Natural scenery that echoes the settings of play—a swimming hole on a river, a mysterious forest to be explored, a cave in a hillside, all become imaginary playgrounds. Family pictures are often favorites, perhaps because they satisfy the child's yearning for love and security. Younger children, especially, enjoy abstract and geometric patterns onto which they project meanings very unlike those an adult might see.

Young children often react in a way which suggests that they do not make as sharp a distinction as adults do between a picture of something and the thing itself. It is almost as though the picture frame is a window through which the child looks; if he likes what he sees, he likes the picture. If what he sees does not interest him, he is bored. One six-year-old in a study of subject matter preference looked at a large number of paintings and said, "I don't like any of them, there is not even one airplane."

Older children, like younger ones, prefer pictures whose content relates to their interests in some way. In the later elementary school years, they expand their range of interest and speculate about the character and values of the people represented in the pictures they see. Their interpretation of what is in the picture will reflect hero worship on the one hand or condemnation on the other. But although these older children are still mainly responding to the content of pictures, they are more able at this stage to deal with aesthetic values.

As children grow older, they become more interested in technique and can de-velop some understanding of how the artist has dealt with design and color. Whereas younger children love strong, gay, diverse, and penetrating colors both for their own pictures and in the works of others, older children often show a taste for monochromatic schemes, and girls especially prefer delicate and subtle colors.

By building on existing interests, as suggested throughout this book, the teacher can help the child to expand his interests and refine his taste.

LEARNING ABOUT ART

Information about an artist's life and about the historical and cultural setting in which he worked can add dimension to his works. It can help children to understand the mode of life, the cultural and artistic traditions, the dominant ideas and values which influenced the artist. And, conversely, it can throw into relief the unique contribution he made, pointing up the qualities which distinguished him from other artists of his time.

Biographical material should present the artist as a human being. Idolizing him makes him unreal, uninteresting, and remote. The obstacles and prejudices artists struggle against, their exultation and despair, and their ultimate recognition, coming to many only after death, can help children to understand the quality of those who have been willing to sacrifice happiness in the conventional sense to satisfy their passion to create.

Under no circumstances, however, should the teacher substitute the acquisition of knowledge *about* a work of art for direct aesthetic response to the work itself. Only vision can discern whatever makes a work of art great. The ultimate emphasis must always be on heightening perception of the qualities that give a work artistic merit.

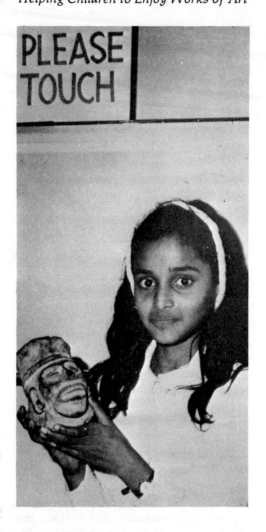

Figure 226. *PLEASE TOUCH. The young child is careful, yet very pleased to be able to "feel" the texture and weight of the mask. It is important that children be permitted to handle beautiful things, either set apart in museums for this purpose or, as the Cleveland Museum of Art tried it in the thirties, to assemble "traveling" exhibits of "touchable" objects to be sent to schools.*[43]

The study of other cultures in social studies presents excellent opportunity for becoming familiar with both the fine art and the folk art of other peoples. Children can learn that art is part of every culture and serves various cultures in many ways. In some, art is invested with magic powers, as in Navaho sand painting. In others, art is used to communicate, as in Egyptian hieroglyphics, or to decorate, as in our own textile designs. Such an approach deepens understanding both of other cultures and of the diverse functions of art.

Objects of everyday life of the past and present help children to understand the influence of use on shape. For example, they can compare the shape of baskets made by California Indians to serve different purposes, such as storing, cooking, and winnowing. They can help develop an understanding of the suitability of various textures for certain uses, and the inventiveness with which man appropriates whatever nature provides, modifying a variety of natural materials for his own use. Decoration used for different objects and by different cultures can be compared. Children can learn that decoration may serve symbolic, aesthetic, or utilitarian purposes.

The architecture of various places and periods can be approached in a similar way, attention being given to the influence of available resources, the level of technology, the function of the building, and the taste of the times.

Art work in different media can be compared with discussion centering on the appropriateness of particular media for expressing the artist's ideas and feelings. Realistic, abstract, and fantastic art can be contrasted. Children can be helped to see ways in which many pictures have elements of all three. Paintings of easily recognizable subject matter may contain abstract elements. Abstractions may use reality as a point of departure. Fantastic scenes may be composed of objects drawn with great accuracy.

Many museums have special educational

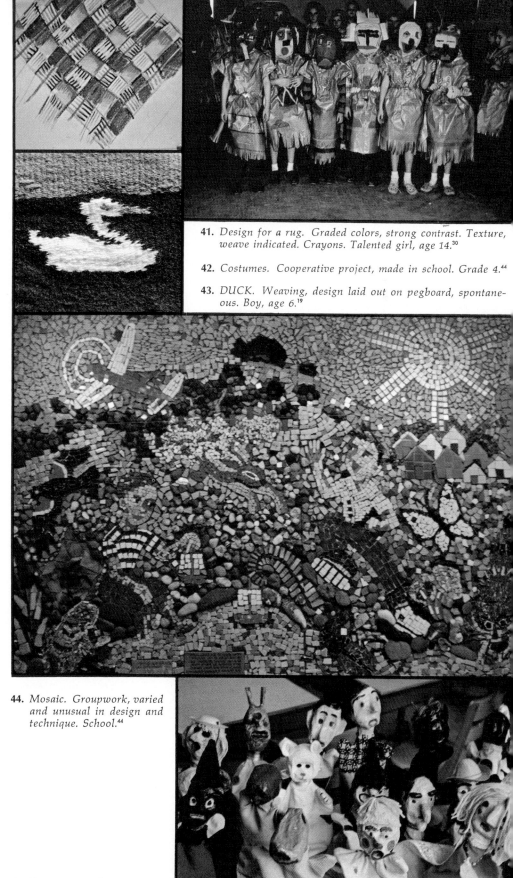

41. *Design for a rug. Graded colors, strong contrast. Texture, weave indicated. Crayons. Talented girl, age 14.*[30]

42. *Costumes. Cooperative project, made in school. Grade 4.*[44]

43. *DUCK. Weaving, design laid out on pegboard, spontaneous. Boy, age 6.*[19]

44. *Mosaic. Groupwork, varied and unusual in design and technique. School.*[44]

45. *Puppets. Made in school. Grade 6.*[44]

46. *Korean, age 6.*[47]

47. *Russian, age 6.*[46]

48. *Hawaiian, age 8.*[47]

49. *Indian, no age given.*[47]

51. *Japanese, ag*

50. *Israeli, age 10.*[47]

programs for children. These programs may include guided tours through special exhibits, films, or other materials to be used in the classroom to help develop enjoyment of art in general or to prepare children to visit a particular exhibit at the museum. Museums often offer classes for children on Saturday. If there is a museum nearby, the teacher should find out how to make the best use of its facilities.

TEACHING ABOUT ART ELEMENTS

Teachers often wonder whether it is worthwhile to teach "art principles" to the class. By "art principles" they mean the generalizations of aestheticians and art critics about relationships that are considered beautiful. To answer this question one must raise a second question, "Will the teaching result in a deeper appreciation of works of art and more beautiful original work?" In most cases "principles" will either fail to "take" with children, or they will operate as rules that restrict the children's freedom. If knowledge of principles were the essential quality needed to produce great art, aestheticians would be the artists. Artists do not create by rules. It is only after they have finished their works that keen observers note how traditional principles have been honored or violated. The merit of the work does not depend either upon respect for rules or upon a willingness to ignore them.

Children have their own sense of balance and rhythm. Young children in particular have a strong disposition toward bilateral symmetry, to the degree that prompts some to put two suns in a picture, although they know very well that there is only one sun in nature (see Figure 89). The principles deduced from adult art are not necessary to

help a child organize all elements into a coherent pattern. He seems to do this intuitively in a characteristically child-like way. Principles rooted in the child's own visual outlook are likely to provide a strong basis for judging both his own work and that of others.

Children's natural enjoyment of color is enhanced by familiarity with some of the properties and effects of color. Children can discuss the way in which different colors make them feel. They can note ways in which man uses color in the home, in apparel, in packaging, and in paintings. They can learn how color protects living creatures from their enemies, why most growing things are green, and why the sky and ocean appear blue.

Older children can study color and light. They can observe how white light is broken up by a prism into the colors of the spectrum. They can compare the effect of a prism to that of rain in producing a rainbow. They can learn why the sky seems to change color at sunset.

Older children are especially interested in mixing colors. They can experiment with mixing color produced by light and color produced by pigment. The primary colors using light are magenta, blue-green, and green. The primary colors using the familiar pigment are red, yellow, and blue. The secondary colors can be mixed from primary colors. With pigment, red and blue produce purple, blue and yellow produce green, yellow and red produce orange, and all three primary colors combined produce brown. A color or hue can be dulled by adding black to produce a tone, or by mixing it with some of its complement, red and green, blue and orange, purple and yellow. Pastel colors are produced by adding white.

Children can observe the use of color to achieve desired effects in paintings. They can observe how colors affect one another, how the same color appears different against different backgrounds. They can compare the palettes of different artists, noting the preference of some for brilliant, contrasting colors, of others for soft, subtle, blending colors, and the seemingly infinite range of possibilities in color relationship.

The references listed provide source material to help the teacher learn more about art and to help her in guiding her pupils.

225. *CRAYONS RESIST FINGERPAINTING.*
Teamwork, crayons and fingerpaints. Made in school. Boys (two), age eight.[50]

SUPPLEMENTARY READING

General Works

Arnheim, Rudolph, *Art and Visual Perception*. Berkeley: University of California Press, 1960.

Barr, Alfred H., *What is Modern Painting?* New York: The Museum of Modern Art, 1956.

Freedman, Leonard, *Looking at Modern Painting*. Los Angeles: The Regents of the University of California, 1957.

Flexarer, James Thomas, *American Painting*. New York: Pocket Books, Inc., 1950.

Gardner, Helen, *Art Through the Ages*. New York: Harcourt, Brace & World, Inc., 1958.

Kepes, Gyorgy, *Language of Vision*. Chicago: Paul Theobald, 1945.

Kuh, Katherine, *Art Has Many Faces*. New York: Harper & Row, Publishers, 1951.

Langer, Susanne K., *Problems of Art*. New York: Charles Scribner's Sons, 1957.

Linderman, Earl W., and Donald W. Horberholz, *Developing Artistic and Perceptual Awareness*. Dubuque, Iowa: William C. Brown Company, Publishers, 1964.

Moholy-Nagy, Laszlo, *The New Vision*. New York: George Wittenborn Inc., 1947.

Read, Herbert, *Art and Industry*. New York: Horizon Press, 1954.

Shahn, Ben, *The Shape of Content*. Cambridge, Mass.: Harvard University Press, 1957.

Books on Color

Healy, Frederick, *Light and Color*. New York: The John Day Company, Inc., 1962.

Itten, Johannes, *The Art of Color*. New York: Reinhold Publishing Corp., 1961.

Books on Design

Emerson, Sybil, *Design: A Creative Approach*. Scranton, Pa.: International Textbook Co., 1953.

Fry, Roger, *Vision and Design*. New York: The World Publishing Co., 1956.

Books for Children

Berry, Anna M., *Art for Children*. New York: Studio Publications, 1952.

Borten, Helen, *A Picture has a Special Look*. New York: Abelard-Schuman Ltd., 1961.

Chase, Alice Elizabeth, *Famous Paintings: An Introduction to Art for Young People*. New York: Platt & Munk, Inc., 1951.

Faulkner, Ray, Edwin Ziegfeld, and Gerald Hill, *Art Today*. New York: Holt, Rinehart & Winston, Inc., 1949.

Farnum, Royal Bailey, *Learning More About Pictures*. Westport, Conn.: Artext Prints, 1957.

Gibson, Katherine, *Pictures to Grow Up With*. New York: American-Studio Books, 1946.

Hillyer, Virgil, and E. G. Huey, *A Child's History of Art*. New York: Appleton-Century Crofts, 1951.

Holme, Bryan, *Pictures to Live With*. New York: The Viking Press, Inc., 1959.

Janson, Horst W., and Dora Janson, *The Story of Art for Young People*. New York: Harry N. Abrams, Inc., 1952.

McKinney, Roland J., *Famous American Painters*. Binghamton, New York: Vail-Ballow Press, 1955.

Ripley, Elizabeth, *Durer*. New York: Oxford University Press, 1958.

——, *Goya*. New York: Oxford University Press, 1956.

——, *Leonardo Da Vinci*. New York: Oxford University Press, 1952.

——, *Picasso*. New York: Oxford University Press, 1959.

——, *Rembrandt*. New York: Oxford University Press, 1955.

——, *Rubens*. New York: Oxford University Press, 1957.

Children's Books about Color

Adler, Irving, *Color in Your Life*. New York: The John Day Company, Inc., 1962.

Daly, Kathleen N., *Colors*. New York: Golden Press, Inc., 1959.

Lionni, Leo, *Little Blue and Yellow*. New York: Ivan Obolensky, Inc., 1959.

Neal, Charles D., *Exploring Light and Color*. Chicago: Children's Press, Inc., 1964.

Periodicals

Architectural Forum. 9 Rockefeller Plaza, New York 20, New York.

Art in America. 635 Madison Ave., New York 22, New York.

Art News. Art News, 32 E. 57th St., New York 22, New York.

Artist Junior. New Haven 11, Conn.

Life Magazine. Time-Life, Inc., Rockefeller Plaza, New York 20, New York.

Teaching Aids

The Metropolitan Museum of Art. *Twelve Portfolios on the Appreciation of Art*, and *Twelve Portfolios on the History of Art*. New York: The Book-of-the-Month Club.

The Museum of Modern Art. *Modern Art Old and New: Teaching Portfolio* No. 3, ed. Rene d'Harnoncourt. New York: The Museum of Modern Art, 1950.

The Museum of Modern Art. *Modern Sculpture: Teaching Portfolio* No. 1, ed. E. C. Osborn. New York: The Museum of Modern Art, 1947.

The Museum of Modern Art. *Texture and Pattern: Teaching Portfolio* No. 2, ed. E. C. Osborn. New York: The Museum of Modern Art, 1949.

The Museum of Modern Art. *Useful Objects Today: Teaching Portfolio* No. 4, ed. Greta Daniel, New York: The Museum of Modern Art, 1955.

Sources of Slides

American Library Color Slide Co., Inc. 222 West 23rd St., New York 11, New York.

Art Council Aids. Box 641, Beverly Hills, California.

Dr. Block Color Productions. 1309 N. Genesee Ave., Hollywood 46, Calif.

Contemporary Slides. 243 East 17th St., New York 3, New York.

Dr. Konrad Prothmann. 2378 Soper Ave., Baldwin, Long Island, New York.

McGraw-Hill Book Co. *The Color Slide Books of the World's Art*. New York, 1963.

The National Gallery of Art. *Survey of American Painting*. Washington, D.C.

Sources of Art Reproductions

Artext Prints, Inc. Westport, Conn.

Dr. Konrad Prothmann. 7 Soper Ave., Baldwin, Long Island, New York.

The Museum of Modern Art. New York.

The National Gallery of Art. Washington, D.C.

CHAPTER TWELVE

Relating Art to Other Areas of the Curriculum

Every area in the curriculum offers opportunity to apply what is gained in art. Visual materials handled with artistry invite the child to look and learn. Aesthetic values can always enhance and need never conflict with the goals of other curricular areas.

All too often, however, teachers seem to forget principles of good teaching of art once the art period is over. Despite the admonitions of art educators, it is not at all difficult to find classrooms in which children are required to color-in stereotyped work-book figures in the hope that work in reading or arithmetic will benefit thereby. One need not go far to find a classroom displaying thirty identical pictures. How many teachers use the art period to make party decorations after a pattern! None of this is necessary. Art can be related to other areas of the curriculum in a manner that serves both.

A good place to begin is in the arrangement of the classroom. Each classroom tells a great deal about the adult and children who use it and about the work they do. It reflects the age of the children and the

233

things that interest them. The classroom is above all a workroom. Materials and equipment must be placed so that they are easily accessible. Traffic lanes must be unobstructed. Learning materials should be placed at eye-level. A cheerful room provides a pleasant place to work. A stark or an overly-decorated room fails to contribute to the learning process. Attractive displays stimulate curiosity. The children's work tells the visitor much about the class and rewards pupils for their effort. A coordinated color scheme carried throughout the room lends a sense of unity to the array of materials displayed.

Below are practical suggestions for using art in many different learning situations. They are intended to serve as a point of departure from which teachers can develop their own ideas, relying on their own creative imagination and that of their pupils.

ART IN THE ROOM ENVIRONMENT

Bulletin Boards

Well-chosen, effectively displayed materials on bulletin boards are visually and intellectually stimulating. It is a good idea to have some materials displayed on the first day of school and to allow open space for new displays as learning progresses.

Upper grade children who have had the experience of helping the teacher set-up bulletin boards and have participated in planning educational displays are ready to take over the main responsibility for them, under the guidance of their teacher. The teacher can help them to decide on a theme or purpose for the display. She can guide them in selecting material related to it and in discarding what is unsuitable. She can show them how to write concise, legible captions, achieve symmetric or asymmetric balance, color harmony, and a sense of unity, and she can help evaluate the completed

display, making adjustments if necessary.

Materials for the bulletin board are drawn from all areas of the curriculum. They may include samples of children's work; charts that inform, remind, direct, record, or test; clippings from newspapers and magazines; a calendar and listing of special dates; collections of photographs, posters, and other materials related to a topic that is being studied. Materials for display may be obtained from audio-visual departments of the school district, libraries, local residents, and commercial concerns, as well as from the children themselves. Visual unity is achieved by mounting unlike shapes on the same size mats and placing more than one item on a mat. Lettering and arrows help tie the parts together. A good way of achieving balance is to place larger and heavier looking elements on the lower half of the board with a larger margin at the bottom.

Modern classrooms have adequate display space. In older classrooms additional space may be gained by stretching corrugated paper, cloth, or wrapping paper over walls; using free standing screens; using masonite, chip board, or flannel boards suspended, mounted or standing; or by hanging wires along the walls from which materials may be suspended.

Select a method of attaching materials that will not mar the materials or damage the non-expendable backgrounds on which they are mounted. Masking tape, doubled over out of sight on the reverse side of display materials, seldom mars wood or painted surfaces. Cellophane tape is not as safe. Sandpaper attached to the back of light-weight materials holds them to flannel surface. Magnets will hold materials against certain metals. Materials can also be held in place with paste, glue, pins, tacks, staples, wall hangers, screw eyes, wire, thread, or string.

Any of the materials and techniques listed previously may be used in mounting.

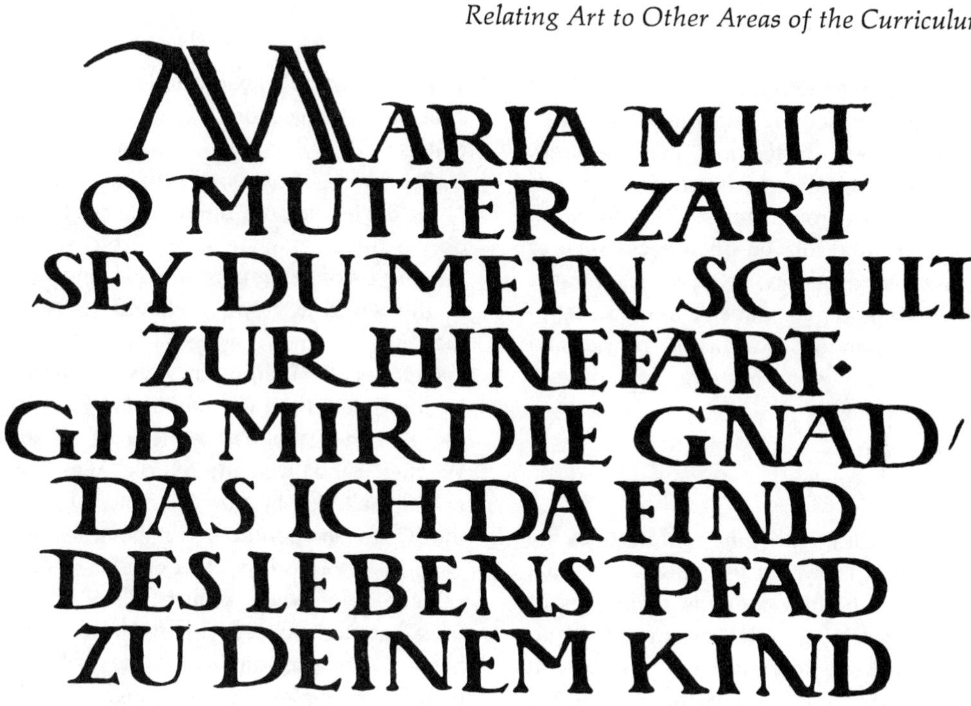

MARIA MILT
O MUTTER ZART
SEY DU MEIN SCHILT
ZUR HINEFART·
GIB MIR DIE GNAD/
DAS ICH DA FIND
DES LEBENS PFAD
ZU DEINEM KIND

Figure 227. *Lettering can be a thing of beauty. It can have the effect of an abstract picture or an intriguing ornamental work of art.*[18]

Bulletin boards can be planned and set up more efficiently if trial lay-out sketches are drawn to scale, using graph paper if desired. The lay-out sketch projected by an opaque projector to the proper size on the bulletin board assures proper positioning. For ease in achieving level arrangements, establish points and lines by use of a yardstick, string, pins, or tape.

Lettering

Although letters are used primarily as a means of communication, the art of lettering, known as calligraphy, is highly developed in Asian countries and practiced in Western countries as well. Lettering on bulletin boards, charts, posters, and the like should enhance the display. Lettering can be done with any of the media described in the preceding chapter. Paper or cardboard letter sets have the advantage of permitting experimentation in spacing. Although letters can be drawn and cut out in

the classroom the process is time consuming and tedious if done with care. Many teachers prefer to purchase sets of ready-made letters, using them directly and as stencils for additional sets of letters.

Mats and Frames

Mats and frames enhance the appearance of two-dimensional materials displayed in groups or individually. In selecting the color for the mat consider the color scheme both of the room and of the item to be mounted. Center items on the mat, or leave a larger margin at the bottom and equal margins on the other sides.

Mats may be made of any kind of heavy paper or cardboard available in the school, used as is, colored evenly, or textured by methods such as stippling, finger painting, sponge printing. If mats are decorated, care must be taken to avoid attracting attention to the mat at the expense of the material matted. The simplest mats are of colored construction paper. They may be used flat or shaped by scoring and folding. Cloth—plain, printed, or textured may be used. Items may be framed with string, yarn, raffia, tape, wire, rope, and the like. Art work is effectively displayed on surfaces such as pressed cork, celotex, or plywood. A frame of wood molding is difficult to construct in the classroom, but, if available, provides an excellent way of calling attention to work of special merit.

Holiday Art

As the year goes by, the room echoes the moods and events of the season. Seasonal colors and holiday symbols remind us of nature's recurring cycles and of the significance of events in nature and in history. It is fitting that traditional symbols be used. But it is important that they not become empty stereotypes.

Each year the meaning of the holidays can be interpreted to children in a deeper way. With young children, holidays can be approached from the point of view of the child. The childhood of famous men, the child's own participation in holiday celebrations, and celebrations of holidays around the world can be reported, discussed, and illustrated. The older children can begin to deal with the more abstract concepts associated with holidays: freedom, peace on earth, gratitude for a bountiful harvest, the renewal of life.

Deeply felt events are not likely to be expressed by hasty and superficial means. It is the teacher's responsibility to help children find adequate means of translating their feelings into art. Materials that encourage a fresh and original interpretation are needed. The story and meaning of holidays can be carried out in any media, using original or traditional symbols.

The listing below is a reminder of the holidays that fall during the school year

and the symbols associated with them, along with suggestions for appropriate activities.

October 12, Columbus Day, commemorating the landing of Columbus at San Salvador in 1492, may be symbolized by the three ships of Columbus, Indians, or a map of the world as it was believed to be at that time.

October 31, Halloween, was celebrated by the Celts as the last day of the year, by the Romans as a harvest festival, as the Witches' Sabbath in the Middle Ages, and as All Hallows' Eve or All Saints' Eve in the Christian tradition. Symbols include witches, broomsticks, black cats, ghosts, spiders, spiderwebs, goblins, devils, bonfires, haunted houses, and symbols of the harvest, such as haystacks, the horn of plenty, and apples. Activities might include making and wearing masks and/or costumes, painting windows with a mixture of starch and tempera, decorating windows with colored cellophane, decorating place mats and cards for a party.

Thanksgiving, now celebrated on the fourth Thursday in November, was initiated by Governor Bradford of Plymouth Colony in 1621, though its roots may be traced to an ancient Hebrew harvest festival. Traditional symbols are: foods, such as turkeys, pumpkins, corn, horns of plenty; the hosts and guests at the first Thanksgiving, the Pilgrims and the Indians; the *Mayflower;* a Colonial fireplace; and families giving thanks together.

On December 25, Christians throughout the world celebrate the birth of Christ. Symbols are derived from the story of the nativity, the teachings of Christ, and from the ancient celebration of the winter solstice.

The art of medieval and renaissance Europe on the nativity theme and the folk art of different cultures, such as the pinata of Mexico, can be presented at the Christmas season. The well-known symbols from the story of the birth of Christ, the motif of "Peace on Earth, Goodwill to Men," the myth of Santa Claus, the winter season and its activities, plants, gaiety, and light find expression in many media.

A pinata can be made by using a light cardboard box or bag as a base and incorporating it, filled with holiday treats, into an animal or bird form made of papier mache or paper sculpture, perhaps decorated with crepe paper.

Paper sculpture angels can drift gracefully on a mobile or stand on a table.

Bells that ring can be made of tin cans or fired clay. Decorative bells can be cut out of aluminum foil.

Individual greeting cards can be made using any one of a variety of techniques. Older children will enjoy using multiprinting techniques to make cards to send to friends.

Windows can be decorated with colored cellophane for stained glass effects.

Ceramic objects can be made as gifts for parents and friends.

Tree ornaments can be made by cutting shapes out of foil and either using them two-dimensionally or shaping them by paper sculpture techniques. Discards with interesting or appropriate shapes, such as egg shells, macaroni, or tooth picks can be arranged and painted. Nature forms, such as pine cones, may be used as is or painted. Carving or modeling techniques can be used to shape ornaments out of a variety of materials.

Three-dimensional stars can be made out of paper drinking straws, dowling, tooth picks, or by modeling and casting, or carving.

During the Christmas season Jewish families celebrate Chanukah, a festival of lights, commemorating a victory for religious freedom. Like Christmas, it is a time for giving gifts to children, traditionally gleaming

coins. Holiday symbols include the menorah, a nine-branched candelabra, and the dreidl, a four-sided spinning top with a letter of the Hebrew alphabet on each side, used in a game of chance. A functional menorah can be made by shaping clay so that it holds nine small candles. Decorations in the shape of a dreidl or a six-pointed star can be made by any appropriate method described in the preceding chapter.

The birthday of Abraham Lincoln, February 12, 1809, is celebrated in many states. He is remembered for his simple humanity and compassion. His contributions to history are expressed through the Emancipation Proclamation and the Gettysburg Address. His humble origins are symbolized by a log cabin, and his days as President by a top hat.

Older children can try their hand at portraits of Lincoln. Younger children can illustrate episodes from his biography in a "movie," joining separate pictures to a large scroll made of a roll of paper attached to two wooden dowels and viewed through a "screen" cut out of the front of a box in which slots have been cut to hold the dowels.

February 14, St. Valentine's Day, heralds spring and is a day for sending messages of friendship and affection. The traditional symbols are hearts, cupids, arrows, birds, and flowers. In all grades, Valentine cards can be made using a variety of materials, including lace-cut paper, tissue paper, and colored cellophane. Older children can work in a group to decorate a box for collecting cards.

The birthday of George Washington, born in 1732, and remembered for his role as a military leader in the War of Independence and the nation's first President, is celebrated on February 22. Of the many paintings of him, the two that are best known are Gilbert Stuart's portrait and Emanuel Leutze's picture of the crossing of the Delaware. The symbols associated with him are the Liberty Bell, cherry tree, and hatchet. Illustrated biographies mounted in a booklet, on a scroll, or on a bulletin board are suitable activities.

In March or April, Christians celebrate Easter, the resurrection of Christ, and Jews celebrate Passover, the escape from bondage in Egypt. Both holidays use symbols of ancient rites of spring. The renewal of life is symbolized by the sunrise, kindling of fires, bunnies, lambs, chicks, nests, baskets of eggs or flowers. The festivity of the season is expressed in Easter bonnets and parades of people in new clothes.

Possible activities for expressing the spirit of the season might be decorating eggs, making egg trees, and making decorated baskets, possibly out of boxes, cottage cheese cartons, woven paper, folded paper.

Mother's Day, celebrated on the second Sunday in May, provides an occasion for presenting mothers with art work. Useful objects, well designed and tastefully decorated, enhance Mother's wardrobe or the family home. Objects that reflect the child's stage of development are likely to be valued for many years. Drawings with ceramic crayons on ceramic objects or colored wall hangings, perhaps ornamented with stitchery, can become mementoes of childhood highly treasured by mothers.

Memorial Day, celebrated on May 30 in northern states and in Virginia, and on other dates in the South, was instituted as a day of remembrance of Union and Confederate dead and now honors all who died for their country. Symbols are those of peace and love of country.

Each child's birthday is a special day for him. Special recognition can be given in many ways, such as a birthday calendar, a special decorated chair in which to sit, a crown to wear while he receives birthday

greetings, and the like. These can be made at the beginning of the year by a group, under the guidance of the teacher, and used throughout the year.

ART IN OTHER SUBJECT AREAS

Visual production in all areas is properly part of the art program. Concern for aesthetic values is as relevant in work that serves other instructional purposes as in work whose purpose is solely to delight the eye.

Some of the many possible applications of art in other areas are described in the pages that follow.

Booklets

Booklets are useful in preserving and sharing collections of written and illustrative material in social studies, health, science, art appreciation, and so on. Booklets can be made in a variety of ways. The simplest method is to fold a large sheet of paper in half and fasten single sheets to the back cover using wire brads or staples. Booklets can also be simply made by stacking several large sheets, folding them in half, and fastening them with a piece of yarn drawn around the fold and tied. Accordion-folded booklets are especially useful in displaying materials simultaneously, as in an illustration of the animals walking two-by-two towards Noah's ark.

The booklet cover may be paper, cardboard, masonite, or other suitable materials. It can be covered with cloth or ornamented paper, or decorated with crayon protected by shellac, crayon resist, paint, or any medium appropriate to the materials of the cover. The booklet may be held together with binder rings, tape, or other fasteners, or sewn with yarn or thread.

Dioramas

Dioramas, panoramas, and peep shows are scenes created on a small scale. They differ from one another in that dioramas have a vertical backing; panoramas are set on an open surface open to view on all sides; while peep shows are enclosed on all sides and viewed through a small opening. Dioramas can be made at grades five and above in connection with social studies, science, literature, or the study of art history. Displays of these types may strive for realism, as in the re-creation of a pioneer fort, or they may be abstract and imaginative, as in the interpretation of fantasy in a story.

Dioramas and peep shows may be contained in any suitable box, such as a shoe or hat box, or be set against a backdrop of paper, chip board, tag board, or other similar materials. The backdrop may be flat or curving. Figures and scenery in the diorama, panoramas, or peep show can be made of modeling material, such as papier mache, clay, salt and flour; paper sculpture, wire, pipe cleaners, mirror, cellophane, twigs, branches, or real objects. Plasticine makes a good base for standing figures. Parts of the display are held together by any appropriate fastener. Water color is good for suggesting sky. Any materials and art techniques may be used.

Murals

Murals, pictures or designs on walls, provide a large format through which many elements may be united around a central theme or a single idea executed in monumental proportions. Murals are usually carried out by several or all members of a class. Murals can be planned and carried out at any grade level, with guidance from the teacher as required by the maturity of the group. Groups whose age and experience enable them to work together smoothly will require considerably less direction than kindergarten class members, for whom it will probably be necessary to assign individual, specific tasks or working areas. Murals can be used in connection with social studies, literature, science, and other areas, showing, for example, the development of transportation, or favorite characters from literature.

A mural takes several days to complete. The first step is discussing the theme, size, location, materials, and techniques to be used, and individual or group responsibilities. Next, trial sketches can be made individually or in groups, a lay-out determined, the finished sketch projected with an opaque projector onto the surface, and the sketch drawn lightly with chalk. Work begins, progresses, is evaluated, adjusted, and finally completed.

The surface of a mural might be butcher paper, wrapping paper, walls, blackboard, cloth, windows, or any material of suitable size and texture. The mural may be carried out using techniques such as collage, paper sculpture, stitchery, crayon and liquid starch, tempera, finger paint, and the like.

Play Production

Play production in connection with language arts or the social studies offers opportunities for art experiences in designing and making costumes and scenery. In puppet plays, the children can make the stage and cast of characters as well.

Costumes need not be elaborate, costly, or time-consuming. An imaginative use of materials to suggest character and period can be as effective as a detailed, literal reproduction. By studying pictures of historic and folk costume, noting their most characteristic details, the essence of the manner of dress of the period and locale can be captured. An understanding of the personality of historic figures or fictional characters can be used in modifying costumes to express particular qualities, such as modesty, flamboyance, slothfulness, elegance.

Costumes may be made of inexpensive or discarded materials such as crepe paper, cheese cloth, old clothes, old sheets, scrap fabrics, boxes, paper bags. The significant details may be added by appliqué, yarn, crayon, printing, or tape. Hats may be made by paper sculpture techniques.

Scenery that enhances the mood of the play can be produced simply and inexpensively in various ways. A back drop can be painted or appliqued with discards. Flats can be made out of refrigerator packing cartons and used as a scene. Scenery can be projected from behind onto a translucent screen, a roll of architect's tracing paper, or a milky plastic sheet. Projection from the front can be used for special effects. Papier maché can be used alone, applied to armatures of wood or chicken wire, or added to old furniture, as in making a chair into a throne.

Puppets

Puppetry is an ancient art, highly developed in many cultures. Puppets can be made and used in classrooms at any grade level. This form of dramatization is especially helpful in gaining the participation of children who are too shy to take part in plays.

Puppets can be made very simply in the lower grades, becoming more elaborate as the children's skill and patience increases. There are several types of puppets. Finger puppets, little puppets fitting on a finger, can be made by drawing faces, and bodies if you wish, on cardboard, paper, tape, or cloth and attaching them by a rubberband on a piece of tape. Push puppets are made by drawing, coloring, and cutting-out paper or cardboard figures and attaching them to a stick with tacks, glue, paste, or tape. Hand puppets, fitting over the hand, can be

Figure 228. *Puppets and marionettes satisfy several art activities. They are instrumental in drama activities, and children become skilful in manipulating them, thus developing expressive gestures. But most of all, it is a satisfying form of sculptural expression.*[43]

made by drawing on an inverted paper bag; modeling a head out of papier maché, or other modeling material, leaving an opening for the child's finger at the base of the head, and attaching a cloth body; using stitchery and appliqué to form features on a sock, mitten, or glove; carving or drawing features on a vegetable; or by modifying the methods described above. Shadow puppets are made like push puppets and are projected by a light source onto the rear of a screen made by stretching an old sheet over a frame.

A puppet stage may be made by cutting an opening out of a large free-standing cardboard box, such as a refrigerator carton, a smaller box placed on a table, or a sheet hung in a doorway, or stretched over a frame, or between poles. The stage can be decorated by tempera, tempera and starch, or cloth or paper collage.

Masks

Masks play a role in many of the cultures about which children will be learning in school. They are worn in the ceremonies of the North American Indians and of many African peoples, in performances in the Orient, at Mardi-Gras celebrations, and at Halloween by children in our own culture.

Masks may be made simply by cutting out eyes and decorating an inverted paper bag with paper sculpture, collage, paint, or crayon. More elaborate ones can be developed on a base made of a cardboard box, laminated papier maché, aluminum foil, cardboard, or tag board, with features drawn or formed with modeling material, or paper sculpture. Additional materials, such as yarn or steel wool can be used to suggest hair. Texture can be added by sprinkling glitter, sand, and the like on a surface covered with glue.

If a protective coating is needed, spray out of doors with plastic, varnish, or lacquer,

Figure 229. *Masks are interesting to make because of the characterization the child can express and the interesting technique with which he can experiment.*[43]

or paint with liquid starch or thin mixture of wheat paste and water.

Conclusion

In the final analysis, the true measure of success in the teaching of art is the extent to which its values permeate life within and beyond the classroom. With artistry the teacher and pupils can create an environment for learning which is responsive to human needs and pleasing to the eye. They can become increasingly aware of the place of art in our own culture and in cultures of other times and places. As an expression of the human spirit, art can serve the teacher as a reminder of the obligation to nurture the creative power within each child.

Ogg, Oscar, *The 26 Letters*. New York: Thomas Y. Crowell Co., 1948.

SUPPLEMENTARY READING

Books on Booklets

Banister, Manly, *Pictorial Manual of Book Binding*. New York: Ronald Press, 1958.

Johnson, Pauline, *Creative Bookbinding*. Seattle: University of Washington Press, 1964.

Town, Lawrence, *Bookbinding by Hand*. New York: Pitman Publishing Corp., 1952.

Books on Bulletin Boards and Display

Randall, Reino, and Edward C. Haines, *Bulletin Boards and Display*. Worcester, Mass.: Davis Publications, Inc., 1961.

Kelley, Marjorie and Nicholas Roukes, *Matting and Displaying the Work of Children*. San Francisco: Fearon Publishers, 1957.

Books on Holiday Art

Koskey, Thomas Arthur, *Bulletin Boards for Holidays and Seasons*. San Francisco: Fearon Publishers, 1958.

Krythe, Marjorie R., *All About American Holidays*. New York: Harper, 1962.

Linse, Barbara B., *Well Seasoned Holiday Art*. San Francisco: Fearon Publishers, 1956.

Maris, Irena, *Holiday Art*. Dansville, New York: F. A. Owen Publishing Co., 1959.

Miller, Bruce, *Let's Celebrate a Holiday*. Riverside, Calif.: Bruce Miller, 1956.

Books on Lettering

Cataldo, John, *Lettering: A Guide for Teachers*. Worcester, Mass.: Davis Publications, Inc., 1958.

Books on Masks

Baranski, Matthew, *Mask Making*. Worcester, Mass.: The Davis Press, 1954.

Wissler, Clark, *Masks*. New York: The American Museum of Natural History, 1946.

Books on Models

Bassett-Lowke, W. J., and Paul B. Mann, *Marvelous Models*. Middlesex, England: Penguin Books Ltd., 1947.

Books on Murals

Kelley, Marjorie, and Nicholas Roukes, *Let's Make a Mural*. San Francisco: Fearon Publishers, 1958.

Randall, Arne W., *Murals for Schools*. Worcester, Mass.: The Davis Publications, Inc., 1956.

Books on Play Production and Puppets

Beaumont, Cyril, *Puppets and Puppetry*. London and New York: The Studio Publications, 1958.

Batchelder, Marjorie, *The Puppet Theater Handbook*. New York: Harper & Row, Publishers, 1947.

Crane, Nancy, *Creative Costumes for the Classroom*. Dansville, N.Y.: F. A. Owen Publishing Co., 1960.

Educational Puppetry Association, *Complete Puppet Book*. London: Educational Puppetry Association, 1956.

Gassner, John, and Philip Barber, *Producing the Play*. New York: The Dryden Press, 1953.

Jagendorf, Moritz, *The First Book of Puppets*. New York: F. Watts, 1952.

Lauchester, Waldo S., *Hand Puppets and String Puppets*. Leicester, England: Dryad Press, 1948.

Merten, George, *The Hand Puppets*. New York: Thomas Nelson & Sons, 1957.

Pratt, Lois H., *The Puppet Do-It-Yourself Book*. New York: Exposition Press, 1957.

Children's Books

Dockstader, Frederick J., *Indian Art in America: The Arts and Crafts of the North American Indian*. Greenwich, Conn.: New York Graphic Society, 1961.

Glubok, Shirley, *The Art of the North American Indian*. New York: Harper & Row, Publishers, 1964.

Honda, Isao, *How to make Origami, the Japanese Art of Paper Folding*. New York: Ivan, Obolensky, Inc., 1959.

Manley, Seon, *Adventures in Making: The Romance of Crafts Around the World*. New York: Vanguard Press, Inc., 1959.

Miles, Charles, *Indian and Eskimo Artifacts of North America*. Chicago: H. Regnery, 1963.

Munsterberg, Hugo. *The Folk Arts of Japan*. Rutland, Vt.: Charles E. Tuttle Co., 1958.

Rasmussen, Carrie, *Fun-Time Puppets*. Chicago: Children's Press, 1952.

United States Committee for U.N.I.C.E.F. *Hi Neighbor*. Books 1 through 5. New York: Hastings House, 1962.

Films for the Classroom

Masks

Making a Mask. International Film Bureau
The Loon's Necklace. Encyclopaedia Britannica Films, Inc.

Filmstrips for the Classroom

Murals

Making a Mural. Young America Films, Inc.

Play production

Art in Our Classroom. We Make Stick Puppets. Encyclopaedia Britannica Films.

Slides for the Classroom

Early American Crafts. Dr. Konrad Prothman, 2378 Soper Ave., Baldwin, Long Island, New York.

References for Illustrations

1. Andree, R., "Das Zeichnen bei den Naturvölkern," *Mitteilungen der Anthropologischen Gesellschaft in Wien*, XVII (1887), 98-106.
2. Beck, W., *Self-Development in Drawing, as interpreted by the Genius of Romano Dazzi*, New York: Putnam's Sons, Knickerbocker Press, 1928.
3. Boutonier, J., *Les Dessins des Enfants*, Paris, Editions du Scarabée, 1953.
4. Burckhardt, H., "Veränderungen der Raumlage in Kinderzeichnungen," *Zeitschrift für paedagogische Psychologie*, XXVI (1925), 352-371.
5. Caroto, Giovanni Francesco, *Fanciullo con pupazzo*, Verona, Italy: Museo de Castelvecchio.
6. Clark, A. B., "The Child's Attitude Toward Perspective Problems," *Studies in Education*, Stanford University (1896-1897), 283-294.
7. *The Complete Letters of Vincent Van Gogh*, Greenich, Connecticut: New York Graphic Society, Vol. 1, 345 (letter No. 224 to Theo).
8. Germann, P., "Zeichnungen von Kindern und Jugendlichen aus dem Waldlande von Nord-Liberia," *Ethnologische Studien*, I (1929), 75-95.
9. Hartlaub, G. F., *Der Genius im Kinde*, Breslau: Ferdinand Hirt, 1930.
10. Hildreth, G., *The Child's Mind in Evolution*, New York: King's Crown Press, 1941.
11. Italian Painting, *The Creators of the Renaissance*, New York: Albert Skira, Inc., 1950, 132, 133.
12. Ivanoff, E., "Recherches expérimentales sur le dessin des écoliers de la Suisse Romande," *Archives de Psychologie*, VIII (1909), 97-156.
13. Japanese Schoolchildren, Exhibit of Prints, Tolman Hall University of California, Berkeley, Spring, 1964.
14. Karrenberg, C., *Der Mensch als Zeichenobjekt, Ein Versuch zur Lösung der Frage: Kann der Mensch Gegenstand des Zeichenunterrichts in der Volksschule sein?* Leipzig: Otto Memnich (Paedagogische Monographien, E. Meumann, ed.), 1910.
15. Kellogg, R., *What Children Scribble and Why*, Palo Alto: Publishers of National Press Books, N-P Publications, 1959.
16. Kerschensteiner, G., *Die Entwicklung der zeichnerischen Begabung*, Munich: Gerber, 1905.
17. Kik, C., "Die übernormale Zeichenbegabung bei Kindern," *Zeitschrift für angewandte Psychologie* (1909), 92-149.
18. Larisch, R., *Unterricht in Ornamentaler Schrift*, 8th ed., Vienna: Oest. Staatsdruckerei, 1922.
19. Lark-Horovitz, B., Private Collection of Children's Drawings.
20. Lark-Horovitz, B., "Interlinkage of sensory memories in relation to training in drawing," *Journal of Genetic Psychology*, XLIX (1936), 69-89.
21. Lark-Horovitz, B., "A Visual memory experiment," in Munro, T., Lark-Horovitz, B., and E. N. Barnhart, "Children's art abilities: Studies at the Cleveland Museum of Art," *Journal of Experimental Education*, XI, No. 2 (1942), 97-155.

22. Lark-Horovitz, B., Barnhart, E. N., and E. M. Sills, *Graphic Work-Sample Diagnosis, An Analytical Method of Estimating Children's Drawing Ability,* The Cleveland Museum of Art, 1939.

23. Leonardo da Vinci, London: Phaidon Press, Ltd., 4th ed., 1951 (reproduction No. 83).

24. Levinstein, S., *Untersuchungen über das Zeichnen des Kindes,* Leipzig: R. Voigtländer, 1905.

25. Lukens, T., "A study of children's drawings in the early years," *Pedagogical Seminary,* IV (1896-1897), 79-110.

26. Luquet, G. H., *Les Dessins d'un Enfant,* Paris; Alcan, 1913.

27. Luquet, G. H., "La narration graphique chez l'enfant," *Journal de Psychologie,* XXI (1924), 183-218.

28. Luquet, G. H., *Le Dessin Enfantin,* Paris: Alcan, 1927.

29. McElwee, E. W., "Profile drawings of normal and subnormal children," *Journal of Applied Psychology,* XVIII (1934), 599-603.

30. Munro, T., Lark-Horovitz, B., and E. N. Barnhart, "Children's art abilities: Studies at the Cleveland Museum of Art," *Journal of Experimental Education,* XI, No. 2 (1942), 97-155.

31. Muth, G. F. "Über Ornamentierungsversuche mit Kindern im Alter von 6-9 Jahren," *Zeitschrift für angewandte Psychologie,* VI (1912), 21-50.

32. Pfleiderer, W., *Die Geburt des Bildes,* Stuttgart: Julius Hoffmann, 1930.

33. Ricci, C., *L'Arte dei Bambini,* Bologna, N. Zanichelli, 1887.

34. Rouma, G., *Le Language Graphique de l'Enfant,* Brussels: Misch and Thron, 1913.

35. Spanish Children's Exhibit with an introduction by Aldous Huxley, 1937-1938.

36. Stern, C., and W. Stern, "Dei zeichnerische Entwicklung eines Knaben vom 4. bis zum 7. Jahr," *Zeitschrift für angewandte Psychologie,* III (1909-1910).

37. Vollbehr, E., "Kinderzeichnungen von Eingeborenen aus den deutschen Kolonien," *Die Umschau,* IVI, No. 36 (1912), 759-762.

38. Weixlgärtner, A., "Kindergraphik," Kie Graphischen Künste, XLV, No. 1 (1922), 1-20.

39. Wintsch, J., "Le dessin comme témoin de développement mental," Zeitschrift für Kinderpsychiatrie, II, No. 3 (1935), 33-44, 69-83.

40. San Francisco Chronicle Collection, 1961-1965.

41. Lark-Horovitz, B., "On Learning abilities of children as recorded in a drawing experiment," *Journal of Experimental Education,* IX, No. 4 (1941), 332-360.

42. Private Collection of Willard Brooks, Fresno, California.

43. Photographs by San Francisco, California, artist-photographers, Rod Mac-Connell and Ruth McNitt.

44. California school districts' contributions: Berkeley, Castro Valley, Canville, Oakland, Richmond, Sacramento, San Francisco, Walnut Creek.

45. Maltoni, M., and G. Venturi, *I Quanderni di San Gersolè,* Prefazione di Calvino, I., Giulio Einudi Editore, Torino, Italy, 2nd ed., 1963.

46. Chaga, L., and A. Mikhailov, *Drawings of Our Children,* Moscow: Sovietsky Kludoznik Publishing House, 1962.

47. Boys Club of Hunters Point, Exhibit of Paintings, Tolman Hall, University of California, Berkeley, 1964.

Indices

Artist and Author Index

Artist and Author Index

Subject Index

Italic numbers refer to page numbers of terms in graphs and tables.
Bold-face numbers refer to terms in caption and to figures not on same text page.
References to numbers of colored figures follow the abbreviation with their numbers.

251

DATE DUE

MY 18 '05			

Please remember that this is a library book,
and that it belongs only temporarily to each
person who uses it. Be considerate. Do
not write in this, or any, library book.